SHELF LIFE

Also by WILLIAM PRITCHARD

Wyndham Lewis

Seeing through Everything: English Writers, 1918–1940

Lives of the Modern Poets

Frost: A Literary Life Reconsidered

Randall Jarrell: A Literary Life

Playing It by Ear: Literary Essays and Reviews

English Papers: A Teaching Life

Talking Back to Emily Dickinson and Other Essays

Updike: America's Man of Letters

SHELF LIFE

Literary Essays and Reviews

WILLIAM H. PRITCHARD

University of Massachusetts Press

AMHERST AND BOSTON

LC 2003002159
ISBN 1-55849-375-1

Designed by Dennis Anderson
Set in Minion by Graphic Composition, Inc.
Printed and bound by The Maple-Vail Book Manufacturing Group

Library of Congress Cataloging-in-Publication Data
Pritchard, William H.
  Shelf life : literary essays and reviews / William H. Pritchard.
      p.   cm.
Includes bibliographical references and index.
    ISBN 1-55849-375-1 (alk. paper)
    1. English literature—History and criticism.   2. American literature—
History and criticism.   I. Title.
  PR99 .P754 2003
  820.9—dc21   2003002159

British Library Cataloguing in Publication data are available

For *Bill Kennick,*
philosopher and friend

Contents

ACKNOWLEDGMENTS

A s with my previous collections, many of these pieces were commissioned by *The Hudson Review,* and I thank once more Frederick Morgan and Paula Deitz for their support.

Christopher Benfey exercised his usual skills as a critical reader who knows what items should be included or left out of such a book. Thanks to him, also to Michael Gorra and Paul Kane for useful suggestions.

Susan Raymond-Fic scanned and keyboarded the manuscript. Lisa Williams copyedited with good sense and a good ear. And although a book of essays and reviews doesn't make publishers' hearts beat faster, Bruce Wilcox, as in the past, has been willing to implement my proposal for gathering up these items.

Thanks finally to various nameless students of mine in Amherst College classrooms who over the decades listened to me talk about and talked with me about most of the writers treated here.

PREFACE

THIS book is the third collection of shorter literary pieces I have thought worth preserving, and like its predecessors, *Playing It by Ear* (1994) and *Talking Back to Emily Dickinson* (1998), focuses on the work of English and American writers, most of them from the just-concluded century. The titles of those previous volumes attempted to advertise principles on which my criticism is based: that what Robert Frost called "ear," as opposed to "eye," reading is essential to any engagement with imaginative writing and that the critic's job is to talk back to the imagination he has been engaged by. I also recommended, in prefacing those volumes, the virtues of humor, of sticking one's neck out, and of writing sentences that could be understood, more or less, by the intelligent reader who is not a professional academic. Intelligent reading and an academic career are, of course, not mutually exclusive, yet as may be noted from perusing the titles of panel topics at the most recent Modern Language Association convention, the vocabulary and interests of many English professors are nowadays directed away from "aesthetic" considerations—away from what T. S. Eliot called, rather stiffly in an early essay, "the elucidation of works of art and the correction of taste." The academic study of "English" is now largely directed toward matters of historical, political, and sociological concern: cultural studies, rather than the study of literature.

Eliot also declared that he wrote for neither a large nor a small audience, but for "the hypothetical Intelligent Man" who does not exist and who is the audience of the artist. His ancestor Samuel Johnson reached out to invoke what he called the Common Reader, "uncorrupted with literary prejudices, after all the refinements of subtlety and the dogmatism of learning." But Eliot's "man" doesn't exist, and—as Frank Kermode has pointed out—Johnson's "common reader" was a much more highly equipped and literate judge of books than is likely to be found in any "common" group today. With an eye toward the present, Kermode suggests that an attempt to revive or construct an appropriate notion of the common reader should look not at "some fictive outsider whose word, it pleases us to say, is our law, but at the students in our class, who, as we are now continually lamenting, know nothing and have never acquired our own need to be on speaking terms with the past." So rather than setting ourselves apart from academic authority by way of justifying what we do as critics and reviewers of books, we might as academics find our justification in the classroom and the attempt to instruct younger minds in the pleasures and powers of more skilled, more humane reading. The effort of addressing and creating common readers is the business of daily conversation in that classroom: as I tell students when we prepare to move into *Paradise Lost* or *The Golden Bowl*, "Prufrock" or *Lucky Jim*, I *need* their cooperative voices and questions, partly because such conversations are the exception rather than the rule in any world outside the one that teacher and students share.

It's no accident, then, that this collection concludes with a section that features some considerations of teachers and teaching. The teacher of mine who is the subject of one essay, Theodore Baird, was a model of what I take the life of reading to be. Though Baird never used the word to describe his way of reading, "disinterested" is an apt characterization of it. The word, in bad favor today, carries echoes of Matthew Arnold's plea that criticism should be disinterested, uncommitted to party or sect. Contemporary critique has it that Arnold's view in fact masked a powerful set of interests of his own— in class, society, politics, religion. In a similar way, the notion that there can ever be such an activity as reading disinterestedly, reading without an agenda, reading purely for the sake of reading, may be equally a delusion, a masking of less pure interests.

To defend such reading, or at least to claim it is possible, admirable or not, I would instance my teacher's voluminous and eclectic labor, as a signal instance of following one's curiosity, the need to find out things, to see whether a writer is worth going on with, whether a book holds up upon rereading, revisitation. My own reading life, less bold and various than Theodore Baird's, has I hope been animated by similar motives and can be seen to manifest a certain serendipity. That, unlike him, I conducted much of my own education through the public channels of writing essays and reviews is for better or worse shown by the present collection. But I would like to think that there may be observed in it a play of taste and subject (Samuel Johnson *and* Raymond Chandler *and* Richard Wilbur) not easily to be classified or explained. Here again the analogy with the classroom holds: although for purposes of organization any course must limit its subject—these writers, not those— the only real continuity I'm interested in is what the students can work out for themselves when they read one damn book after another. As a teacher, that is, I play down the thematic links by which someone organizing a course can make it "go together," at least in someone's head. My impulse, rather, is to make the sequence of books show some of the waywardness, confusion, and surprise that characterize my reading life outside the classroom. A skeptical eye might see such "disinterestedness" as but a mask over an interest in making students have a reading life that resembles mine. But I can live with that.

A final, prefatory thought: Philip Larkin's "Continuing to Live" contains the following pronouncement:

> And once you have walked the length of your own mind, what
> You command is clear as a lading list.
> Anything else must not, for you, be thought
> To exist.

I've walked a good portion of my mind's length, and what seems not to exist there in any observable way is the passion to be political. Aside from being a registered Democrat and casting a vote at least when national elections come round, I am on the sidelines, take no active stake in improving the environment, ameliorating social injustice, or striving for gender equality. Most of the time I can't even be sure what it is I "really" believe about the public issues and crises that daily solicit our attention. My life has been spent in largely escaping those issues, such escape made possible by the tenured security of the ivory tower where, in the main, no one has told me what I must or must not do.

It is in literature and music where that escape has been made most satisfyingly. The rhythm of my mind, my inner life, is such that it can be kept awake and busy by the run of a Brahms piano capriccio, a lyric by Yeats or Cole Porter, a hymn (words and music) by Arthur Seymour Sullivan, a trivial song from World War II ("My Dreams Are Getting Better All the Time"), or an obscene limerick by Anon. In rationalizing my failure as a citizen, then, I have recourse to pleading that one can't do everything and that my preoccupation with poems, novels, classical music, jazz, and playing the piano has crowded out less selfish concerns. There have been a few exceptional spirits who combine in their work the worlds of politics, ideas, literature, music—I think of Bernard Shaw or Kenneth Burke, more recently of Irving Howe (a ballet-goer) or Edward Said (a pianist)—but it's hard to think of very many. At any rate, this miscellany of pieces, the earliest written in 1965, the latest just yesterday, is assembled in the spirit of Frost's wish that a college should dispose its students forever to look for a book side to everything. If a reader of this book comes away convinced that the author never left college, I won't be disappointed.

POETRY AND POETS

THERE is a thirty-five year span between the items in this section, but I see no large revisions in the way I think about, like to talk about, poets and poetry. "Frost in His Letters," first delivered as a lecture at a Frost conference held at Bread Loaf, Middlebury College, is a demonstration that Frost's "poetry" is as much evident in his epistolary behavior as in his poems. I didn't know at the time the good news that his letters, out of print for decades, will be published by Harvard University Press as part of a larger project—under the general editorship of Robert Faggen—of bringing out Frost's work. "*A Witness Tree* and Frost's Biography," also delivered at a conference, this one at Winthrop College in South Carolina, is an attempt to extend the appreciation (made earlier in my *Frost: A Literary Life Reconsidered*) of the great opening sequence of poems in that late volume. It was also concerned to demonstrate the crudity of Jeffrey Meyers's effort, in his biography of Frost, to "explain" the poems by using events from the poet's life.

"Reading *The Waste Land* Today" makes a case for taking less seriously the larger, cultural interpretations Eliot's poem has elicited, and emphasizes rather the immediate pleasures and excitements experienced as we move through Eliot's verse. My reading is doubtless a partial one—certainly it doesn't take adequate account of "What the Thunder Said," the poem's closing section. But the comparison of Eliot to Ben Jonson in terms of the essay Eliot wrote on that poet just prior to writing *The Waste Land* still seems to me important, and commentary over the past thirty years hasn't made enough of it.

The appreciations of Richard Wilbur and James Merrill, both graduates, like me, of Amherst College, are instances of provincial satisfaction that aren't, I trust, merely provincial. The Wilbur essay originated in a talk I gave about *The Beautiful Changes,* his first book of verse, on the occasion of its fiftieth anniversary. The short review of Merrill celebrates the publication of his *Collected Poems.* The pieces on Robert Graves and L. E. Sissman were occasioned by a posthumous edition of Sissman's collected poems and the final volume of a three-volume biography of Graves by his nephew. The Sissman collection is out of print, but a selection of his poems, *Night Music,* edited by Peter Davison, appeared in 1999. A three-volume edition of Graves's *Complete Poems* is available from Carcanet Press, Manchester, U.K.

The essay on R. P. Blackmur as a critic of poetry dates from 1967, when I was much under his spell. Although the spell has worn off a bit over decades, it is good to be reminded of how passionately and fully Blackmur gave himself to the elucidation of poetry, especially modern poetry.

Frost in His Letters

F<small>ROST</small> in his letters: we might ask about the title, its appropriateness as a subject of study, of literary commentary. How many English or American writers can plausibly be approached as if their "letters" were a genre worth taking seriously for the special pleasures and rewards to be found there? Academic libraries fill up with multi-volume collections of letters by the great writers—Wordsworth, Dickens, Charlotte Brontë, Tennyson, Hardy, Bernard Shaw, Henry James—but who reads them, much less owns them? (James, maybe, in a one-volume selection from the four volumes.) As a young student of literature, I had it implanted in my mind by no less an authority than Lionel Trilling that there were two great writers of letters in English—Keats and D. H. Lawrence. There's certainly a case to be made for each, though who wants to work through the nine volumes of Lawrence's letters that have now been published? Unless they're subsidized, university-sponsored collections of letters surely have no appeal for publishers: fifteen years ago Houghton Mifflin published Randall Jarrell's letters, wonderfully engaging pages I found them, which sold poorly. (Robie Macauley, then an editor at Houghton Mifflin, told me that only Flannery O'Connor's letters had made it into paperback.)

Surely Frost's letters have not been clamored for by readers who presumably love his poetry, at least not to the extent that Frost's publisher was willing to keep them in print. Lawrance Thompson's *Selected Letters* and Louis Untermeyer's collection of Frost's letters to him, both published by Holt in the year after Frost's death, have been out of print for decades, along with the valuable *Family Letters of Robert Frost,* edited by Arnold Grade. The *Library of America* has usefully printed some pages of letters dealing especially with matters of poetic form and Frost's "theory" of verse. Other publishers of his poetic contemporaries have done better by them, keeping Pound's and Stevens's letters in print, as well as the first and only volume published so far of T. S. Eliot's. I want to direct these remarks not—if I may draw a danger-ous distinction—at the "content" of Frost's letters, at what he "had to say" about poetry or love or heroism, but at the distinct and memorable way he said those things. The distinction is dangerous, of course, in the way that any separation of form and content simplifies and makes less rich the poem, the paragraph, the sentence in question. But by way of comparison with his peers in their correspondence: Eliot and Pound give us direct news and gos-sip about the London literary world; Wallace Stevens takes us on long walks with him and tells us what he saw—later on he will explicate his own poems, often at tedious length. By contrast Frost's epistolary style is teasing, indirect, sometimes rather opaque, making us feel that perhaps we're missing some-thing, the point maybe. In this he follows the style of his prose in the few es-says he wrote: you never know quite which way he will jump, and sometimes you're not sure you've jumped with him in the right direction. What *is* the right direction, one asks?

In formulating his theory of poetry in 1913 in England, he insisted, to his sounding-boards John Bartlett and Sidney Cox back in America, that sen-tence sounds, in and out of poetry, must "unmistakably" show a reader how to voice "the posture proper to the sentence": "Never if you can help it write down a sentence in which the voice will not know how to posture *specially,*" he wrote Bartlett. But there may be some ambiguity here. Is Frost, as poet, mainly anxious to help the reader get the poem, the line, the special posture "right"? Or is it conceivable that he might also, even primarily, be interested in contriving, in his own voice, a posture so special as to confuse the reader—to leave him in the dust? In and out of the letters, from the begin-ning, there is an emphasis on wiliness ("ain't I wily," he once wrote); on his own complicated forethinking ("I am not undesigning"); and on collapsing presumed opposites together ("I am never so serious as when I am joking"). Think collaterally of the more than one occasion on which he held up "The Road Not Taken" as a tricky poem. Thompson says in his introduction to the letters that in this poem Frost was carrying himself in the manner of Edward Thomas, who on their walks in England kept regretting the road he had taken and thinking of the other one and what might have been. Thompson tells us that Frost sent the poem to Thomas in manuscript, hoping that "his friend would notice how the poem pivots ironically on the sentimental phrase, "I shall be telling this with a sigh." Edward Thomas missed it, says

Thompson, because "the irony had been handled too slyly, too subtly," and he thinks Frost was similarly disappointed when American readers missed the "pivotal irony" of the poem. Yet in Thompson's following paragraph he quotes Frost saying in a letter about his own writing, "I should like to be so subtle at this game as to seem to the casual person altogether obvious." And he indulged in what sounds like a boast to Untermeyer when he writes that "I bet not half a dozen people can tell who was hit and where he was hit by my Road Not Taken."

And of course it wasn't just a question of "The Road Not Taken" being a poem where Frost was too sly or subtle in his irony. Consider the final stanza of "Tree at My Window"

> That day she put our heads together
> Fate had her imagination about her,
> Your head so much concerned with outer,
> Mine with inner, weather.

Who would like to stand up and describe the special posture of "Fate had her imagination about her," to say just how serious or how humorous it is? Are seriousness and joking the same for Frost?

> They cannot look out far,
> They cannot look in deep,
> But when was that ever a bar
> To any watch they keep?

I needn't go into the difficulty critics and readers have had with *that* assertion—of just how to weigh it. The best Randall Jarrell could do was to address the "tone" of the last lines and immediately qualify that with "or rather, their careful suspension between several tones, as a piece of iron can be held in the air between powerful enough magnets." To say further how or why that suspension is "careful" was a task Jarrell didn't take on. I'm suggesting, in other words, that Frost's deepest impulse as writer of poems and prose was (to use Jarrell's metaphor) suspended between the desire not to be "caviare to the crowd," to reach out rather to all sorts and kinds of readers, and a contrary desire to be altogether unobvious to the casual—that is, to most—readers: to hold back, to *not* say all he could and he would, to *not* unfold a tale that would tell all.

1.

In his *T. S. Eliot and Prejudice,* Christopher Ricks has a valuable comparison of Frost to Eliot by way of indicating the often undramatic quality of tone in Eliot's poetry. Ricks quotes Frost's 1913 Fourth of July letter home to Bartlett about the sound of sense, and after some examples of that sound ("You mean to tell me you can't read? I said no such thing. Well read then. You're not my teacher.") Frost writes "Those sounds are summoned by the audile imagination and they must be positive, strong, and definitely and unmistakably indicated by the context. The reader must be at no loss to give his voice the posture proper to the sentence." Ricks calls this insistence "one half of the truth," and notes that although "Frost's poems are often less single-minded than this, as a commentator on poetry he is indeed single-minded." But Frost in his letters is many things besides a commentator on poetry, although he is never far from that subject, and one way of distinguishing his correspondence from that of his poetic contemporaries is to suggest how much doublemindedness there is in his writing.

Consider a couple of sentences from letters to Susan Hayes Ward in 1894, after the magazine she edited (the *New York Independent*) had accepted "My Butterfly" for publication, the first such acceptance Frost had received. He thanks her profusely—"It is just such a letter . . . that I have been awaiting for two years"—then draws back, or moves in a more complicated direction: "Yet the consideration is hardly due me. Take my word for it that poem exaggerates my ability. You must spare my feelings when you come to read these others, for I haven't the courage to be a disappointment to anyone." What is the exact special posture of this? How "positive" and "strong" is its unmistakable tonal indication? "Take my word for it that poem exaggerates my ability"—what sort of "word" is this she's supposed to take? Does it help to call the word "tongue-in-cheek" or "ironical"? Not much, for what mainly comes across, especially in that oddly unexpected verb "exaggerates," is a cool elegance that is not unhumorous and that is at variance with what the words literally say, yet created only through their distinctive way of saying. Spare my feelings, he warns her when she reads other work he is sending her ("Two of these are the returned poems and the other is no better"), since "I haven't the courage to be a disappointment to anyone." Is that what it takes to disappoint people—more courage than one has? Again irony, tongue-in-cheek, saying one thing while meaning another, are only the roughest handles to grab on to the felicity of that yoking of courage and disappointment. Six months or so later, back from his excursion in Virginia's Dismal Swamp, he thanks Susan Ward for printing "My Butterfly," then clears his throat and backs off into a new paragraph: "Before proceeding further I perceive I must assume an attitude, or else endanger the coherency of my remarks,—for my natural attitude is one of enthusiasm verging on egotism and thus I always confuse myself trying to be modest." Part of this fussing is no more, perhaps, than the self-consciousness of a young man, sending off his wares for inspection by a person in a position to publish them. But the final sentence has the pleasure of an originality beyond nervousness: granted, it's not uncommon for someone to admit he's enthusiastic, perhaps egotistical in that enthusiasm; but then the unexpected conclusions—"Thus I always confused myself trying to be modest." The only way, evidently, to be clear rather than confused, is to assert yourself, egotistical as that way may be.

I have noted the inadequacy of ready-made labels like "irony" to deal with Frost's distinctive epistolary style. Since we may call that style, safely if vaguely, a humorous one, it's worth remembering what Frost had to say about humor as it bore on himself. The saying comes in a letter to Untermeyer, probably the correspondent who over the years, beginning in 1915 when Frost returned from England, called forth the poet's most extravagant and complicated performances. In a letter of 10 March 1924, Frost addressed himself to the meaning of "style" in prose or verse. It indicates "how the writer takes himself and what he is saying," and Frost proceeds to exemplify it by briefly and pungently characterizing the ways different writers like Stevenson, Swinburne, Emerson, Thoreau, Whitman, Carlyle ("whose way of taking himself simply infuriates me"), and Longfellow "took" themselves. Then a new paragraph:

> I own any form of humor shows fear and inferiority. Irony is simply a form of guardedness. So is a twinkle. It keeps the reader from criticism. . . . At bottom the world isn't a joke. We only joke about it to avoid an issue with someone to let someone know that we know he's there with his questions: to disarm him by seeming to have heard and done justice to his side of the standing argument. Humor is the most engaging cowardice. With it myself I have been able to hold some of my enemy in play far out of gunshot.

If asked to name, on the basis of these sentences, *Frost's* style—how he "took" himself—we could do it by lifting another sentence from the same letter, in which style is figured as "the mind skating circles round itself as it moves forward." "Style" is the way a writer "carries himself toward his ideas and deeds"; it is a product of "superfluity."

The vigorous skating round himself that goes on in Frost's letters, their "superfluity," is a virtuoso activity in which words are continually slipping out of their stable meanings at the command of the performer who puts new twists on them. In the sentence above ("I own any form of humor shows fear or inferiority"), words that usually have a less than admirable ring—especially for a tough guy like Frost—turn out to be necessary attributes of "any form of humor" and they join "irony" as the respectable constituents of a defensive style that, even as you scarcely notice it, turns into a subtle and effectively offensive one called "guardedness." The process seems wholly analogous to the moment at the end of his *Paris Review* interview when he muses on what's meant by "inspiration":

> It's just the same as when you feel a joke coming. You see somebody coming down the street that you're accustomed to abuse, and you feel it stirring in you, something to say as you pass each other. . . . It's him coming toward you that gives you the animus, you know. When they want to know about inspiration, I tell them it's mostly animus.

To recap a bit: humor or irony is a way of showing "fear and inferiority"; it is a kind of "guardedness," an "engaging cowardice" employed to hold the enemy "in play far out of gunshot." How much of this is "objective" thinking and how much is it a deeply subjective response to life, with its roots in Frost's biography? Surely it has much to do with his extreme wariness about other people—with his "overactive" imagination ("I am never not working," he loved to say), ever alert to the possibilities for embarrassment, for defeat, or perhaps victory, in human encounters ("You see somebody coming down the street that you're accustomed to abuse"). It may have something to do with the years of relative isolation in his twenties when the shy and fiercely proud young man held himself and his gift apart from other people and from the world—that world where people seemed to be "disallowing" him, achieving more than he by graduating from college and establishing themselves in one or the other solid occupation. But Frost had, in his isolation, a vantage point: "And if by noon I have too much of these, / I have but to turn on my arm and lo, / The sunburned hillside sets my face aglow."

With Elinor, he can share a vantage point on the world that is neglecting them, as in "In Neglect":

> They leave us so in the way we took
> As two in whom they were proved mistaken
> That we sit sometimes in a wayside nook
> With mischievous, vagrant, seraphic look
> And *try* if we cannot feel forsaken.

What a lovely way to keep the enemy in play and out of gunshot—to wield those three words that never before came within remote proximity of one another: "mischievous, vagrant, seraphic." Here is indeed inspiration, the animus well breathed, as those adjectives brilliantly suggest the concentrated waywardness, the wandering mischief of Frost's humorous fantasies.

Sometimes those fantasies, as spun out in his correspondence, are so fiercely concentrated on undoing the enemy that it feels as if something like gunshot were in fact about to happen: the reader laughs, sort of, but feels contorted in so doing. Frost once wrote his eldest daughter, Lesley, who had been bothered by what he terms as some "co-occupants" of her New York City apartment. Frost provided free-of-charge advice on how to deal with them, "to set them back temporarily if not get rid of them entirely":

> You can get in a kerosene can a gallon of gasolene (price 36 cts) and pour, literally pour, it into every crack and corner of the wood work of the bed or cots and soak the canvas of them all along where it is nailed to the wood. Don't wet the mattresses: they are as uninhabited as the moon. You must do the deed very early in the day when no light or fire is lit in the room or going to be for a good many hours—that is till the gasolene has had time to evaporate and get out the windows. You can leave the windows open for the day. I say this only for your own comfort for the time being. . . . You may have to buy a cheap kerosene can. It is the best thing to buy the gasolene in and to put the stuff on with. Don't spare it. Make the wood bubble. Go over the beds twice perhaps. Then open the windows and get out.

He adds in a final note, "This is the kind of letter I should hate to mail at the Franconia postoffice for fear Salome would open it for her amusement and keep it as a memorial for our private affairs." (He mailed it from the post office in Arlington, New Hampshire.) It took this reader some time to realize that the co-occupants were not obstreperous roommates, to be summarily dealt with, but stubborn bedbugs who would succumb only to liberally laid-on gasoline. Doubtless Frost's advice was good practical sense; yet isn't there a relish in his laying it out ("Don't spare it. Make the wood bubble") that goes beyond what a more ordinary father might have suggested his child should do? Frost, as father, delights in making mischief, in exuberantly, and with superfluity, imagining the end of such an insidious foe.

A quieter but no less deadly form of aggression occurs in a 1914 letter from England about the behavior of the Georgian poet W. H. Davies, who had been visiting Frost's friend Wilfrid Gibson. I've already referred to it in my book on Frost, but want to introduce it again here since it so perfectly expresses a central part of the Frostian epistolary temperament. He says that Davies had lately "disgusted" the Gibsons, then adds:

> His is the kind of egotism another man's egotism can't put up with. He was going from here to be with Conrad. He said that would be pleasant because Conrad knew his work *thoroughly.* After waiting long enough to obscure the point we asked him if he knew Conrad's work *thoroughly.* Oh no—was it good? We told him yes. He was glad we liked it.

There is a lot stirring, or rather bubbling, here. A less playful, more self-righteous spirit than Frost would have had Davies's egotism simply impossible to put up with, as if to say "you and I, reader, are not ourselves egotistic but generously open to other people." But Frost surprises us with bringing in "another man's egotism," as if Davies's egotism were of the sort a mere ordinary egotist can't put up with. What's special about Davies's egotism? Perhaps it is his imperviousness to his betters, if not to Frost then surely to Joseph Conrad. Davies's patronizing of Conrad comes through by Frost wickedly repeating and emphasizing the word "thoroughly," as in "he knows my work *thoroughly,*" and there is also the surprise appearance of the altogether unobvious, unexpected verb "obscure," as in "after waiting long enough to obscure the point," suggesting that the trap set for Davies was of the most subtle kind, set by a plural "we"—although we're willing to blame Frost for all the inspiration. Then there is the fine, totally deadpan rendering of Davies's unawareness that Conrad might have a touch of egotism as well: ". . . we asked him if he knew Conrad's work *thoroughly.* Oh no—was it good? We told him yes. He was glad we liked it." That last, mock-childish sentence, which gets the proper order of things all confused, is especially to be cherished. Extremely aggressive humor then, but at the same time delivered deadpan with an oddly muted, restrained distance about it, so as not to dignify Davies too much by assaulting him too directly, with too obvious a scornful tone of contempt. We remember Frost remarking in his notebooks about the cliché "dry humor" that it was "the kind of humor that doesn't seem to appreciate itself. I wish all literature were as dry in the same sense of the word." One of the main ways of ensuring that this humorous play with W. H. Davies will be sufficiently "dry," is to suppress all "wet" feelings of obvious indignation and jealousy—to avoid such easily nameable special postures by making the tone more of a monotone, harder to get at, "cooler" than a heated rejoinder would have been. Frost never grew any more subtle at that game than in this letter home about a rival poet.

2.

Rarely in his letters did Frost address the subject of letter writing; he complained to his former student Bartlett in 1916 that he had too many people to write to and would rather see them in the flesh, then added "Of course there's a whole lot about the art of writing that none of us there ever masters. We all remain duffers and properly dissatisfied with ourselves. . . . It is touch and go with any of us. Now we get it for a little run of sentences and now we don't." Getting "it" for that little run, being on what we call a roll, is what the poet aspires to, and letter writing becomes something really satisfying, an "art," when it is analogously poetic—when the writer is making] "his own words as he goes," rather than depending on words already made "even if they be his own." (to Cox, 1914). One of the things that distinguishes Frost from his contemporaries, Eliot and Stevens and Pound, is that however dissatisfied he may be with his current academic affiliation at Amherst or Michigan or wherever, he invariably reaches out to the classroom as a place where, even though most of the time he and his students are "duffers" and properly dissatisfied with themselves, there can occur at moments something quite different, a little run of making words count. It is exciting to listen (and that is the right verb for it) to Frost when, pursuing some point or argument in fairly ordinary ways, he suddenly rises to a different, indeed a higher plane, as he does in this letter to his Amherst colleague George Whicher. The apropos is Bread Loaf, and Frost is proposing some teaching of creative writing that (Thompson tells us) paved the way for the Bread Loaf Writers' Conference in 1926. In the letter Frost makes various assertions about how the teacher should converse with his class, should turn from correcting grammar in red ink to "matching experience in black ink, experience of life and experience of art." Then this:

> The writing he has nothing to say to fails with him. The trouble with it is that it hasn't enough to it—of Heaven Earth Hell and the young author. The strength of the teacher's position lies in his waiting till he is come after. His society and audience are a privilege—and that is no pose. On the rare occasion when he goes after his pupils it will be to show them up not for what they aren't but for what they are. He will invade them to show them how much more they contain than they can write down; to show them their subject matter is where they came from and what in the last twenty years they have been doing.

I am moved by these sentences, partly because to my mind they are the assumption that underlay the Amherst course in freshman composition (taken and taught by me) designed by Theodore Baird, on whom Frost's influence was profound. One needn't assent to Frost's rule that students should be "gone after" only on the rare occasion; Baird went after them all the time. The crucial sentence is the one that says such invasion is for the purpose of showing students "how much more they contain than they can write down." But—and this Frost doesn't make explicit—writing that has something "*to it*" will attempt to express that "more," will be so bold as to contain "Heaven Earth Hell" as imagined by "the young author." I don't know any other modern poet who talks like this, or who would publish, in the *Atlantic Monthly* in 1951, a series of apothegms titled "Poetry and School," in which he treats the subject of how to deal with poetry in the classroom, indeed why it is *in* classrooms more than outside them. (I invariably begin my course in freshmen English—"Reading, Writing, Criticism"—with these declarations, such as "We go to college to be given one more chance to learn to read in case we haven't learned in High School. Once we have learned to read the rest can be trusted to add itself unto us." ("Hanging around until you catch on" was another way he put it.)

If I appear to be straying from my subject of Frost in his letters, I think the impression is only apparent. My aim is to suggest how Frost is a most interesting teacher in his letters and that his epistolary relation to his correspondents and to us can be usefully thought of as that of teacher to student or pupil or learner or ephebe, and that the nature of the instruction is extremely indirect, complex, poetic, as it seeks to show how much more there is to us than we realized. It may be of help to distinguish Frost's procedure from the tell-it-like-it-is one of Ezra Pound's. I am thinking of Pound's short manifesto, "The Teacher's Mission," not, to be sure, a letter, but no different from the kind of instruction furnished in the vigorous letters Pound wrote. He announces in his opening paragraph that "a nation's writers are the voltometers and steam-gauges of [a] nation's intellectual life," "recording instruments" that if they falsify reports can do great harm: "If you saw a man selling defective thermometers to a hospital, you would consider him a particularly vile kind of cheat," says Pound, then goes on to announce that this kind of cheating and falsifying has been going on for the last fifty years in America. He is there to blow the whistle, for he knows that "the mental life of a nation is no man's private property. The function of the teaching profession is to maintain the HEALTH OF THE NATIONAL MIND. He insists that it is only by comparing particular passages from artists that true knowledge may be gained, prejudices and shibboleths discarded, and a healthy society ensue—especially if (it is 1934) a vicious economic system is revamped. In this and other essays and in much of the poetry of the *Cantos,* Pound's is a mind without ambiguity, a mind that believes there are no two ways about anything—except the right and the wrong one—and that he is there to extirpate the latter since he knows what the former is. The village explainer, said Gertrude Stein, good if you are a village, if not, not. Of course there was a lot of "village" in American literary culture, and Pound's explanations of and to it were often tonic, to say the least. But they were utterly unlike Frost's approach to things, as demonstrated quite wonderfully in the following passage from a letter to Sidney Cox, a disciple of Frost's who sometimes tried to get a little closer to the master than Frost preferred:

> I'd like to put it to you while you are still young and developing your procedure if you don't think a lot of things could be found to do in class besides debate and disagree. Clash is all very well for coming lawyers politicians and theologians. But I should think there must be a whole realm or plane above that—all sight and insight, perception, intuition, rapture. . . . Having ideas that are neither pro nor con is the happy thing. Get up there high enough and the differences that make controversy become only the two legs of a body the weight of which is on one in one period on the other in the next. Democracy monarchy; puritanism paganism; form content; conservatism radicalism; systole diastole; rustic urbane; literary colloquial; work play. I should think too much of myself to let any teacher fool me into taking sides on any one of those oppositions.

I don't know what, if anything, Cox had said to provoke this train of thought; it surely has something to do with Frost's lingering battle with what he called "Meiklejaundice." Alexander Meiklejohn, the recent president of Amherst College, believed—as Frost saw it—in the replacing of "learning" by "thinking" and that—(Frost had written Untermeyer two years previously—"by thinking [the students] meant stocking up with radical ideas, by learning they meant stocking up with conservative ideas." In that letter Frost said about one of his Amherst classes, "We reached an agreement that most of what they had regarded as thinking . . . was nothing but voting—taking sides on an issue they had nothing to do with laying down."

The letter to Cox develops a notion of what might go on in the liberal arts classroom besides dialectic, and here it seems to me Frost's recommendation is wholly relevant to what still happens, or doesn't happen, in our college classrooms at the end of the century. The title of one of his prose essays is "Education by Poetry," but this letter to Cox proposes something like Education *as* Poetry. It is very different not only from the instructive debate and disagreement that Meiklejohn promoted or that a latter-day liberal philosopher like Martha Nussbaum espouses (she is for the classroom whose members confront one another with their different ideas and rationally work things out by active "thinking"). It is different also from the Poundian method of instruction, in which a specimen from, say, Tennyson is placed next to one of, say, Donne, by way of illustrating something about one poet's superior use of image or diction.

Frost's aspiration is rather toward what I once called "Elevated Play," and this play takes place both in a good poem (as he conceived it) and in the classroom when "a little run of sentences" shared between teacher and students comes into being. One of Frost's favorite words for it is "performance," and the successful poem was "some sort of achievement in performance" that went along with, was the product of, a "feat of association." As he put it in the *Paris Review* interview, "All thought is a feat of association: having what's in front of you bring up something in your mind that you almost didn't know you knew. Putting this and that together. That click." In just how many classes was the click likely to occur? There is no unimpeachable testimony about Frost's classroom, but one suspects it was a rather disorderly place, a kind of Liberty Hall where on many days the students, and probably their teacher, would be hard-pressed to say just what happened and whether it profited those in attendance. But of course such "failure" in education, in teaching, is routine only for those who, like Frost, pitch their aspiration very high indeed—choose something like a star.

3.

In the space remaining I want to consider three moments in Frost's correspondence where the writer, the teacher, the wily veteran of holding other people—enemies but friends as well—in play and out of gunshot, has been himself seriously wounded, stricken by the death of his nearest and dearest. Between 1934 and 1940 he lost three members of his family: his wife Elinor and their children, son Carol and daughter Marjorie. The first to go was Marjorie, who after giving birth to a daughter caught an infection in the hospital and struggled for seven weeks until she died. Frost wrote Untermeyer shortly after the event, and I excerpt the letter:

> No death in war could more than match it for suffering and heroic endurance. Why all this talk in favor of peace? Peace has her victories over poor mortals no less merciless than war. Marge always said she would rather die in a gutter than in a hospital. But it was in a hospital she was caught to die after more than a hundred serum injections and blood transfusions. . . . Never out of delirium for the last four weeks. . . . The only way I could reach her was by putting my hand backward and forward between us as in counting out and saying with over-emphasis *You*—and—*Me.* The last time I did that, the day before she died, she smiled faintly and answered "All the same," frowned slightly and made it "Always the same." . . . Everything she said, however quaint and awry, was of an almost straining loftiness. It was as if her ruling passion must have been to be wise and good, or it could not have been so strong in death. . . . We thought to move heaven and earth—heaven with prayers and earth with money. We moved Nothing. And here we are Cadmus and Harmonia not yet placed safely in changed forms.

There are many things at work in this moving letter, the noblest I know written after such an event, but three of them are of particular note. Humorous play, undesirable in such a situation, gets only the briefest nod, in that bitter joke about war and peace. (The allusion is to Milton's "To the Lord General Cromwell"—"Peace hath her victories / No less renowned than war.") The letter strives to bring out Marjorie's heroism by noting the quality and tone of her speech, even in delirium: the correction of "all" to "always" (in "always the same") and the insistence on the elevated nature of her discourse, which "was of an almost straining loftiness." "Get up there high enough," Frost said about the classroom, and you will put that class into another realm, above controversy and disagreement. Marjorie Frost was straining toward that realm, and her father tries to help her with his posthumous words. Finally, the man, the teacher, who has been able to move nothing, is left with only poetry as consolation, such as Callicles' beautiful lyric from Arnold's *Empedocles on Etna*:

> Far, far from here,
> The Adriatic breaks in a warm bay
> Above the green Illyrian hills; and there
> The sunshine in the happy glens is fair,
> And by the sea, and in the brakes.

There in those woods live "two bright and aged snakes," Cadmus and Harmonia, "In breathless quiet, after all their ills." They had seen, "In Thebes, the billow of calamity / Over their own dear children roll'd, / Curse upon curse, pang upon pang." But unlike it is in the poem, Frost and Elinor are still in Thebes, "not yet placed safely in changed forms." The effort in this remarkable letter is finally toward a kind of sad self-instruction, one that ends with a feat of association—education by poetry, education *as* poetry—both futile and yet all there is to reach out to: only that.

Four years later, in March of 1938, Elinor Frost died of a heart attack, and two weeks later her husband wrote the following words to his (at that time) good friend, Bernard DeVoto:

> I suppose love must always deceive. I'm afraid I deceived her a little in pretending for the sake of argument that I didn't think the world as bad a place as she did. My excuse was that I wanted to keep her a little happy for my own selfish pleasure. It is as if for the sake of argument she had sacrificed herself to give me this terrible answer and really bring me down in sorrow. She needn't have. I knew I never had a leg to stand on, and I should think I had said so in print.
>
> All the same I believe a lot of mitigating things, and anything I say against the universe must be taken with that qualification. I always shrank from hearing evil of poor little Edgar Allen Poe and my reason was when I come to search it out of my heart, that he wrote a prose poem out of those lovely old lines

> Stay for me there I will not fail
> To meet thee in the hollow vale.

What is more he used a cadence caught from the Exequy to make the whole of his poem The Sleeper. Never mind that he couldn't be tender without being ghoulish. You have to remember he was little Edgar Allen Poe.

To be fair in representing this four-paragraph letter, it has an opening paragraph about Frost's loneliness and a closing one about arrangements for the funeral in Amherst. But the really interesting parts are the two middle paragraphs I quoted, notable for the quite indirect way Frost conducts himself, first with the conceit that Elinor's death was a terrible answer to his own pretense that the world wasn't so bad a place as Elinor (an atheist) thought it was. "She needn't have" given him this terrible answer—needn't have died, as it were—since he knew the truth already. Then the business about Poe. Why, we might ask, as a more ordinary human being/letter writer might have done, didn't Frost just quote those two lines from King's "The Exequy" as illustrative of his private promise to Elinor—"Stay for me there; I will not fail / To meet thee in that hollow vale"? My, admittedly speculative, guess is this: that just as Poe "couldn't be tender without being ghoulish"—some lines from Poe's "The Sleeper" read as follows:

> My love, she sleeps! Oh may her sleep,
> As it is lasting, so be deep!
> Soft may the worms about her creep!

(one of the worst triplets I know of)—so Frost couldn't be tender without being just the least bit wicked, or at least humorously debunking of the competition, of some other poet's attempt to deliver moving utterance in the face of death. It won't do for Frost simply to elevate himself and Elinor through the nobility of Henry King's lines; he needs as well to cast an ironic eye on something lower down the scale, on the bathetic attempt of "little Edgar Allen Poe" to rise to authentic feeling. At the beginning of the Poe paragraph, Frost reminds DeVoto that he, Frost, "believes a lot of mitigating things," and that anything he says "against the universe must be taken with that qualification." If in these terms you believe a lot of mitigating things, then you are obliged to complicate and play around with any special posture of sorrow that might too nakedly and sincerely reveal your suffering soul. The effort at self-instruction is never more strongly made than in a seemingly final moment like this one, in which, as we like to say, words can't express how . . . , etc. But if poetry is the renewal of words, forever and forever, then expression is not to be given up on. "Humor is the most engaging cowardice," he had written, and even in these extreme moments of self-analysis something like humor shows its head. Or at least, some positive gesture of control, of mastery, in which the grief-stricken survivor may repose, momentarily, in a stay against confusion.

My final example is from a letter, again to Untermeyer, about Carol Frost's death by suicide (he shot himself). In the letter Frost writes "I took the wrong way with him. I tried many ways and every single one of them was wrong." He had tried to get his son to ease up on himself "and take life and farming off-hand." Frost then turns critically on his teacherly penchant: "Yesterday I was telling seven hundred Harvard freshmen how to live with books in college. Apparently nothing can stop us when we get going." But, he says, from now on he is "disqualified" from giving counsel. Then, following a description of Carol's son's heroic behavior in calling the police and standing by, Frost ends as follows:

> I failed to trick Carol or argue him into believing he was the least successful. That's what it came down to. He failed in farming and he failed in poetry (you may not have known). He was splendid with animals and little children. If only the emphasis could have been put on those. He should have lived with horses.

An absolutely astonishing thing, it has always seemed to me, to write about your dead son; but especially striking, or Frostian, in the way it recovers itself at the end, after castigating himself for failing in every way with that son and for pretending that he, Frost, can tell anyone how to live. Then to end the letter with that short, final pronouncement—"He should have lived with horses." "Never if you can help it write down a sentence in which the voice will not know how to posture *specially*," he said twenty-six years previously. I should hate to be challenged to describe the special posture of that last sentence about Carol, to weigh the exact tone in which it is to be said. Once again, Frost's practice was richer, more confusing, than his theory; and when, as with these three letters about the death of loved ones, the human being is most challenged to "say something" ("Say something we can take to heart and when alone repeat"), then the challenge to rise to something like poetry made itself poignantly felt. Poetry was a deed, he liked to say, and that

old-fashioned word crops up tellingly in some final lines from a poem, and
my conclusion today:

> Only when love and need are one,
> And the work is play for mortal stakes,
> Is the deed ever really done
> For heaven and the future's sakes.

New England Review, Spring 1999

A Witness Tree and Frost's Biography

In a 1975 essay, where I proposed Frost's "The Wind and the Rain" as his best "unknown" poem, I also claimed that the opening ten poems in *A Witness Tree*, 1942 ("The Wind and the Rain" is one of them) constitute the most impressive sequence of poems to be found anywhere in the poet's work. The sequence, I wrote, contained "extremes of delicate tenderness and of shocking brutality," and its pervasive melancholy reached a depth not hitherto encountered, or to be encountered again, in Frost. Two accounts of the biographical circumstances out of which *A Witness Tree* emerged have caused me and perhaps others to think again about that book, especially its opening sequence, and about the degree to which a poet's art can be more fully understood and appreciated when we learn more about the life experiences that surround and motivate it. My comments here are directed toward clarifying, or at least exploring further, these matters of literary and biographical criticism.

1.

I should begin by acknowledging with gratitude the first of these two accounts, Donald Sheehy's 1990 essay, "Refiguring Love: Robert Frost in Crisis, 1938–1942," by far the most subtle and penetrating treatment of Frost's life in the years following his wife Elinor's death in 1938, up through the publication of *A Witness Tree* in 1942. Those years include, most saliently, his relationship with Kathleen Morrison, officially his secretary, unofficially and surely his lover, and the most important "other" in his life in those four post-1938 years. During them, Frost composed some of the best poems in *A Witness Tree*, also his great essay "The Figure a Poem Makes" that prefaced his *Complete Poems* (1949). Mr. Sheehy's claim for the opening sequence in *A*

Witness Tree is similar to mine, but sets it more richly within the biographical nexus:

> Taken in its entirety, the opening section of *A Witness Tree* is a major triumph of Frost's career, rivaled in its sustained power and human complexity only by *North of Boston*. To read it exclusively as a record of personal experience is, of course, to diminish its poetic accomplishment, but to approach it without recognizing it to be a poetic chapter of personal crisis and resolution is finally to devalue the emotional and psychological achievement that it represents. If a career is a progress both public and private, then for no poet more than for Frost were the two moments so inextricably linked.

This is admirably and tactfully said, and it invites us to investigate more fully the extent to which it's possible to read this sequence "as a record of personal experience."

The other recent effort to make a case for *A Witness Tree* in its biographical circumstances is to be found in Jeffery Meyers's 1996 biography of Frost, whose most revelatory chapter is one that treats Frost's relations with Kay Morrison. What Sheehy's essay did with tact and complication, Meyers approaches in his typically blunt, free-swinging way, providing us with a you-are-there glimpse of the poet and his new love. In a key paragraph he describes the consummation of their relationship, and the single footnote to this paragraph refers us to Robert Newdick's unfinished biography of Frost—in which Frost spoke to Newdick about being "fearful" of the "arrangement with Kay"; also, more germanely, we are referred to Lawrance Thompson's unpublished "Notes on Frost." It is presumably from the latter source, unless Meyers is inventing things, that enables him to write as follows: "Troubled and excited by their long walks in the woods, [Frost] took along condoms (which he had been reluctant to use with Elinor)." There follows, and in quotation marks, "Then Frost began making passionate love to her and found that she was willing. . . . All he had to do was to take off her drawers and consummate an urge that seemed mutual." Meyers makes things even more exciting by alluding to a figure from "The Figure a Poem Makes": "Frost rode on her own melting." He concludes the paragraphs with two sentences I am unable to fathom: "Frost wrote that no one could object to being legally wed when the marriage was consummated naked in bed. But it is an entirely different matter when you have sex out of doors with no clothes off but drawers."

At the conclusion of this chapter about Kay Morrison—whose love affairs with Bernard DeVoto, a hired man named Stafford Dragon, and with Thompson himself are detailed—Meyers writes three-and-a-half pages in which he reveals "the real meaning of *A Witness Tree*." Of course such a phrase as "real meaning" should in itself be enough to alert readers that some activity other than sensitive criticism of lyric poetry is going on. As usual, Meyers is of no two minds in his judgments, telling us that the first ten poems of *A Witness Tree* under the rubric "One or Two," take up "the question of whether Frost will be alone or joined with Kay." (Meyers neglects to mention that Frost's previous collection, *A Further Range* [1936], organized its poems under the rubrics "Taken Doubly" and "Taken Singly.") "The ten poems express, directly or indirectly," Meyers goes on, "his love for Kay." Meyers thinks that the first of them, "The Silken Tent" "describes, with the greatest possible delicacy, the conflict between Kay's bondage and freedom as she is pulled, loosely by Ted in marriage or tightly by Frost in love." By way of indicating an aspect of the poem's great delicacy, Meyers instances Frost's use of the word "guys" ("So that in guys it gently sways at ease") as "a triple pun on ropes, mockery, and men." So much for delicacy. Among other poems mentioned by the biographer is "The Most of It," which "describes Frost's longing for and response to Kay." Presumably Frost identified with the great buck who "creates an orgasmic waterfall, so that his mate can make The Most of It." As for "Never Again Would Birds' Song Be the Same," its final line—"And to do that to birds was why she came"—"concludes on a bold sexual pun," suggesting that "as the lady's voice intensified the birds' song, so Kay's sexual passion inspired the words that made this poem."

"The poem must resist the intelligence / Almost successfully," wrote Wallace Stevens, and Frost himself either as man or poet had no wish to be too easily found out. In a letter of 1929 he addressed the question of how much personal material should go into one's poems:

> Everybody knows something has to be kept back for pressure and to anybody puzzled to know what I should suggest that for a beginning it might as well be his friends, wife, children, and self. . . . Poetry is measured in more senses than one: it is measured feet but more important still it is a measured amount of all we could say an we would. We shall be judged finally by the delicacy of our feeling of where to stop short.

The trouble with Meyers's account of these *Witness Tree* poems is that it doesn't know where or when to stop short. The poems don't resist his intelligence "almost successfully"; indeed they don't resist it at all. Or so he presumes, insofar as their real and true meaning can be grasped and stated as easily and quickly as it takes to desubtilize them by plugging their lines and imagined situations into real-life equivalents named "Kay," or "orgasmic waterfall." The question remains, what exactly has one understood by so penetrating the poems' language in order to extract their real meanings? The answer is, I'm afraid, not very much. And even Meyers would probably agree that establishing the crucial biographical importance of the love between Frost and Kay Morrison does not mean perforce that we must put a high value on the poems supposedly resulting from it. We might also remind ourselves that *A Further Range,* dedicated to Elinor Frost, contained poems as major to the Frost canon as "Two Tramps in Mud Time," "Desert Places," "The Strong Are Saying Nothing," "Neither Out Far Nor In Deep," "Design," "Provide, Provide," and the lovely, underappreciated "Iris by Night." It is not as if Frost in the 1930s had entered or declined into some rut in which he did no more than rework old themes or perform his bardlike functions as public entertainer.

Yet the sequence in *A Witness Tree* is something special. After two epigraph-like and rather enigmatic short poems, "Beech" and "Sycamore," we have the following: "The Silken Tent," "All Revelation," "Happiness Makes Up in Height for What It Lacks in Length," "Come In," "I Could Give All to Time," "Carpe Diem," "The Wind and the Rain," "The Most of It," "Never Again Would Birds' Song Be the Same," and "The Subverted Flower." After this sequence the final four poems in "One or Two" are a falling-off, although "The Quest of the Purple-Fringed," written much earlier, is exquisite. Perhaps the use of that adjective about this poem in praise of the orchis (or rather, as George Monteiro has suggested, the gentian), may suggest the difference between it and the earlier ten poems:

> I felt the chill of the meadow underfoot,
> But the sun overhead;
> And snatches of verse and song of scenes like this
> I sung or said.
>
> I skirted the margin alders for miles and miles
> In a sweeping line.

The day was the day by every flower that blooms,
But I saw no sign.

Yet further I went to be before the scythe,
For the grass was high;
Till I saw the path where the slender fox had come
And gone panting by.

Then at last and following him I found—
In the very hour
When the color flushed to the petals it must have been—
The far-sought flower.

There stood the purple spires with no breath of air
Nor headlong bee
To disturb their perfect poise the livelong day
'Neath the alder tree.

I only knelt and putting the boughs aside
Looked, or at most
Counted them all to the buds in the copse's depth
That were pale as a ghost.

Then I arose and silently wandered home,
And I for one
Said that the fall might come and whirl of leaves,
For summer was done.

With reference to the man's discovery of the flower he has been seeking, Frank Lentricchia called it "the purest celebratory moment in Frost's poetry," and surely it is a lovely one, a lyric instance of song that ends itself as fully as Frost ever ended any poem. It doesn't invite a search for some key that might unlock it; it is not a "conflicted" poem, and if, as Frost claimed, everything written is as good as it is dramatic, I take "The Quest of the Purple-Fringed" to be a small exception to that rule. Or at least its dramatic component—in the sense of some argument or complication going on between voices in the poem—is small: it has an "I" whom we can trust, who is telling us a small story of discovery that has a beginning, middle, and end. It *settles*, admittedly in a slightly melancholy way, rather than unsettles; in this it is distinguished from the earlier sequence in *A Witness Tree*.

Those ten poems are neatly divided in half, five of them with an "I" speaking out of a dramatic situation whose level of realization varies, though in none of them is it as strongly located in place and time as is "The Quest of the Purple-Fringed," or as it was in earlier Frost poems like "The Tuft of Flowers," "The Wood-Pile," or "Two Look at Two." Perhaps the most conventionally "dramatic" of the first-person poems from "One or Two" is "Come In," with its familiar prop of man confronting dark woods ("Into My Own" began all that) and debating whether or not to enter them. What's most familiar about "Come In" is the play of tone by which the speaker declines the thrushes' blandishment, first by making much of their song, although in a way that hedges slightly—"Almost like a call to come in / To the dark and lament"—then more emphatically declining the invitation in two stages: "But no, I was out for stars: / I would not come in," followed by the admission that it wasn't an invitation at all—"I meant not even if asked, / And I hadn't been." Joseph Brodsky made much of the poem, in a line-by-line exposition, but ended up with translating, disappointingly, the title into a meaning—"I am afraid, the expression 'come in' means die"—rather than pointing out how Frost the trickster once more, in the language of "One Step Backward Taken," "saved myself from going." For all its cleverness, I find "Come In" perhaps the most predictable poem in the sequence.

Of course, thinking sequentially about the ten poems isn't an inevitable or even necessary way of proceeding: they can be read individually, without regard to juxtapositions; or they can be put with poems from earlier volumes by way of establishing thematic and other relationships. But if we care at all about Frost's literary career with its order of published volumes, and if we take seriously the order in which, within the individual volume, Frost arranged the poems, then there appears to be visible a grouping of these ten poems by way of how they approach subject and reader. The first two, "The Silken Tent" and "All Revelation," are impersonal pronouncements that propose universal or mythic, revelatory disclosures. They are followed by five more personal disclosures, especially as concerned with the lyric speaker's feelings about present and past, time, change, and death. Four of these five are told in the first person; "Carpe Diem," told in the third person, nevertheless belongs with the others in tone and theme. Then follow "The Most of It," "Never Again Would Birds' Song . . .", and "The Subverted Flower": large, parable-like declarations that refuse to declare themselves quickly or unambiguously.

As for how these poems have been valued, relative to one another, the nod goes clearly to the third-person ones, which tend to get anthologized. (Interestingly enough, Randall Jarrell, in "To the Laodiceans," where he made lists of Frost's best and second-best poems, included only "The Most of It" and "I Could Give All To Time.") Richard Poirier has made the strongest case for the closing three poems, claiming that they suggest, as did Frost's earliest ones in *A Boy's Will*, "That consciousness is determined in part by the way one 'reads' the response of nature to human sound." He also claims that by placing "Never Again . . ." between "The Most of It" and "The Subverted Flower," "Frost once again revealed his deep commitment to married love as a precondition for discovering human 'embodiments' in nature." Poirier is eloquent about both "The Most of It" and "Never Again . . ." and his phrase, in referring to "The Most of It," about that poem's "large but wavering mythological context" suggests to me that, especially with reference to the second adjective, the formulation may be of use in thinking about not just "The Most of It" but the whole *Witness Tree* sequence.

"Wavering"—restless, playing or moving to and fro, swaying, hesitating, faltering, unsettled in opinion—these filial relatives in the "wavering" family have often been invoked by readers of Frost who are responding to the moral and human doubleness that informs his situations and concerns. The principle of wavering informs the last poem from Frost's earlier volume *Mountain Interval* (1916), "The Sound of the Trees":

> I wonder about the trees.
> Why do we wish to bear
> Forever the noise of these
> More than another noise
> So close to our dwelling place?
> We suffer them by the day
> Till we lose all measure of pace,
> And fixity in our joys,
> And acquire a listening air.
> They are that that talks of going
> But never gets away;
> And that talks no less for knowing,
> As it grows wiser and older,
> That now it means to stay.
> My feet tug at the floor
> And my head sways to my shoulder

> Sometimes when I watch trees sway,
> From the window or the door.
> I shall set forth for somewhere,
> I shall make the reckless choice
> Some day when they are in voice
> And tossing so as to scare
> The white clouds over them on.
> I shall have less to say,
> But I shall be gone.

From the beginning of his career, it was not only the sound of trees but more centrally the sound of sense that the real poet cultivated and the good ear-reader attended to, having acquired a listening air. There is no diminishment of this commitment to sound in the *Witness Tree* poems; indeed, the more we reread them, the more familiar we become with their "content," the more we marvel at the rhythmic life and variety of their sentence sounds. And the more they add up to an achieved "wavering," from one poem to the next and within individual poems. Which makes biographical accountings for them, such as Meyers's of how "Kay" inspired this one, or how that one is "about" Frost and her, less and less to the point.

2.

By way of demonstration, I shall make some remarks about the prosodic rhythms of some of these poems, neglecting—perhaps to the point of folly—their content, my purpose being no more or less than to bring out the strange originality, even for the always original Frost, of their aural inventiveness. In "The Silken Tent," we have an Elizabethan sonnet, consisting of a single sentence which, like the tent's central cedar pole, is "loosely bound," at least to the extent where Judith Oster, at the outset of her rigorously exhaustive grammatical analysis of it, admits that "the sentence comes perilously close to going out of control with the multiplication of subordinate clauses." Attempts to paraphrase "The Silken Tent," by way of unpacking its content, inevitably feel lame and uninteresting and tend to sound like this one: "The ties to 'everything on earth the compass round' reveals her awareness and concern for all people and the whole scope of experience." Let us call it rather a poem that's extremely beautiful as you perform it, say it aloud, but from which there is nothing to take away, at least insofar as thoughts about either a woman or a tent. In fact, you could even say there's no woman in the poem, and no tent either. For "The Silken Tent" is fictive music played out through a grammar complicated and elusive enough so as to provide no easy and direct way out to the world, to action, to human beings, to a woman—whether she is named Elinor Frost or Kathleen Morrison. In his preface to *King Jasper* Frost once considered the question of how or whether a poem leads to action. "Surely art can be considered good only as it prompts to action," says a young man to Frost. "How soon, I asked him. But there is danger of undue levity in teasing the young."

"All Revelation," which Reuben Brower writes well about in his still useful book, *The Poetry of Robert Frost,* is an especially challenging poem, certainly one I've never spoken about with confidence. In calling it Frost's "most symbolist poem," Brower seems to acknowledge the air of equivocation that characterizes it. Brower calls the final line—"All revelation has been ours"—an achieved answer "to the doubts and wonders expressed in the exclamation that concludes the second stanza—"Strange apparition of the mind!" But though he thinks "All Revelation" is "Frost's most vigorous answer to the larger question of the relation between mind and reality," he immediately qualifies the claim by finding an "irony" that remains in "asserting so limited a revelation." And he warns us not to suppose Frost "has reached a firm conclusion or final position in this or any poem."

This lack of a firm position is of course what so annoyed Yvor Winters about Frost's poetry generally, and though few of us are likely to accept his strictures on Frost's limitations as a poet, Winters identified something crucial to the poetry. It may be indicated by some words from a letter Frost wrote to Leonidas Payne in answer to Payne's question whether, in "Mending Wall," Frost's intention was fulfilled "with the characters portrayed and the atmosphere of the place." "I should be sorry," wrote Frost in reply, "if a single one of my poems stopped with either of those things—stopped anywhere in fact. My poems . . . are all set to trip the reader head foremost into the boundless." He went on in the same letter to speak of his "innate mischievousness," a mischievousness that we find in programmatically playful poems like "Mending Wall" or "Departmental," but just as much in the lyric soundings of affirmation—the large declarations in *A Witness Tree* about "countless silken ties of love and thought," or of how "All revelation has been ours." A reader who doesn't "trip" over them, not just on a first or second reading but permanently, won't be propelled into the boundless, a place where it's not reassuring to be, but which is our true and real destination in Frost's best work.

In "I Could Give All to Time," fifth poem in the sequence, a propelling into something like the boundless occurs in the third stanza, two earlier ones having described the inexorable leveling action of "Time" on all things. Now the man, just because he knows all about Time's effects, is impelled to resist them:

> I could give all to Time except—except
> What I myself have held. But why declare
> The things forbidden that while the Customs slept
> I have crossed to Safety with? For I am There,
> And what I would not part with I have kept.

In that final stanza we see those capital letters, hear that ringing human affirmation (which Randall Jarrell compared to the affirmation at the close of Yeats's "Dialogue of Self and Soul") but get tripped up when we attempt to specify or analyze exactly *what* has been declared. We are left instead with the mischievous, double-edged Customs metaphor and the unparticularized "what" of the final line—"And what I would not part with I have kept."

In that same essay of Jarrell's on Frost, he speaks of how some Frost poems might be considered "slight," yet says that the sigh we give after we read them isn't a slight one. In these terms, perhaps the two slightest poems in the sequence are "Happiness Makes Up in Height for What It Lacks in Length," and "Carpe Diem." Both are slim poems to the eye, twenty-four and twenty-six lines long, respectively, written in trimeter—"Happiness," in trimeter couplets; "Carpe Diem," unrhymed. Trimeter tends to be "monotonous," says *The Princeton Encyclopedia of Poetic Terms*, and its "tripping" potential, especially in couplets, might seem to make for triviality rather than for lyric depth. Yet Yeats uses it—without couplets—in some of his finest verse: in "Easter, 1916," "The Tower," part 3, and "In Memory of Eva Gore-Booth and Con Markiewicz." Frost had exploited trimeter with success in "The Sound of the Trees," and in "Happiness . . ." he also manages to portray a wavering and meditative imagination at work, arriving at "wisdom" over the course of, through the figure of, the poem ("It begins in delight and ends in wisdom. The figure is the same as for love"—"The Figure a Poem Makes"). He achieves his effects, in this poem, mainly by playing the sense units against the couplet rhyme and overriding the couplet's closure. It is an excellent me-

ter for poems designed to "trip the reader," since it has in its feel a "tripping"
rhythm, reluctant (in Frost's words) to "stop anywhere":

> Oh, stormy stormy world,
> The days you were not swirled
> Around with mist and cloud,
> Or wrapped as in a shroud,
> And the sun's brilliant ball
> Was not in part or all
> Obscured from mortal view—
> Were days so very few
> I can but wonder whence
> I get the lasting sense
> Of so much warmth and light.
> If my mistrust is right
> It may be altogether
> From one day's perfect weather,
> When starting clear at dawn,
> The day swept clearly on
> To finish clear at eve.
> I verily believe
> My fair impression may
> Be all from that one day
> No shadow crossed but ours
> As through its blazing flowers
> We went from house to wood
> For change of solitude.

It is a poem of three sentences, the first completing itself with line eleven, the
second with line seventeen, then sweeping on to end the third in line twenty-
four. As with the way the couplets succeed one another, there's a sense of irregularity about the sentence units, and both these qualities help to create
the illusion of a mind exploring the past, rather than owning an attitude toward it all made up in advance:

> I verily believe
> My fair impression may
> Be all from that one day
> No shadow crossed but ours
> As through its blazing flowers

> We went from house to wood
> For change of solitude.

No punctuation at the ends of lines; slightly off rhymes like "ours / flowers" and "wood / solitude": it is an example of what Milton in the note he added to *Paradise Lost* called "the sense variously drawn out from one Verse into another." In Frost's words from "The Figure a Poem Makes," a "clarification of life" has been achieved, but just barely, and not one, as he put it, "such as sects and cults are founded on."

Similarly with "Carpe Diem," which Poirier treats sketchily and rather condescendingly as "inadequate to the mixed complications it proposes to sort out." On the contrary, it seems to me a highly adequate way of thinking about time present and time past, and as with "Happiness . . . ," its adequacy—call it rather its beauty—is intimately connected with the movement of its verse. Instead of rhyming couplets, each line has a feminine ending (stress on the penultimate syllable) that contributes to the irregularity and informality of rhythm. There is also a playful jamming-up of words that echo, sometimes duplicate, one another—both within and at the ends of lines—perhaps by way of suggesting the crowding, confusing present that defeats our imagination. The poem opens with a rather creaky personification, "Age," who takes it upon himself to instruct a pair of youthful lovers (though not to their faces) on how to seize the day. After Age does his number, Frost takes over the poem and instructs Age on the way things happen in real life, rather than in the commonplaces and conventions of literary wisdom. Simple enough, but it is made complicated and complexly satisfying by the way the language is worked:

> Age saw two quiet children
> Go loving by at twilight,
> He knew not whether homeward,
> Or outward from the village,
> Or (chimes were ringing) churchyard.
> He waited (they were strangers)
> Till they were out of hearing
> To bid them both be happy.
> "Be happy, happy, happy,
> And seize the day of pleasure."
> The age-long theme is Age's.

> 'Twas Age imposed on poems
> Their gather-roses burden
> To warn against the danger
> That overtaken lovers
> From being overflooded
> With happiness should have it
> And yet not know they have it.
> But bid life seize the present?
> It lives less in the present
> Than in the future always,
> And less in both together
> Than in the past. The present
> Is too much for the senses,
> Too crowding, too confusing—
> Too present to imagine.

Three "happy"s succeeding one another in a line is almost enough in itself to demonstrate the fatuity of Age's advice, and immediately after he says his little piece, Frost plays with Age's personified status by turning it back on him—"The age-long theme is Age's"—before delivering a seven-line, unpunctuated sentence that makes a tricky, quite subtle sound of sense:

> 'Twas Age imposed on poems
> Their gather-roses burden
> To warn against the danger
> That overtaken lovers
> From being overflooded
> With happiness should have it
> And yet not know they have it.

The play with "overtaken / overflooded," the repetition at line ends of "have it," guarantees that Frost's sense will be sounder than Age's simple "Be happy, happy, happy." The play continues in the poem's final eight lines—another sentence—with "the present" concluding three of the lines and introducing something of an aural vertigo ("Too crowding, too confusing") from which we emerge only in the final line. There "present," now no longer "the present," becomes instead an adjective nested within the line and replaced at its end with the weighted verb "imagine." One thinks, by contrast, of the weighty, toneless annunciation of Eliot in the opening lines of "Burnt Norton"—"Time present and time past / Are both perhaps present in time future, / And time future contained in time past." Indeed a comparison between Eliot and Frost could well be conducted by juxtaposing "Carpe Diem" and the beginning of "Burnt Norton" ("He plays eucharist, I play euchre," Frost once said about his rival.)

No wonder then that Frost critics often look up from the analytical task, clear their throats, and admit how difficult it is to perform that task without heavy-handedness. Even so resourceful an interpreter as Poirier says at one point that some of Frost's poems are beyond us, not quite understandable. A recent essay on the poet by Jason Mauro speaks of how hard Frost makes us work, how the reader "must strain to keep things from splitting apart," and notes that Frost's genius "works at teasing out the duplicitous, complex nature of any utterance, any sentence, any word." Judith Oster, before launching her commentary on "The Most of It," says "This is a poem that eludes any definite interpretation or response." This elusiveness, which I believe to be part of the greatness of these *Witness Tree* poems, is there in "The Most of It" not despite but because of its forthright, declarative sequence of assertions, right down to "And that was all"—which says everything, and nothing in particular. It is there as well in "Never Again Would Birds' Song Be the Same," through the opposite of declarative forthrightness, in a sonnet that begins, cagily, "He would declare and could himself believe," then follows such conditionals with subtle qualifiers like "Admittedly," "Be that as may be," "Moreover," and "probably."

As for "The Subverted Flower," final poem in the sequence, Frost liked to say—in his "devilish" way and while not reading the poem aloud—that it was about "frigidity in women." The poem may have originated from an incident involving him and Elinor, though Poirier suggests that it is more a nightmare, a symbolic dream-enactment of something terrible. Meyers says that it "obliquely describes their passionate sex life" but doesn't demonstrate how it does so "obliquely." An important part of that obliqueness I attribute to its meter, which is again trimeter (not the four-stressed line Poirier hears), here rhymed in an irregular, off-balanced way that gives it the shimmering strangeness of fairy tale (I quote the poem's second half):

> It was then her mother's call
> From inside the garden wall
> Made her steal a look of fear
> To see if he could hear

And would pounce to end it all
Before her mother came.
She looked and saw the shame:
A hand hung like a paw,
An arm worked like a saw
As if to be persuasive,
An ingratiating laugh
That cut the snout in half,
An eye become evasive.
A girl could only see
That a flower had marred a man,
But what she could not see
Was that the flower might be
Other than base and fetid:
That the flower had done but part,
And what the flower began
Her own too meager heart
Had terribly completed.
She looked and saw the worst.
And the dog or what it was,
Obeying bestial laws,
A coward save at night,
Turned from the place and ran.
She heard him stumble first
And use his hands in flight.
She heard him bark outright.
And oh, for one so young
The bitter words she spit
Like some tenacious bit
That will not leave the tongue.
She plucked her lips for it,
And still the horror clung.
Her mother wiped the foam
From her chin, picked up her comb
And drew her backward home.

Brower, in his remarks on the poem, says that the girl's horrified "discovery" of her lover's sexuality is rendered with some of D. H. Lawrence's hard purity. Yet when he quotes to illustrate this, Brower omits the very lines that are to me supremely and relentlessly memorable:

A girl could only see
That a flower had marred a man,
But what she could not see
Was that the flower might be
Other than base and fetid:
That the flower had done but part,
And what the flower began
Her own too meager heart
Had terribly completed.

In one of his best formulations, Frost has said that there should be more than disagreement and debate in a classroom: "Clash is all very well for coming lawyers, politicians and theologians. But I should think there must be a whole realm or plane above that—all sight and insight, perception, intuition, rapture. . . . Get up there high enough and the differences that make controversy become only the two legs of a body." I have written before about Frost's "elevated play" and these lines from "The Subverted Flower," for all the terror of their content, are a great instance of both elevation and play, in the face of the unspeakable. At such a moment, and in these poems from the section of *A Witness Tree* most clearly connected to Frost's life experiences of love and death, he reaches the realm or plane where a reader, rather than explaining things biographically or otherwise, must prepare to be tripped head foremost into the boundless.

The Cambridge Companion to Robert Frost, edited by Robert Faggen.
New York: Cambridge University Press, 2001

Reading *The Waste Land* Today

My TITLE suggests the difficulty. Does anybody except some dutiful under-graduate in a modern poetry course actually sit down now and "read" *The Waste Land?* Eliot's poem is one of the most memorizable ever written; whole sections can be reeled off in an instant, with hardly a thought; every-one knows that Mr. Eugenides comes after Sweeney and Mrs. Porter and leads inevitably into the typist and her young man carbuncular. Such knowl-edge is easy to come by because of the many conveniently memorable shifts in verse form and speaking posture that provide landmarks, plain and un-avoidable; indeed, it exists so firmly in the ear that one's own determination to read it is often defeated when, as the eye moves carefully down the page, the poem suddenly begins to sing away beyond the reach of the sight, and it becomes impossible to attend visually to any one group of lines—we have already been swept well past them. A more disturbing possibility is that the poem does not exist to be read at all—as something with a beginning and end between which an action is presented—but is simply there to be under-stood or known as a cultural monument to Sterility, or what in my student days was called Lack of Communication in the Modern World. Comfortably ensconced in some college armchair, we regarded *The Waste Land* highly, learning from it that modern life was sordid and that people couldn't really communicate with each other, no matter what it may have seemed like. To-day the poem's immediate relevance to students, and perhaps to poetry readers in general, has decreased; in comparison with the instant life of a Frost lyric, or the quirky expansiveness of a Stevens meditation, *The Waste Land* seems—at least to an American reader—too much *the* modern poem to be quite believable. The same person who reads *Four Quartets* with de-voted attention and deeply stirred feelings may find himself embarrassed in dealing with the earlier poem. And as we disdain vulgar paraphrases of it—

a poem about sterility in the modern world—there is still something uncertain or unconvinced in our acceptance of it: what do we accept it *as*, what do we admire it *for*? An early reviewer who claimed, in mockery of Edmund Wilson's adulatory review of it, that the poem "is another agonized outcry, perhaps, against the Eighteenth amendment and the Volstead Act" can probably be refuted. But beyond that certainty, what possibilities remain for reading *The Waste Land*?

In trying to name some of these possibilities and address once more a famous, almost half-century-old poem, I may seem to be guilty of an attempt to set all previous commentators straight.[1] Let me emphasize, then, that I'm not interested in scoring off other critics, only in criticizing their vocabularies in the interests of one I think flexible enough to serve the poem in a way it deserves. Without dealing or dispensing with such matters as the Notes, anthropological dimensions, or the published manuscript, I want to plunge into the middle of the poem, indeed into the middle of "The Fire Sermon," and ask how a reader confronts such an ordinary event in *The Waste Land* as the Smyrna merchant:

> Unreal City
> Under the brown fog of a winter noon
> Mr. Eugenides, the Smyrna merchant
> Unshaven, with a pocket full of currants
> C.i.f. London: documents at sight,

---

1. The following is a list of the main critical accounts of *The Waste Land* that my argument deals with. The essays by Cleanth Brooks (in *Modern Poetry and the Tradition*) and F. R. Leavis (*New Bearings in English Poetry*) are well known, as is F. O. Matthiessen's *Achievement of T. S. Eliot*. Stephen Spender's remarks are in his *The Destructive Element*, and R. P. Blackmur's "Anni Mirabiles" (in which he discusses the poem) has been reprinted in A *Primer of Ignorance* (New York: Harcourt, Brace & World, 1967). Hugh Kenner's *The Invisible Poet* is probably the best single book on Eliot. Two approaches to *The Waste Land* are basically similar to the one I am suggesting, although their particular interests and emphases differ from mine: these are A. L. French's "Criticism and *The Waste Land*" in the Australian *Southern Review* (1964) and C. K. Stead's valuable account of Eliot in *The New Poetic* (London: Hutchinson University Library, 1964). Reference is also made to David Craig, "The Defeatism of *The Waste Land*," *Critical Quarterly* (Autumn 1960), and to John Peter, "A New Interpretation of *The Waste Land*," *Essays in Criticism* (July 1952). Essays by Richard Poirier ("T. S. Eliot and the Literature of Waste," *New Republic* [May 20, 1967]) and Hugh Kenner ("Eliot and the Literature of the Anonymous," *College English* [May 1967]) should also be looked up, though I have not made special reference to them in this essay.

Asked me in demotic French
To luncheon at the Cannon Street Hotel
Followed by a weekend at the Metropole.

This passage is probably not a prime candidate for inclusion in anybody's treasury of precious lines from Eliot's verse. They don't move us deeply, as the phrase is, don't—in Eliot's own language—arouse a host of inarticulate feelings. Confronting such a passage for the first time, a reader might scratch his head: nothing particularly difficult here, and yet—what does it add up to? A literary experience or just words? In the attempt to answer these questions he might well consult someone who knows, and if he turned to Cleanth Brooks's widely influential analysis in *Modern Poetry and the Tradition*, he would find the following exposition of Mr. Eugenides:

> He is a rather battered representative of the fertility cults; the prophet, the seer, with only one eye.
> The Syrian merchants, we learn from Miss Weston's book, were, along with slaves and soldiers, the principal carriers of the mysteries which lie at the core of the Grail legends. But in the modern world we find both the representatives of the Tarot divining and the mystery cults in decay. . . . Mr. Eugenides, in terms of his former function, ought to be inviting the protagonist into the esoteric cult which holds the secret of life, but on the realistic surface of the poem, in his invitation to "a weekend at the Metropole" he is really inviting him to a homosexual debauch. The homosexuality is "secret" and now a "cult" but a very different cult from that which Mr. Eugenides ought to represent. The end of the new cult is not life but, ironically, sterility.

Thus Mr. Eugenides fits beautifully into the overall scheme of the poem, which we may be impressed by if we regard Eliot's notes as profound, take Jessie Weston and the Fisher King very seriously, and believe that modern sterility should be opposed to ancient vitality. Cleanth Brooks warns us that his "scaffolding" is not to be substituted or mistaken for the poem itself; the difficulty comes when a reader who masters the scaffolding then goes back to the poem itself. Isn't it possible that his experience of Mr. Eugenides will be in exactly the terms Brooks has provided: "a rather battered representative of the mystery cults in decay" or (more excitingly) a "homosexual debauch"? The critic's feeling is that Mr. Eugenides *ought* to represent a better cult than he does, and that this is an unfortunate commentary on him and on the modern world. What he is "really" doing, in Brooks's terms, is something profoundly symptomatic, profoundly symbolic.

My question is whether there is a way of taking the literary event called Mr. Eugenides that grows naturally out of "the poem itself" rather than out of Eliot's notes or a scaffolding such as Brooks's. And my answer is a decided yes, if we let the poetry do its work on us while regarding these appendages with less than full seriousness. For, in himself, Mr. Eugenides is unforgettable—not as unforgettable perhaps as Sweeney, Mrs. Porter and her daughter, or the young man carbuncular, but reasonably so. The means employed to render him are extraordinarily simple and direct: what we know and remember of him is essentially put forth in two lines—"Unshaven, with a pocket full of currants / C.i.f. London: documents at sight"—and no one forgets these lines. Whether the currants are a symbol of the drying-up of fertility cults is a question that need not occur to the reader engaged in apprehending the Smyrna merchant unmistakably for what he is. This apprehending is an immediate, uncomplicated operation, just as is the ease with which one might play the game of naming some unknown but unmistakable figure in real life: "Look, there's Mr. Eugenides, see!" *The Waste Land* invites us to move out from its vividly drawn portraits into life, invites us to indulge ourselves in the delights of seeing how real people conform to their literary counterparts. The ease with which we can do this, and the admitted superficiality of the operation, is possible mainly because there is absolutely nothing to figure out about Mr. Eugenides. He has no character, no motives, no ghost in the poetic machine which constitutes his identity: "C.i.f. London, documents at sight." Is he "really" inviting the narrator to a "homosexual debauch"? The question is as beside the point as would be any attempt to penetrate the secrets of Mr. Eugenides' supposed character. What there is of him is all there, instantly revealed on the surface of the poem, then lodged in our ears and imaginations; a reader who follows Brooks's lead and says that the merchant is a "rather battered representative of the fertility cults" has committed himself to a story no more to be found in the poetry than is the homosexual debauch. Mr. Eugenides has his rightful importance in *The Waste Land*, but it is felt through the authority and skill by which the words interact to create him, rather than through some symbolic function he is supposed to fulfil. I would argue that an approach to the poem along "superficial" lines such as these is preferable for our own life as readers of it, and also very likely in harmony with what Eliot may have been up to in composing it. But before commenting further on other parts of the poem, and considering possible objections to this way of reading, I want to make some more general speculations about Eliot's creative art in the poem. If crucial moments can be accounted for in terms he himself has given us, there is no reason not to make use of them, especially if they seem more light and serviceable than the heavy anthropological baggage the poem has carried for so long.

I

Thirty years ago Stephen Spender observed that the characters in *The Waste Land* were psychologically crude, and without developing it he made the very telling remark that "one of the most astonishing things about Eliot is that a poet with such a strong dramatic style should seem so blinded to the existence of people outside himself." Yet, Spender continued, "the effect of his poetry depends very largely on his blindness." A. L. French has put a similar charge to the poem by questioning just how much of "modern life" it is really interested in. Isn't there a difference, Mr. French asks, between a poem that is seriously engaged by, interested in, exploratory of, the phenomena of modern life, and one which uses the phenomena to achieve certain highly stylized poetic effects whose brilliance is not in the least a condition of the poet's moral insight into the society he looks at? I believe that both Spender and A. L. French direct our attention to matters the poet was himself concerned with until he wrote the poem and effectively concealed them behind a smoke-screen of notes. The best criticism of *The Waste Land* was written by Eliot *before* he wrote the poem itself—let alone the notes—and is to be found in the essay on Ben Jonson published originally in November 1919 and collected in *The Sacred Wood* a year later.

It will be remembered that Eliot calls Jonson an unread classic of English literature because his poetry is "of the surface": unlike Shakespeare's "the polished veneer of Jonson reflects only the lazy reader's fatuity; unconscious does not respond to unconscious; no swarms of inarticulate feelings are aroused." As for the relation of this poetry to "life": "Jonson's drama is only incidentally satire, because it is only incidentally a criticism upon the actual world." Eliot went on to argue that such satire issues from no precise emotional attitude or precise intellectual criticism of the actual world; when compared with Swift, Molière, the Flaubert of *Education Sentimentale*, all to one degree or another manifesting a ruling faculty of "critical perception, a commentary upon experienced feeling and sensation," Jonson's relation to the actual world is more "tenuous" and therefore less directly satirical. Eliot calls his art "creative" satire, an art that is superficial in the best sense since

> the superficies of Jonson is solid. It is what it is: it does not pretend to be another thing. . . . We cannot call a man's work superficial when it is the creation of a world; a man cannot be accused of dealing superficially with the world he himself has created; the superficies is the world. Jonson's characters conform to the logic of the emotions of their world. It is a world like Lobatchevsky's; the world created by artists like Jonson are like systems of non-Euclidean geometry. They are not fancy, because they have a logic of their own; and this logic illuminates the actual world, because it gives us a new point of view from which to inspect it.

It will be noted that Eliot doesn't attempt to say how the new point of view illuminates the actual world, nor can he describe the exact nature of that "energy"—rather than "human life"—which elsewhere in the essay he says informs Jonson's characters. And we notice language reaching its limits as he makes a final attempt to summon up the reality of Jonson's creative satire and discovers "a kind of power . . . which comes from below the intellect, and for which no theory of humours will account." No theory of anything, it might be added; but the "kind of power" is creatively evoked by Eliot's own prose as it salutes the "titanic show" that is Jonson's work, a show which in its "brutality, lack of sentiment, polished surface, handling of large bold designs in brilliant colours . . . ought to attract about three thousand people in London and elsewhere."

Even with the boost Eliot's essay gave him, Ben Jonson has not in the last fifty years attracted three thousand people in London or elsewhere. But, of course, Eliot was not simply talking about Jonson here; and the poem which appeared three years after the essay has attracted a good many more than three thousand readers. Let us therefore appropriate Eliot's language about Jonson and apply it to *The Waste Land:* the poem then becomes a titanic show, run by a showman who draws upon resources in the language and in himself of great power and energy. In this titanic show, characters and scenes are drawn in strong and simple outlines; a solid superficies presents itself for inspection, behind which no murky and ambiguous depths beckon to be plumbed. If this showman is a satirist, he is a creative one, his satire only incidentally a criticism of life, of the "modern" world, and springing from no precise intellectual criticism of that world. To read such a poem adequately we must become correspondingly creative, our criticism of the poem a commentary on experiencing the imaginative life of a particular artifact. We cannot fall back on what Eliot is saying about the modern world, because that "saying" is wholly identified with the order of words that is *The Waste Land*. And efforts to extract meanings from the poem by translating events into more general intellectual and symbolic terms would be performed at the peril of making the tenuous and indirect relation between poem and world much more direct than it is.

II

The objection can be raised that, whether or not we view the poem as springing from some precise intellectual criticism of the modern world (as Eliot claimed Jonson's satire did not), it most certainly does issue in a precise emotional attitude toward that world (as Eliot also claimed Jonson's did not). That is, what holds together the various portraits or events in *The Waste Land* is Eliot's repulsion or horror or disgust at the facts of post-war civilization; furthermore, that Mr. Eugenides and the other characters are static assemblages of fragments that have been carefully selected and juxtaposed, much as are the portraits in an Augustan satire, to make a general point about something or other.[2] Any lack of a third dimension, of psychological depth, would simply be a consequence of the method: we are not meant to become involved in understanding Mr. Eugenides, since "he" is but a highly selective group of details designed to make a vivid point about modern life. By this argument, a precise intellectual and emotional attitude or criticism would emerge from the careful way in which all the portraits were integrated to form a consistent tone toward the horror of it all. By way of meeting this objection, we can note that Eliot, in writing about Jonson's satire, was at pains to express his own sense of Jonson's selectivity—Eliot calls it "simplification":

> The simplification consists largely in reduction of detail, in the seizing of aspects relevant to the relief of an emotional impulse which remains the

2. For an excellent account of Augustan satiric technique, see William H. Youngren, "Generality in Augustan Satire," in *In Defense of Reading*, ed. Reuben A. Brower and Richard Poirier (New York: Dutton, 1962).

same for that character, in making the character conform to a particular
setting. This stripping is essential to the art, to which is also essential a flat
distortion in the drawing; it is an art of caricature, of great caricature, like
Marlowe's. It is a great caricature which is beautiful; and a great humour,
which is serious. The "world" of Jonson is sufficiently large; it is a world of
poetic imagination; it is sombre. He did not get the third dimension, but
he was not trying to get it.

Nor was Eliot: consider the lines depicting the "neurasthenic" lady from the
first part of "A Game of Chess":

> Above the antique mantel was displayed
> As though a window gave upon the sylvan scene
> The change of Philomel, by the barbarous king
> So rudely forced; yet there the nightingale
> Filled all the desert with inviolable voice
> And still she cried, and still the world pursues,
> "Jug Jug" to dirty ears.
> And other withered stumps of time
> Were told upon the walls; staring forms
> Leaned out, leaning, hushing the room enclosed.
> Footsteps shuffled on the stair.
> Under the firelight, under the brush, her hair
> Spread out in fiery points
> Glowed into words, then would be savagely still.

The way in which "she" conforms to her particular setting is unmistakable;
the "distortion" is to be found in the artfully aggressive manipulation and
"stripping" of the actual world into an awful coherence, into a "sombre"
world of poetic imagination. If getting the third dimension in art involves an
achieved illusion of sustained life, or of a character who acts and suffers, who
changes and modifies himself in a way we often describe by the term "dramatic," then Eliot, like Jonson, doesn't get the third dimension. As the lady's
hair glows into fiery points, then into the fiery words that follow ("My nerves
are bad to-night. Yes, bad. Stay with me. / Speak to me. Why do you never
speak. Speak."), while the narrator remembers that those are pearls that were
his eyes and goes on to sing the Shakespeherian Rag, our sympathetic interests and involvements are severely limited, in fact simply not there at all. Instead we are thrilled and excited by the alternation of sharp and hopeless
questions with knowing and hopeless narrative comment; any developing

sense of sympathetic engagement with "her" situation is absent. Abruptly after a few more lines, her act in the titanic show concludes itself: we move on to hear about Lil's husband without so much as a backward glance at the poor lady with her hair down.

But then doesn't this portrait of a lady make a vivid point about modern life, about the hopelessness and sterility of a certain kind of overbred, stifling, enclosed existence? Certainly the vividness with which she is rendered is not in dispute; the question is whether it is possible for vivid verbal creations of this sort—in Eliot's own critical terms, the caricatures of creative satire—to be diagnostic of the actual world as well, to embody or represent or enact some mature criticism of life? It is probably in the typist scene from "The Fire Sermon" where this question can be best confronted. Readers who expect or demand the third dimension in poetry might well be bothered by the way in which the ladies in "A Game of Chess" are neatly juxtaposed—high and low—and then bid goodnight to, their act concluded. But the typist passage—the point at which the poem clicks along most brilliantly and is most memorizable—is the point above all where readers have been most outraged at the human inadequacy of what they see as Eliot's attitude toward love in the modern world. In an essay titled "The Defeatism of *The Waste Land*," the post-Lawrentian critic David Craig points out how the "sordid" details of the typist passage are out of key with the ornamental resonance of its diction, thus that Eliot's "conscious literariness is working . . . more to hold at arm's length something which he personally shudders at than to convey a poised criticism of behaviour." Leaving aside the matter of where in modern poetry we would look to find poised criticism of behavior, or indeed whether it is essential to good poetry, let me say that what Craig sees as the crippling defect in Eliot's poem is to me its radical virtue. Here are the lines:

> Out of the window perilously spread
> Her drying combinations touched by the sun's last rays,
> On the divan are piled (at night her bed)
> Stockings, slippers, camisoles, and stays.
> I Tiresias, old man with wrinkled dugs
> Perceived the scene, and foretold the rest—
> I too awaited the expected guest.
>
> He, the young man carbuncular, arrives,
> A small house agent's clerk, with one bold stare,

One of the low on whom assurance sits
As a silk hat on a Bradford millionaire.
The time is now propitious, as he guesses,
The meal is ended, she is bored and tired,
Endeavours to engage her in caresses
Which still are unreproved, if undesired.
Flushed and decided, he assaults at once;
Exploring hands encounter no defence;
His vanity requires no response,
And makes a welcome of indifference.

   . . . .

She turns and looks a moment in the glass,
Hardly aware of her departed lover;
Her brain allows one half-formed thought to pass:
"Well now that's done: and I'm glad it's over."
When lovely woman stoops to folly and
Paces about her room again, alone,
She smooths her hair with automatic hand,
And puts a record on the gramophone.

It is most certainly true that the passage puts forth no "poised criticism of behaviour" of the sort Craig expects satirists to provide. But is anything being "satirised" here at all in a critical or moral way? Whether or not Eliot "personally shudders" at clerks or typists, that shudder is not there in the verse; and so the reader isn't tempted to shake his head sadly over a sterile or loveless union. On the contrary, we experience a flawless, stunning presentation of behavior: simplified, caricatured if you will, giving us no complex insights into either typist or young man, setting forth no precise intellectual or emotional attitude toward them, indulging in no moral censure or praise of them. The poetry is of great beauty, using that unfashionable word in the sense of Eliot's own description of Jonson's creation: "It is a great caricature which is beautiful."

To praise the typist passage in these ways is the opposite of admiring its "style" while admitting it to be unsatisfactory in human terms; it is intensely satisfactory in the way all beautiful pieces of imaginative work are. Only when a critic is bent on translating the poetry into what it *really* is saying about people in the modern world do "details" become "sordid," and the verse is accounted for as prompted by a shudder of distaste. In this passage there is nothing sordid, nothing to avert our eyes from, to feel squeamish in the face of. As Hugh Kenner exclaimed about the young man carbuncular: "If he existed, and if he read these words, how must he have marvelled at the alchemical power of language over his inflamed skin!" The exclamation could be extended to *The Waste Land* as a whole, since it is a poem that demands no response so much as one that is akin to the heroic admiration we give Volpone or Mosca or Sir Epicure Mammon—literary creations no more representative of the actual world of Ben Jonson's time than are Madame Sosostris, Mr. Eugenides, and the typist representative of Eliot's time. It is needless to remind ourselves how much modern literature is built on the third-dimensional principle that to know all is to forgive all: Eliot's art in *The Waste Land* is in this sense non-psychological; it lacks complex diagnosis of the modern world and sympathetic insight into the citizens of it. But the alternative is not some airily aesthetic posture in which we simply amuse ourselves, since what Eliot has done in this passage, and in other typical ones from the poem, is so to elevate the mundane, the unheroic ("Flushed and decided, he assaults at once, / Exploring hands encounter no defence") as truly to make us admire something for the first time. Where but in this poet, so often patronized or chastised for his ascetic and stuffy disregard of sex, could one find a comparable presentation of a sexual encounter? Yeats would richly mythologize or dramatically moralize it; Stevens would exfoliate it into sheer sound, or conjure over it; Frost (in "The Subverted Flower") would darken it, harshen it; Williams, for all his doctrinal immediacy, would use it for something beyond itself. We don't need to pick sides, only to admit that Eliot's presentation is what it is—a vibrant instance of the kind of poetic knowledge that suffices.

Other consequences follow from reading *The Waste Land* in the spirit I have been suggesting. Just as we should be wary about claiming, without plenty of qualifications, that the poem "satirizes" anybody or criticizes modern life, so the whole issue of present and past, modern versus ancient times—the "what have we lost?" syndrome—deserves as much skepticism directed at it. Red herrings such as whether the Thames was really idyllic or really dirty in Spenser's time ("Sweet Thames run softly till I end my song") can be dispensed with once we admit how equally beautiful, cigarette ends and all, the Thames is made by Eliot's poem: ("The river's tent is broken: the last fingers of leaf / Clutch and sink into the wet bank. The wind / Crosses the brown land, unheard. The nymphs are departed.") Another Thames that never was on sea or land. But if few critics now claim that the poem casts it-self wholly on the side of ancient glories against modern sordidness, the im-plications of seeing the poem in these terms still haven't been faced. John Pe-ter asks whether the Elizabeth and Leicester section of "The Fire Sermon" is "a simple contrast between Elizabethan glamour and modern drabness or a parallel between Elizabethan coquetry and modern philandering":

> Elizabeth and Leicester
> Beating oars
> The stern was formed
> A gilded shell
> Red and gold
> The brisk swell
> Rippled both shores
> Southwest wind
> Carried down stream
> The peal of bells
> White towers
> > Weialala leia
> > Wallala leialala

The question is an inescapable one if we approach the poem ready to ma-nipulate the ancient-modern terms; but Peter can answer it only by saying that his quite different interpretations are not "mutually exclusive." The real question is, mutually exclusive or not, do these interpretations, or any inter-pretation, bear any possible relevance to the crisp, slender music of the sec-ond Rhinemaiden's poetry whose relation to the actual world is even more tenuous and indirect than that of the typist or the neurasthenic lady? It may well be that responsive assimilation of a poetic moment such as this one must be conducted in ways that have little or nothing to do with interpreta-tion as it is often brought to bear on modern verse. And F. O. Matthiessen's often-quoted phrase about *The Waste Land* exhibiting a "music of ideas" should be employed only after admitting how very unlike "ideas" are what emerge from the portraits and passages of this poem.

With this caveat in mind we can bring together and conclude these sug-gestions about reading *The Waste Land* by inspecting the climactic moment in "What the Thunder Said," where some awful resolution seems to be at hand:

What is that sound high in the air
Murmur of maternal lamentation
Who are those hooded hordes swarming
Over endless plains, stumbling in cracked earth
Ringed by the flat horizon only
What is the city over the mountains
Cracks and reforms and bursts in the violet air
Falling towers
Jerusalem Athens Alexandria
Vienna London
Unreal

A woman drew her long black hair out tight
And fiddled whisper music on those strings
And bats with baby faces in the violet light
Whistled, and beat their wings
And crawled head downward down a blackened wall
And upside down in air were towers
Tolling reminiscent bells, that kept the hours
And voices singing out of empty cisterns and exhausted wells

The last eight lines were once chosen by R. P. Blackmur as a great example of what he termed the "sensual metaphysics" of poetry. He testified to their effect in the following manner: "The exegetes tell us, and it is true, that we are in the Chapel Perilous and the Perilous Cemetery is no doubt near at hand, and it may be as one of the exegetes say that we hear something like the voice of John the Baptist in the last line. But for myself, I muse and merge and ache and find myself feeling with the very senses of my thought greeting and cries from all the senses there are." Whether you admire (as I do) this flight, or deplore it as a piece of Blackmurian doubletalk, it gets at the central issue the poem presents to the reader: how the exciting brilliance of Eliot's language overwhelms and renders of little account not only direct moral commentary about civilization, the modern world, but also the mythic structures that provide the poem's scaffolding. It is "no doubt true" we are in Chapel Perilous, but of course the whole force of Blackmur's rhetoric is to suggest that we aren't there in any sense that matters. Instead the astonishing mingling of beauty and terror as the bats crawl head downwards and the towers toll upside down is the creation of a verse that unites great impulsive movement with artfully poignant and clinging rhymes (towers / hours—the voice lingers over the words but also pushes ahead) to achieve a toneless rhythm of annunciation. There is nothing complex to puzzle out, no deep idea to be gradually understood through repeated readings: it is all grandly there. In Eliot's language about Jonson, it forms a "large bold design in brilliant colours" that brings together in harrowing metamorphosis various elements of the titanic show we have witnessed.

Whether the rains arrive too late or just in time, whether significance should be attributed to the narrator's shoring fragments against his ruin— these are questions it would clearly be difficult to answer, and perhaps they need not even be asked. What the thunder finally says is not quite as impressive as what the poem has been saying all along, particularly at the climactic upside-down vision just considered. And if "Shantih shantih shantih" fails to incorporate the wisdom of the East into the poem, it seems ungracious to ask for something more adequate. Reading *The Waste Land* is not like reading a dramatic novel or lyric in which we keep pressing on to find out what happens next. And so if certain parts of the poem are weaker than other parts, they need not be the occasion for overmuch regret or head-shakings about lack of unity. For all its obvious difference, Wordsworth's *Immortality Ode* provides a useful analogue of a poem all of whose parts cannot be equally admired and also of a poem which we do not read from beginning to end with a sense of ever widening or deepening expectation and knowledge, though Wordsworth probably meant it to be read that way. Those who object to the public postures of the ode are saying that they are uneasy about the way it puts Wordsworth on the stage as a performer. But if we love parts of the poem enough, it's likely we may come to have feelings about blemishes ("a six years' darling of a pygmy size") that are not simple ones of either approval or disdain. Finally, I think we can take F. R. Leavis's famous remark about *The Waste Land* exhibiting no progression in a somewhat different sense than he meant it, understanding it not merely as a description of how the poem lacks a dramatic development, but as a name for the poem's formal cause as well. It is the nature of creative satire, animated by energy and lacking the third dimension, to lack also the kinds of human resolutions we look ahead to, live through, in more complexly human kinds of literature. After all is said and done, *The Waste Land*, like Eliot's idea of poetry in general, "is what it is and not another thing." And Blackmur reminds us that, for

Eliot, poetry was also a mug's game and a superior form of amusement. With these definitions in mind, when we listen again to the voices crying out on life through the poem in their bizarre and unforgettable ways, we are moving closer to that thing *The Waste Land* is.

Essays in Criticism, April 1969

Richard Wilbur: *The Beautiful Changes*
Fifty Years On

THE POET we honor today published his first book of poems fifty years ago this month when Reynal & Hitchcock brought out *The Beautiful Changes*. Its forty-three poems constituted a claim on poetry readers' attention that the career of books to follow would only intensify. In the course of his review, a few years later, of Richard Wilbur's second volume, *Ceremony*, Randall Jarrell was (as ever) witty at the expense of what he thought—in that volume—was the poet's over-cautiousness, his willingness to settle, in football terms, for six or eight yards rather than go for the long gain. Yet in the course of lecturing Wilbur, Jarrell called him "the best of the quite young poets writing in this country." Jarrell made a list of older poets that included Robert Lowell, Elizabeth Bishop, Karl Shapiro, Theodore Roethke, and Delmore Schwartz (although Lowell was only four years Wilbur's senior), and he might have added John Berryman and himself to the list, although in 1947 neither had published poems that compared in density, wit, and formal grace with the ones in *The Beautiful Changes*.

But I don't plan to speak much as the literary historian, or even as the critic concerned to provide new readings and interpretations of old poems. These remarks will be selectively appreciative rather, brief rather than lengthy, and begin with my discovery of Mr. Wilbur back in the early 1950s. I can't remember the first poem that really registered with me but suspect it was "Museum Piece," from *Ceremony*:

> The good gray guardians of art
> Patrol the halls on spongy shoes,
> Impartially protective, though
> Perhaps suspicious of Toulouse.

Here dozes one against the wall,
Disposed upon a funeral chair,
A Degas dancer pirouettes
Upon the parting of his hair.

See how she spins! The grace is there,
But strain as well is plain to see.
Degas loved the two together;
Beauty joined to energy.

Edgar Degas purchased once
A fine El Greco, which he kept
Against the wall beside his bed
To hang his pants on while he slept.

That seemed to me and still seems invigoratingly irreverent, celebrating the beauty and energy of art that is too much for its good gray guardians; celebrating also the casual irreverence with which a genius of energy like Degas treats a masterwork. But it was that last line—"To hang his pants on while he slept"—that gave me a kick. The same sort of kick delivered by lines, also from a quatrain poem, this one in *The Beautiful Changes,* called "Folk Tune." It begins with Paul Bunyan, and goes on to consider some other legendary characters:

When Bunyan swung his whopping axe
The forests strummed as one loud lute,
The timber crashed beside his foot
And sprung up stretching in his tracks.

He had an ox, but his was blue.
The flower in his buttonhole
Was brighter than a parasol.
He's gone. Tom Swift has vanished too,

Who worked at none but wit's expense,
Putting dirigibles together
Out in the yard, in the quiet weather,
Whistling behind Tom Sawyer's fence.

I found a fine expense of wit in having Tom Swift put his dirigible together behind Tom Sawyer's fence, so I came originally to Wilbur by an unlikely way, by way of satiric, punchy poems in quatrains not all that much different from T. S. Eliot's sharp wit in his own quatrain poems.

When I reached Harvard graduate school in 1954, Wilbur was teaching at Wellesley and preparing for publication the poems that would make up his third, influential book, *Things of This World* (1956). He was also doing a fair number of poetry readings in the Boston area—at Harvard's Sanders Theater, at the Poet's Theater in Cambridge, at Wellesley College. It was of course the great age of poetry readings (just as the '50s were a great age for literary study), and I remember how much I looked forward to them—to hearing, as I did, Frost, Eliot (just missed Wallace Stevens), Marianne Moore, William Carlos Williams, Robert Graves, John Crowe Ransom, Robert Penn Warren, Robert Lowell—but to Wilbur more often than any of these, and always with the sense that I'd gotten my money's worth (of course the readings were free) and that each of his successive performances was better than the one before. The poems I heard at those readings in the '50s were, predominantly, the ones he'd just been writing and that were about to appear in *Things of This World:* "Altitudes," with its evocation of Emily Dickinson and "a wild shining of the pure unknown / On Amherst"; "Piazza de Spagna"; "Mind," the poem after Francis Jammes's "A Prayer to Go to Paradise with the Donkeys"; "A Baroque Wall-Fountain in the Villa Sciarra"; and above all, the title poem—"Love Calls Us to the Things of This World." So even though I owned a secondhand copy of *The Beautiful Changes* (purchased for a buck from the library of one Scott Spear, whoever he may be), I knew most of the poems in that book far less well than I did later ones.

Indeed, when I began to prepare these remarks, I was amazed at how inadequate my grasp was of much in *The Beautiful Changes,* how carelessly and lazily I had read and reread many of the poems. And how too credulously I had accepted Jarrell's account—admittedly, he had *Ceremony* particularly in mind—of how much of Wilbur's poetry "consents too easily to its own unnecessary limitation." Addressing Wilbur in the spirit of William Blake, Jarrell wrote: "You never know what is enough unless you know what is more than enough." In fact, reading through *The Beautiful Changes* brings the discovery of how much "more than enough" its forty-two poems contain. Blake said in another of his proverbs of Hell, "The road of excess leads to the palace of wisdom," and in this first volume Wilbur took long steps down that road. His first published poems, in their diction and vocabulary (have you used "hebetude," "legerity," "bavardage," "danseuse," "maculate," "retractility," "rogaume," or "ponderation" recently?), their elaborateness and variety of stanza form, are not only excessive, they are often about the idea of excess—of just how much is enough, or too much, or too little. (Blake's final proverb of Hell is "Enough / or Too Much.")

"Praise in Summer," the book's penultimate poem, is a good example of such seeing doubly:

> Obscurely yet most surely called to praise,
> As sometimes summer calls us all, I said
> The hills are heavens full of branching ways
> Where star-nosed moles fly overhead the dead;
> I said the trees are mines in air, I said
> See how the sparrow burrows in the sky!
> And then I wondered why this mad *instead*
> Perverts our praise to uncreation, why
> Such savor's in this wrenching things awry.
> Does sense so stale that it must needs derange
> The world to know it? To a praiseful eye
> Should it not be enough of fresh and strange
> That trees grow green, and moles can course in clay,
> And sparrows sweep the ceiling of our day?

This is the poem of a man who, on army service in World War II, packed up in his old kitbag (along with his troubles) a copy of Gerard Manley Hopkins's poems. But it seems a shade more mischievous than its precursor. Like so many of Wilbur's efforts, back then and later on, it presents a case—how poets praise summer in extravagant metaphor—then, in the wondering seventh line, seems to turn on such wrenching things awry in favor of sanity, a just appreciation of things as they are, of the sheer facts that trees grow green and moles do their work in the earth. But do moles really "course in clay?" A little derangement there, and the final line that looks to be in apposition to the previous one deranges things even more: "And sparrows sweep the ceiling of our day." It's not just that there are wrenchings of sound as "sparrows" "sweep" "ceiling," but that the metaphor proposed is every bit as extravagant, as "deranging" as the earlier ones that were rejected. The doubleness of "sweep" here is surely mischievous, since we don't just think of sparrows in flight but think also of how something the opposite of a floor is getting swept by them. Almost unbeknownst to itself, the poetic imagination improves on nature rather than simply mirroring it—maybe even blasphemes by saying more than should be said (Enough / or Too Much). And of course there is a great deal more that *could* be said in praise of the play made with the sonnet structure, the ingenuity of the rhyme scheme and so forth.

It may not have been until the publication in the 1970s of *Opposites* (and later *More Opposites*), children's poems to be read by adults, that Wilbur's humor and verbal fun became fully apparent. (*The Disappearing Alphabet* [1997] is a further demonstration of his humorous mastery.) But from the beginning, he has written with a comic wit in which serious "themes"—like the one about what imagination adds to reality—are worked up in a purely pleasurable way. I have in mind, as example of this sort of wit, "The Walgh-Vogel," a poem about a large, heavy, flightless bird now extinct, if it were not for the poet who brings him/her back to life:

> More pleasurable to look than feed upon,
> Hence unconserved in dodo-runs, the round,
> Unfeathered, melancholy, more than fifty pound
> Dodo is gone,
>
> Who when incarnate wore two token wings
> And dined on rocks, to mock at mockeries.
> Empowered now by absence, blessed with tireless ease,
> It soars and sings
>
> Elated in our skies, wherever seen.
> Absolute retractility allows
> Its wings be wavy wide as heaven; silence endows
> Its hoots serene
>
> With airy spleenlessness all may unhear.
> Alive the dodo strove for lack of point,
> Extinct won superfluity, and can disjoint
> To joy our fear.
>
> Dive, dodo, on the earth you left forlorn,
> Sit vastly on the branches of our trees,
> And chant us grandly all improbabilities.

"Improbabilities," "superfluity," "disjoint," "endows," "retractility," "empowered," and "unconserved"—this melancholy bird is treated in a diction that does it proud, so proud one doesn't want to be superior and call the mode Mock Heroic. The myth of how, after the dodo left us, our earth was as forlorn as it feels at the end of Keats's Nightingale ode—the lovely understanding of the dodo's melancholy strivings, its lack of "point"—is set forth in ample, spacious stanzas that sometimes run on from one to the next, then suddenly come to a full stop at unobvious places. Frost talked about how he loved to *lay* the words into the poetic line, and one feels such a pleasure here in the beautifully accurate placement and pace of language that so magnificently preserves the dodo, right down to an expressive alliterative invoking it: "Dive, dodo, on the earth you left forlorn, / Sit vastly on the branches of our trees. / And chant us grandly all improbabilities."[1]

Next, an example of a poem in which the same "theme" is treated in a quite different manner, more personal and humanly serious, the poem from *The Beautiful Changes* I've been most pleased to discover, this time through, how much I liked—"My Father Paints the Summer":

> A smoky rain riddles the ocean plains,
> Rings on the beaches' stones, stomps in the swales,
> Batters the panes
> Of the shore hotel, and the hoped-for summer chills and fails.
> The summer people sigh,
> "Is this July?"
>
> They talk by the lobby fire but no one hears
> For the thrum of the rain. In the dim and sounding halls,
> Din at the ears,
> Dark at the eyes well in the head, and the ping-pong balls
> Scatter their hollow knocks
> Like crazy clocks.
>
> But up in his room by artificial light
> My father paints the summer, and his brush
> Tricks into sight

---

1. In a note to the poem, Wilbur acknowledges its source in a description of the dodo by Sir Thomas Herbert, a seventeenth-century traveler. Speaking of the rareness of certain "feathered creatures" he encountered on the island of Mauritius, Herbert writes: "I will name but some, and first the dodo; a bird the Dutch call *walgh-vogel:* her body is round and fat, which occasions the slow pace or that her corpulence; and so great as few of them weigh less than fifty pound: meat it is with some, but better to the eye than stomach; such as only a strong appetite can vanquish: but otherwise, through its oyliness it cannot chuse but quickly cloy and nauseate the stomach, being indeed more pleasurable to look than feed upon."

The prosperous sleep, the girdling stir and clear steep hush
Of a summer never seen,
A granted green.

Summer, luxuriant Sahara, the orchard spray
Gales in the Eden trees, the knight again
Can cast away
His burning mail, Rome is at Anzio: but the rain
For the ping-pong's optative bop
Will never stop.

Caught Summer is always an imagined time.
Time gave it, yes, but time out of any mind.
There must be prime
In the heart to beget that season, to reach past rain and find
Riding the palest days
Its perfect blaze.

Part of its appeal to me is that, in the midst of a book of fanciful often fabulous objects and characters, we suddenly meet someone as unadorned with poetic trappings as "my father." The fact that Lawrence Wilbur was indeed a painter adds to the touch of intimacy. But that's as far as the personal revelation goes, since this is not a poem about a father and his son, except insofar as they share an assumption about what art does to nature. "Nature" is there in the opening two stanzas the thrumming rain brings with it—as *I* can remember it happening at summer hotels on rainy days—the hollow knocks of ping-pong balls, something to pass the time. Meanwhile, upstairs the father/painter is busy by "artificial light" (the light of artifice) turning, in Sir Philip Sidney's formulation, a brazen world into a golden one, into the prosperity of "A summer never seen," "a granted green" in that telling four-syllable line ending the stanza. The fifth stanza, in its fabulous translations and transformations of Summer, is just a little beyond me, but I regain my hold with the beautiful first line of the final stanza: "Caught Summer is always an imagined time," the way art catches anything only by doing something to time, stopping or tricking it, playing with the phrase "time out of mind" so as to turn it into "time out of any mind." It is yet one more example, like the chanting of the dodo, of "improbabilities."

Speaking of improbabilities, it is worth reminding ourselves how improbably exciting those immediate post–Second World War years were for

American poetry and poets. Of course there were distinguished names
adding to their store: Frost's *Steeple Bush* and Stevens's *Transport to Summer,*
both published in the same year as *The Beautiful Changes;* William Carlos
Williams's *Paterson,* Book 1 (1946); Pound's *Pisan Cantos* (1948). And there
was the up-and-coming younger generation: Bishop's *North & South* (1946);
Lowell's *Lord Weary's Castle,* of the same year; Karl Shapiro's *Trial of a Poet*
(1947); Berryman's *The Dispossessed,* and Jarrell's *Losses* (both 1948). Auden
was holding culture together in New York, especially in the famous picture
of the 1948 party at the Gotham Book Mart for the Sitwells. Among those in
attendance were, of course, Stephen Spender, Roethke, Richard Eberhart,
Marianne Moore in her funny hat, Elizabeth Bishop, Delmore Schwartz,
Jarrell looking especially feline and supercilious, and other privileged invi-
tees from the literary community, with Auden above them in the rear, sitting
on a book ladder. Two years previously Auden had gone up to Cambridge
to deliver the Phi Beta Kappa poem, "Under Which Lyre," that contains two
perfect stanzas welcoming back the servicemen to university and college
campuses:

> Encamped upon the college plain
> Raw veterans already train
>   As freshman forces;
> Instructors with sarcastic tongue
> Shepherd the battle-weary young
> Through basic courses.
>
> Among bewildering appliances
> For mastering the arts and sciences
>   They stroll or run,
> And nerves that never flinched at slaughter
> Are shot to pieces by the shorter
>   Poems of Donne.

Shapiro and Jarrell and Lowell wrote about Europe under the shadow of the
just-concluded war. Wilbur did his service in the European theater, and it
shows in a number of poems from *The Beautiful Changes* that have Europe
and the war as background or spectral presence. I am thinking of "Mined
Country," (a very up-to-date subject fifty years later, it turns out), "On the
Eyes of an SS Officer," "Place Pigalle," "The Peace of Cities," and my favorite
of these, "First Snow in Alsace":

The snow came down last night like moths
Burned on the moon; it fell till dawn,
Covered the town with simple cloths.

Absolute snow lies rumpled on
What shellbursts scattered and deranged,
Entangled railings, crevassed lawn.

As if it did not know they'd changed,
Snow smoothly clasps the roofs of homes
Fear-gutted, trustless and estranged.

The ration stacks are milky domes;
Across the ammunition pile
The snow has climbed in sparkling combs.

You think: beyond the town a mile
Or two, this snowfall fills the eyes
Of soldiers dead a little while

Persons and persons in disguise,
Walking the new air white and fine,
Trade glances quick with shared surprise.

At children's windows, heaped, benign,
As always, winter shines the most,
And frost makes marvelous designs.

The night guard coming from his post,
Ten first-snows back in thought, walks slow
And warms him with a boyish boast:

He was the first to see the snow.

The English critic and entertainer, Clive James, who wrote a lively, mainly appreciative account of Wilbur's poetry, especially his earlier work, thinks this poem goes soft at the end and fobs us off with an "orgy of consolation," "the exact verbal equivalent of a Norman Rockwell cover painting." But no, no orgy here, much too elegant and subtle for Rockwell's heart-whopping messages. It's true that the night guard may be thinking back, perhaps, to a Rockwell full-snow frontispiece for the *Saturday Evening Post* his parents in Cincinnati subscribed to. But how far from orgiastic sentimentality is the poem's ending can be seen in how its terza rima suddenly concludes itself, so simply and monosyllabically declarative: "He was the first to see the snow." In this poem, Nature, in the vestments of falling snow, drapes and transforms the works of man—ammunition piles and ration stacks—into sparkling combs and milky domes. It's an illusion of course, one of Nature's grand stunts. But the poem is faithful enough to the illusion to render it unfalteringly through the march of the verse.

There are few poems in *The Beautiful Changes*—indeed few in the Wilbur canon—that don't rhyme. One of the most interesting, indeed one of the most—perhaps *the* most—passionate poem in his first volume, eschews it in favor of a long-lined emphatic style of address that invests much in its subject, a subject (I venture to say) no lyric poet previously celebrated, or if one of them did it was under a less forthright title than "Potato":

> An underground grower, blind and a common brown;
> Got a misshapen look, it's nudged where it could;
> Simple as soil yet crowded as earth with all.
>
> Cut open raw, it looses a cool clean stench,
> Mineral acid seeping from pores of prest meal;
> It is like breaching a strangely refreshing tomb:
>
> Therein the taste of first stones, the hands of dead slaves,
> Waters men drank in the earliest frightful woods,
> Flint chips, and peat, and the cinders of buried camps.
>
> Scrubbed under faucet water the planet skin
> Polishes yellow, but tears to the plain insides;
> Parching, the white's blue-hearted like hungry hands.
>
> All of the cold dark kitchens, and war-frozen gray
> Evening at window, I remember so many
> Peeling potatoes quietly into chipt pails.
>
> "It was potatoes saved us, they kept us alive."
> Then they had something to say akin to praise
> For the mean earth-apples, too common to cherish or steal.
>
> Times being hard, the Sikh and the Senegalese,
> Hobo and Okie, the body of Jesus the Jew,
> Vestigial virtues, are eaten; we shall survive.

What has not lost its savor shall hold us up,
And we are praising what saves us, what fills the need.
(Soon there'll be packets again, with Algerian fruits.)

Oh, it will not bear polish, the ancient potato,
Needn't be nourished by Caesars, will blow anywhere,
Hidden by nature, counted-on, stubborn and blind

You may have noticed the bush that it pushes to air,
Comical-delicate, sometimes with second-rate flowers
Awkward and milky and beautiful only to hunger.

"Potato" is the only poem in *The Beautiful Changes* that is dedicated, that is "for" someone, in this case André de Bouchet, friend of the Wilburs, and evidently the animating force behind the publication of these poems by Reynal & Hitchcock. (M. de Bouchet is said, by Wilbur, to have read over the manuscript at the behest of Charlee Wilbur, kissed the poet on both cheeks, and announced that the poems must be published.) Ever since the time when a mutual friend of mine and Wilbur's, David Ferry, singled out "Potato" for me, I've admired it, though never known quite what to do with or say about it, except read it aloud. We can admire the alliterative, strongly-stressed pattern of lines, sometime five, even six, stresses to a line. And admire as well the wonderfully surprising modulation, in a new key, to that "remembering" in stanza five where an "I" is introduced who remembers those wartime evenings, perhaps was there himself peeling quietly away as if he were Walt Whitman. "Potato" is what Frost would call an "extravagance," though not an extravagance about grief, but an extravagant, affirming, unironic view of things, making those things mean more than at first they seem to, paying heed to the "hidden counted-on, stubborn, and blind virtues" possessed by some things of this world if only we will passionately possess them. I don't know that I have got "Potato" right (I know it's not spelled with a final "e"), but it is surely, at some level, a hymn of thanks to survival, to surviving things like World War II. It seems to me at any rate an achievement, indeed a life-enhancing one.

I've been attempting to describe some of the ways, the kinds of verbal performance that make *The Beautiful Changes* such a marvel, such a marvelous book. And not just marvelous "for a first book of poems." Among these performances there is the rugged, ballad-like directness with which the death of an American original like Tywater is set forth: "And what to say of him, God knows; / Such violence, and such repose." Or there is the witty inquirer into metaphor, into poetry, who asks, in "Praise of Summer," "Does sense so stale that it must needs derange / The world to know it?" Or the exquisitely amusing hymner of superfluity and tireless ease who instructs his subject to "Dive, dodo, on the earth you left forlorn." There is the believer in artifice, in artificial light, as the only light able to trick us into new kinds of seeing and apprehending: "Caught summer is an imagined time, / Time gave it, yes, but time out of any mind." And there is the grave, chastened observer of first snow who remembers that the soldiers its eyes are filling have been dead only a little while; that, as in "Potato," we shall survive," but only by acknowledging and praising our natural proclivities and imperfections—all of us mean earth-apples, too common to cherish and steal. In conclusion, and without further commentary, there is Richard Wilbur the love-poet, what I hope I'm not mistaken in judging to be, as well as its title poem, the most personal, intimate one in this first book and perhaps in the many ones he would go on to write.

> One wading a Fall meadow finds on all sides
> The Queen Anne's Lace lying like lilies
> On water; it glides
> So from the walker, it turns
> Dry grass to a lake, as the slightest shade of you
> Valleys my mind in fabulous blue Lucernes.
>
> The beautiful changes as a forest is changed
> By a chameleon's tuning his skin to it;
> As a mantis, arranged
> On a green leaf, grows
> Into it, makes the leaf leafier, and proves
> Any greenness is deeper than anyone knows.
>
> Your hands hold roses always in a way that says
> They are not only yours; the beautiful changes
> In such kind ways,
> Wishing ever to sunder
> Things and things' selves for a second finding, to lose
> For a moment all that it touches back to wonder.

James Merrill Collected

ALTHOUGH 2001 has some months to go, the literary event of the year has occurred with the publication of James Merrill's *Collected Poems*. Collected rather than complete, since not included is his volume-length epic, *The Changing Light at Sandover*. But it contains enough to keep a reader busy for months, years: ten volumes, ranging from *First Poems* published in 1951, four years after his graduation from Amherst College, to *A Scattering of Salts*, brought out soon after his death in 1995. In addition there are about two hundred pages of material only the Merrill expert will be familiar with—translations, uncollected and unpublished poems, including a final few written when he was near death. As a physical object, the nine-hundred-page volume is a beauty: handsomely bound and sewn, with black pages separating the individual collections and with Thomas Victor's photo of Merrill wrapped around the spine of a mostly black dust-jacket on which appears the poet's name in large, lavender letters. The lavender motif—alluding to Merrill's homosexual preference—is extended to the opening and closing pages and to a silk bookmark, all in all a state-of-the-art project designed by the resourceful Chip Kidd. In a time when one is invited to plunk down twenty-five dollars for any old novel, the forty-dollar pricing of *Collected Poems* is a bargain.

In fact, the book is priceless. For what immersion in Merrill's life work of poems brings us is the conviction that, taken together, the volumes of beautifully wrought verse he gave us make up what we must call—vaguely but unmistakably—a world, one capacious enough to allow endless opportunities for moving around in, for surprise, for continued discovery. About the

Collected Poems, by James Merrill, edited by J. D. McClatchy and Stephen Yenser. New York: Knopf, 2001.

creation of that world, Merrill was astonishingly prophetic when, in his early thirties, he wrote "A Tenancy," the concluding poem in *Water Street* (1961) the book in which we hear for the first time the deepened range of a poetic voice. The poem begins with Merrill recalling a March afternoon in 1946 when, having turned twenty, he proposes a "bargain with—say with the source of light":

> That given a few years more
> (Seven or ten or, what seemed vast, fifteen)
> To spend in love, in a country not at war,
> I would give in return
> All I had. All? A little sun
> Rose in my throat. The lease was drawn.

"A Tenancy" ends with the now "leaner veteran" of fifteen years later being visited by three of his friends and contemplating his identity as a poet:

> If I am host at last
> It is of little more than my own past.
> May others be at home in it.

This pledge of hospitality offered the reader was to be observed for the next thirty-four years, as the world of Merrill's poetry expanded and complicated itself but never ceased to imagine a listening reader, someone who cared enough to tune in to the unfailingly regular broadcasts.

The best critic of Merrill's work has been Helen Vendler (her collected reviews of him would make an excellent book), who has more than once spoken to the "Mozartian" spirit of his work. She is referring to its comic nature, comedy of course being a most serious matter; indeed Alexander Pope wanted life to be "a long, exact, and serious comedy," and Vendler names as Merrill's three great precursors in English verse, Pope, Byron, and W. H. Auden. These poets may well be the greatest technicians of our language (we don't think of Shakespeare or Wordsworth as technicians, even though their employment of words is brilliant). It's also on record that Merrill's contemporary, Richard Wilbur, has called him "the most dazzling technician we have"—this compliment paid by a fellow graduate of Amherst who might himself with equal justice be called the most dazzling technician we have. But the word is dangerous, since it can invite the demeaning adjective "mere" (a "mere" technician, "merely" technique), so to rescue Merrill from the impeachment we should recall T. S. Eliot's observation that "we cannot say at what point 'technique' begins or where it ends." In other words, it won't do to hive off the dazzling employment of words from anything supposedly more serious.

By way of suggesting how impressive a technician James Merrill was and how fully that technique served to create a compelling human presence, I will adduce a single poem, "The Victor Dog," published in *Braving the Elements* (1972):

> Bix to Buxtehude to Boulez,
> The little white dog on the Victor label
> Listens long and hard as he is able.
> It's all in a day's work, whatever plays.
>
> From judgment, it would seem, he has refrained.
> He even listens earnestly to Bloch,
> Then builds a church upon our acid rock.
> He's man's—no—he's the Leiermann's best friend,
>
> Or would be if hearing and listening were the same.
> *Does* he hear? I fancy he rather smells
> Those lemon-gold arpeggios in Ravel's
> "Les jets d'eau du palais de ceux qui s'aiment."
>
> He ponders the Schumann Concerto's tall willow hit
> By lightning, and stays put. When he surmises
> Through one of Bach's eternal boxwood mazes
> The oboe pungent as a bitch in heat,
>
> Or when the calypso decants its raw bay rum
> Or the moon in *Wozzeck* reddens ripe for murder,
> He doesn't sneeze or howl; just listens harder.
> Adamant needles bear down on him from
>
> Whirling of outer space, too black, too near—
> But he was taught as a puppy not to flinch,
> Much less to imitate his bête noire Blanche
> Who barked, fat foolish creature, at King Lear.
>
> Still others fought in the road's filth over Jezebel,
> Slavered on hearths of horned and pelted barons.

His forebears lacked, to say the least, forbearance.
Can nature change in him? Nothing's impossible.

The last chord fades. The night is cold and fine.
His master's voice rasps through the grooves' bare groves.
Obediently, in silence like the grave's
He sleeps there on the still-warm gramophone

Only to dream he is at the première of a Handel
Opera long thought lost—*Il Cane Minore.*
Its allegorical subject is his story!
A little dog revolving round a spindle

Gives rise to harmonies beyond belief,
A cast of stars . . . Is there in Victor's heart
No honey for the vanquished? Art is art.
The life it asks of us is a dog's life.

It is one of the poems ("Matinées" and "The *Ring* Cycle" are others) in which his inwardness with music is patent. It is learned and difficult, but not obscure, and it has elicited surprisingly little comment, perhaps because—misleadingly, I think—critics deem it so light-spirited as to be the opposite of profound. "The Victor Dog" is a poem of forty lines, in ten stanzas rhyming ABBA. It is spoken by the Poet, the one on whom nothing is lost, who knows and sees and hears all, and to whom it is our privilege and pleasure to listen. If the lines quoted earlier from "A Tenancy"—the poem in which Merrill pledged himself to his art—are gravely thoughtful, those in "The Victor Dog" crackle with witty fireworks, to describe which the adjective "playful" is woefully inadequate. "Bix to Buxtehude to Boulez" is, for openers, a line no one came close to writing previously, showing an aural quickness of association, which, once "Bix" is sounded, moves inevitably to "Bux[tehude]" then (with the sound of "hude") to "*Boulez.*" There is a sheer pleasure in pronouncing the names of these three B's of the composer-performer world.

Merrill's own performance in the first three stanzas seems especially packed with what Frost named as the essential constituents of poetry—"this thing of performance and prowess and feats of association." Merely to note the ABBA rhyme pattern suggests nothing about how delightfully "off" are the first and fourth line-rhymes of these stanzas: Boulez / plays; refrained /

friend; same / *s'aiment.* Auden was expert at slanting his rhymes, but Merrill's rhyming is even more inventive, more fun (especially in the same / *s'aiment* rhyme where the words look so very different). Then there is the pacing: Frost said he was interested in how he could "lay" sentences into lines of verse; Merrill's three stanzas contain seven sentences—of, respectively, three, one, one, two, two, a half, and two and a half lines—with the effect of keeping us off-balance, surprised at the way a line does or doesn't conclude itself in a full-stop period. These off-beat happenings help generate changes of voice: from the mock-casual "It's all in a day's work, whatever plays" (the play on "work" / "play" is so casual as to be scarcely discernible); to the mock-thoughtful "From judgment, it would seem, he has refrained"; to the deadpan coupling of the Christian church's laying its foundation on a rock ("*Tu es Petrus*") with the 1970s acid rock that the dog refrains from judging, just listens to. My favorite moment is the mock correction of phrase in "He's man's—no—he's the Leiermann's best friend," the reference here being to the final song in Schubert's *Winterreise,* a strange, ghostly one about a hurdy-gurdy man.

As always with lines from Merrill's poems, there is more to be said, and I refrain from further lunges at explanation. (But what about "the Schumann Concerto's tall willow hit / By lightning"? Do we need to hear the opening theme in the third—or the first—movement?) Yet the poem is more than one devilishly clever stroke after another, since it also has a development, a little narrative that broadens into an exquisitely touching finality of statement:

> The last chord fades. The night is cold and fine.
> His master's voice rasps through the grooves' bare groves.

That is what it is like to hear the record-player's needle having come to the end of the piece and moving through "grooves' bare groves" as they revolve. Suddenly we are precipitated into the lovely conceit of the little dog's dream, involving discovery of the hitherto undiscovered opera *Il Cane Minore* (slant-rhymes with story), at which point the poet, caught up in the dream ("life's allegorical subject is his story") is moved to state the ultimate mystery of how going round and round the spindle produces the splendors and sadness of music. Such "harmonies beyond belief" that call forth a mid-line breaking-off (. . .) and a poignant question not to be answered: "Is there in Victor's heart / No honey for the vanquished?" Or rather, answered only by the bare truths that end the poem:

> Art is art.
> The life it asks of us is a dog's life.

Merrill went to his writing desk every morning, led the dog's life of writing, in order to give us the richness of his music.

Merrill's art is to give rise to harmonies beyond belief without ever raising his voice—as Eliot, Yeats, Robert Lowell raised their voices. He once said on the subject that "If you were taught that it's not polite to raise your voice, it's very hard to write like Whitman," and we may be grateful that he didn't attempt the barbaric yawp. In this restraint he most resembles that other "technician," Wilbur, who has also avoided loud affirmations or negations, believing (in the words of Merrill's "The Thousand and Second Night") that "Form's what affirms." Merrill and Wilbur, along with Anthony Hecht, all roughly the same age, seem to me our great formal poets, each brought up on high modernist predecessors, but also responsive to the quieter voicings and ceaseless wit of a Frost, an Elizabeth Bishop. Like Frost and like Bishop, these successors are committed to narrative, to writing poems with a "plot," a development that, however difficult it is to track (and with Merrill it is often extremely difficult if not impossible), is committed to making something we call, for lack of a better word, *sense.* (Here the three poets differ from their contemporary John Ashbery, who just goes on in his merry way making nonsense.)

Merrill's poems have denouement; they twist and turn in the motions of an imagination working something out. His practice and subjects as a poet have been remarkably continuous: one does not talk of "development" in the twenty-three years of work that followed "The Victor Dog." We may recall Oscar Wilde, declaring that only mediocrities develop, but note as well that unlike, most impressively, Robert Lowell's, Merrill's art is not made out of the dramatic presentation of self-struggle, action and reaction, the taking on of successive Yeatsian masks. He claims furthermore never to have thought of his homosexuality as an "issue," either in the poems or outside them. As the social stigma lessened or disappeared altogether in the 1970s, Merrill was not on the battlements: "I stood still and the closet disintegrated," he remarked: "I don't believe in being the least militant about it." His final three volumes, published after the closet disintegrated (*Late Settings, The Inner Room,* and *A Scattering of Salts*), are books this reader has scarcely begun to assimilate, and they contain some of his very best poems.

Perhaps, in the manner Randall Jarrell liked to employ when dealing with a poet's life work, it is permissible to name about twenty-five poems for which in my judgment Merrill should be most remembered. In more or less chronological order, then: "The Black Swan," "The Country of a Thousand Years of Peace," "Mirror," "An Urban Convalescence," "For Proust," "Getting Through," "Annie Hill's Grave," "A Tenancy," "The Thousand and Second Night," "Time," "The Broken Home," "Matinées," "Up and Down," "The Victor Dog," "Lost in Translation," "Clearing the Title," "Days of 1941 and '44," "The House Fly," "Santorini: Stopping the Leak," "Investiture at Cecconi's," "Farewell Performance," "Nine Lives," "The *Ring* Cycle," "Family Week at Oracle Ranch," "164 East 72nd Street," "Overdue Pilgrimage to Nova Scotia," "Self-Portrait in Tyvek™ Windbreaker." Add to these two of the last poems he wrote that conclude this volume, "Christmas Tree" and "Days of 1994."

To call these last poems rehearsals for death puts it too bluntly only if the moving affirmations in which they end are ignored. "Days of 1994," the last of many "Days of" poems he wrote, concludes with the notion of waking in a tomb "Below the world" and enumerates some of "the thousand things / Here risen to if not above / Before day ends":

> The spectacles, the book,
> Forgetful lover and forgotten love,
> Cobweb hung with trophy wings,
> The fading trumpet of a car,
> The knowing glance from star to star,
> The laughter of old friends.

And—if possible—even more movingly because more wittily, there is "Christmas Tree," an account by the tree of being "brought down from the cold mountain," "warmly" taken in and dressed by the world, put under the spell of love and human hospitality. But the tree knows how different is what lies ahead, and seamlessly the speaking voice becomes the poet's from his hospital bed ("a primitive IV / To keep the show going"). He imagines "the stripping, the cold street, my chemicals / Plowed back into the Earth for lives to come." But it is too much to be dwelt on and the voice ends instead with "No dread. No bitterness," naming its surroundings even as they vanish:

> Dusk room aglow
> For the last time
> With candlelight.

Faces love lit,
Gifts underfoot.
Still to be so poised, so
Receptive, still to recall, to praise.

The tenancy, drawn up in 1946, was about to expire; the tenant remained in his lines, ever poised, receptive, recalling and giving praise.

CHRISTMAS TREE

      To be
        Brought down at last
From the cold sighing mountain
Where I and the others
Had been fed, looked after, kept still,
Meant, I knew—of course I knew—
That it would be only a matter of weeks,
That there was nothing more to do.
Warmly they took me in, made much of me,
The point from the start was to keep my spirits up
I could assent to that. For honestly,
It did help to be wound in jewels, to send
Their colors flashing forth from vents in the deep
Fragrant sables that cloaked me head to foot.
Over me then they wove a spell of shining—
Purple and silver chains, eavesdripping tinsel,
Amulets, milagros: software of silver,
A heart, a little girl, a Model T,
Two staring eyes. The angels, trumpets, BUD and BEA
(The children's names) in clownlike capitals,
Somewhere a music box whose tiny song
Played and replayed I ended before long
By loving. And in shadow behind me, a primitive IV
To keep the show going. Yes, yes, what lay ahead
Was clear: the stripping, the cold street, my chemicals
Plowed back into the Earth for lives to come—
No doubt a blessing, a harvest, but one that doesn't bear,
Now or ever, dwelling upon. To have grown so thin.
Needles and bone. The little boy's hands meeting
About my spine. The mother's voice: *Holding up wonderfully!*

No dread. No bitterness. The end beginning. Today's
   Dusk room aglow
   For the last time
   With candlelight.
   Faces love lit,
   Gifts underfoot.
Still to be so poised, so
Receptive. Still to recall, to praise.

Amherst, Summer 2001

Robert Graves Remembered

Robert Graves is in the great tradition of eccentric English writers (Sterne and Peacock, Carlyle and Ruskin come to mind), full of the most outrageous convictions and certainties, treated by some as a holy fool to be worshiped, or at least licensed; ignored by others as a prolific but minor talent now on the verge of being forgotten. Over the seventy or so years of his active writing life—he died at age ninety, in 1985—Graves produced scores of novels, literary commentary, and mythological creations, the most famous of which are perhaps *I Claudius,* an agreeable historical fiction, if you like that sort of thing; and *The White Goddess,* his "historical grammar of poetic myth," in which this reader has made no headway. But first and last Graves was a lyric poet, gifted with one of the finest ears audible in English verse and with a command of the plain style as impressive as Jonson's or Swift's or Landor's. In particular, he has been admired as a love poet who left a number of treasures dedicated to the celebration of the goddess from whom true poets receive their birthright and power.

This third volume of a biography of Graves by his nephew, Richard Perceval Graves, was published in England three years ago and is the completion of a ten-year project. The work he has put into it may be suggested in this volume by the eighty pages of reference notes that conclude it. No one, I suspect, is likely to clamor for further fact about the life of Robert Graves; indeed, all but the most fanatic Gravesian, if there are any around, will feel glutted by the yearly parade of people, writings, travels, mishaps, and triumphs that form the narrative of these pages. Since Graves was senile during the final decade of his life (he wrote no poems after 1975), there's an in-

---

Robert Graves and the White Goddess, 1940–1985, by Richard Perceval Graves. London: Weidenfeld and Nicolson, 1995.

evitable sag in the biographer's account, and the chapters toward the end became very brief indeed.

Graves, having finally gotten himself free of (or ditched by) Laura Riding, his collaborator, mentor, and first muse—who among her other accomplishments managed to convince him to abstain from sex with her for many years—fell in love with Beryl Hodge in 1937. Accordingly, Beryl left her husband, Alan (also a collaborator of Graves's), and in 1940 began to live with Robert. They were eventually married, after their divorces became final, and Beryl bore him four children (he also had four by his first wife, Nancy Nicholson). After living for a time in Devon, they moved back to the house in Deyá, Majorca, where Graves and Riding had lived in the 1930s. Beryl appears to have been nothing less than heroic, certainly long-suffering, in her adherence and loyalty to Graves, as she permitted him, over the next decades, to take on (not simultaneously) the four attractive younger women whom he would convert into muse-figures, embodiments of the White Goddess.

R. P. Graves remarks about his uncle's marriage to Beryl that, "everything was so much more secure and settled: which did not suit Robert at all." You can't be a wife-mother and a magic muse as well, was the brilliant rationalization Graves acted upon and brought off successfully. On occasion this made for awkward dinner-table moments: "Shut up, I want to hear Judith," he once instructed Beryl when she interrupted something the first muse, Judith Bledsoe, might have been about to utter. Under the influence of the most aggressive and erratic of these female goddesses, Cindy Lee (a.k.a. Amaelia Laracuen Lee), Graves was at one point on the verge of leaving Beryl, but someone's cooler head prevailed and Cindy went off to get in various kinds of trouble on her own.

Graves knew about everything, including how a woman who had had two miscarriages might avoid a third: "Clear out all rubbish from the house (backs of drawers, under stairs etc. between May 14 and June 14) and burn it, unless classifiable as salvage, in the backyard." Primroses for the Goddess and "a handful of pearl barley laid on a raised stone" would also help. And in fact Joanne Simon, the recipient of this advice, proceeded successfully to bear a child. Worried about a perceived increase in the number of homosexual men, Graves laid it to heredity and environment, "but largely because men now drink too much milk." This is a factor few of us had considered as crucial to sexual orientation.

Predictably, he was scornful of Yeats's occult learning ("rubbish borrowed from the planchette"), and Yeats was one of the reigning modern poets he attacked—along with Eliot, Pound, Auden, and Dylan Thomas—in the infamous Cambridge Clark Lectures of 1965, "These Be Your Gods, O Israel." Graves set himself firmly against modernism as he found it in these poets, although in the lectures he also managed to make contemptuous references to Milton, Dryden, Pope, Gerard Manley Hopkins, and D. H. Lawrence. He thought of modernist poetry as, in R. P. Graves's words, "directed mainly by American expatriates in London and Paris against the English poetic traditions," and his preferred modern poets were Frost, e. e. cummings, and John Crowe Ransom. One sees why Philip Larkin includes Graves in his own list of worthy moderns.

It's perhaps too much to ask that a nephew should have an ironic purchase on his uncle, but I would have welcomed, on occasion, a slightly colder eye being cast on the great man's utterances and activities. And though R. P. Graves from time to time quotes a poem by Robert, it's usually done with only the most minimal comment of approval, or simply with no comment at all. Although the last decades of his life contain the White Goddess poems (the most famous of which is "To Juan at the Winter Solstice"), which Randall Jarrell thought his richest and most magical, my own sense is that while he never lost his facility and poetic nerve, the poems that have permanently lodged themselves were written earlier, between roughly 1915 and 1935, and are basically epigrammatic ("emblematic," Donald Davie shrewdly pointed out). I mean such ones as "Lost Love," "Warning to Children," "The Cool Web," "Love in Barrenness," "Sick Love," "Flying Crooked," "The Devil's Advice to Story-Tellers," and, most succinctly, "Love without Hope":

> Love without hope, as when the young bird-catcher
> Swept off his tall hat to the Squire's own daughter,
> So let the imprisoned larks escape and fly
> Singing about her head, as she rode by.

The combination of rhyme, strong syntax, and impeccable rhythm is there to admire in many of his poems, but certainly much less so in the later work, especially in the two hundred and more pages of lyrics in his final collection, *Poems 1975*.

For readers interested in Graves but not prepared to wade through three volumes of his life, there is an excellent alternative to R. P. Graves in Miranda

Seymour's one-volume, critically sophisticated biography of 1995. Still, and along with its predecessors, R. P. Graves's concluding volume is a labor of love and scholarship, and whenever a mere critic like myself is moved to annoyance or disbelief at some Gravesian pronouncement, it is well to remember that such is the trouble with Genius. After all, you can't find too much fault with a man who once admitted that, for him, falling in love with a woman was as easy as falling in love with his big toe; or who worked hard and well every day, year after year; or who managed to be good friends with Ava Gardner (she attended his memorial service). How could such a combination of sense and nonsense, love and callousness, critical brilliance and critical fatuity exist in one man? Graves provided his own answer for us in the final couplet of "The Devil's Advice to Story-Tellers": "Nice contradiction between fact and fact / Will make the whole read human and exact."

Boston Sunday Globe, September 13, 1998

L. E. Sissman: Innocence Possessed

THE publication of this volume is a major event in the history of recent American poetry; for in it L. E. Sissman emerges as a most interesting poet and surely the most undervalued of those who began their careers in the 1960s, a decade (in America at least) overpopulated by poets while under-critical about the art of poetry. From the preface to this volume, ably edited by his literary executor, Peter Davison, and from Sissman's collection of his occasional journalism (*Innocent Bystander,* 1975), we can piece together the main events of his life.

Louis Edward Sissman was born in Detroit on New Year's Day, 1928, an only child. The major recorded fact of his youth is unquestionably his service as a "quiz kid" on a never-to-be-forgotten (by some of us) American radio program of the 1930s and 1940s. Sissman's forte was spelling; at the age of thirteen he won the National Spelling Bee in Washington, and one is reminded of J. D. Salinger's Glass family, whose radio show was called *It's a Wise Child.* Sissman entered Harvard in 1944, was rusticated in 1946, and become a stack boy in the Boston Public Library. Readmitted in 1947, he graduated as Class Poet, married, then divorced, sought his fortune in business in New York, returned after a few years to Boston, worked at a series of jobs (including selling vacuum cleaners in northern Vermont), eventually settled in the advertising business, remarried (happily) in 1958, and in 1963 began seriously to write poetry once more. Then, in November 1965, he was told that he had Hodgkin's disease—the "incurable Hodgkin's Disease," as Robert Lowell called it in his *Life Studies* poem about Uncle Devereux. Sissman's doctor did his best to cushion the blow:

Hello, Darkness: The Collected Poems of L. E. Sissman, edited by Peter Davison. New York: Little, Brown, 1978.

"But be glad
These things are treatable today," I'm told.
"Why, fifteen years ago—" a dark and grave-
Shaped pause. "But now, a course of radiation, and"—
Sun rays break through. "And if you want X-ray,
You've come to the right place."
. . . .
                        But bland
And middle-class as these environs are,
And sanguine as his measured words may be,
And soft his handshake the webbed, inky hand
Locked on the sill, and the unshaven face
Biding outside the window still appall
Me as I leave the assignation place.

"Dying: An Introduction," the poem from which these lines are quoted, was my introduction to Sissman's work, encountered by chance while leafing through a magazine; and I remember being surprised and disturbed by it—my realization being that this was not just something "made up", that the poem's "I" was undeniably speaking of its creator's "appalling" experience. Yet the final section of "Dying: An Introduction" was called "Outbound" and felt oddly and poignantly exhilarating. Released from the doctor's office, Sissman, now introduced to his own death, walks a Boston November street that, of all things, smells like spring. Meeting some college students, he is thrown back to his freshman year at Harvard, twenty-one years before, when he discovered for the first time "the source / Of spring in that warm night." So it is with truly a new lease of life that he now, two decades later, sees the November evening, the street, the college girls "As, oddly, not as sombre / As December, / But as green / As anything: / As spring."

Sissman had been assembling his poems with a book in mind, but the new, awful fact of Hodgkin's disease made all the difference to his art. As Mr. Davison says in his preface, "For the rest of his life he wrote like one possessed of a knowledge remote from most of us, the knowledge of real time." "Dying: An Introduction" became the title of his first volume in 1968; it was soon followed by *Scattered Returns* (1969) and *Pursuit of Honor* (1971). Since these were the years when many American poets (Ginsberg, Levertov, Bly, Rich) were using verse to express their detestations of the Vietnam War and the state of the union, and when both zany and portentously toneless voices expressed themselves without reference to any metrical pattern, Sissman's wryly intelligent humor (employed mainly in rough-and-ready iambic pentameters, with occasional bouts of rhyming) looked formally old-hat and insufficiently national or global in its aspirations. At least it did to some of my college students who found his second volume too clever, too fancy, too ironically expert. And so it was, for them.

Scattered Returns contained some less than flattering glimpses of the younger generation countering culture, as in "Visiting Chaos," which begins

> No matter how awful it is to be sitting in this
> Terrible magazine office and talking to this
> Circular-saw-voiced West Side girl in a dirt-
> Stiff Marimekko and lavender glasses, and this
> Cake-bearded boy, in   short-rise Levi's, and hearing
> The drip and rasp of their tones on the softening
> Stone of my brain . . .

and ends with the poet's decision, though not made with certainty, that at least it is better than being dead. But usually Sissman's poems are without animus. Mr. Davison describes him as writing like "an innocent man possessed," and I would emphasize the latter term since Sissman was possessed by his past, the people he knew and cared about, the seasonal cycle, the ways in which we age and harden and sometimes burst out into sudden glory. Such concerns inform the long sequence, "A War Requiem," in which vignettes and panoramic sleights like the following from "Rosedale Theatre, 1938" pass before our eyes:

> The first big feature ends;
> We trade reactions and gumballs with friends
> Above the marching feet of Movietone,
> Which now give way to a twin-engine plane
> That lands as we half watch, and Chamberlain
> Steps out, in his teeth, Homburg, mustache,
> A figure of some fun. We laugh and miss
> His little speech. After the Michigan-
> Ohio game, Buck Rogers will come on.

This is precisely and sensitively right about what it was like to go to the Saturday afternoon matinée as an American ten-year-old back then. The poetry does not matter: Sissman's typical attempt is, like Movietone, to keep events in motion—with a minimal deference to "form" and a disinclination to attempt dramatic lyrics with an "I" at the center, experiencing and learning from the experience. In this he resembles—though the comparison seems an unlikely one—Edwin Arlington Robinson, rather than, say, Frost or W. C. Williams. Robinson, a fine and subtle humorist who was disinclined to dramatize himself in complex ways, is the subject of an affectionate poem of Sissman's describing him as "implicit in the inward town" (Head Tide, Maine) where he was born. Sissman frequently makes an analogous attempt to "hide out in the Hideout of my memory," as the last poem from "A War Requiem" has it. While hiding out unsuccessfully from his country's "unlovely recent history," he watches snow lance against the window, then sees

> By luck, a leisurely and murderous
> Shadow detach itself with a marine
> Grace from an apple tree. A snowy owl,
> Cinereous, nearly invisible,
> Planes down its glide path to surprise a vole.

This could not be seen at Rosedale Theatre, 1938, but it is as compelling as Buck Rogers, more real than Chamberlain, and no more explicit in its declared "meaning" than either.

But the most splendid and chilling things in the collection are found in its posthumous section, especially in three poems—"Homage to Clotho: A Hospital Suite," "Cancer: A Dream," and "Tras Os Montes"—from the final "Hello, Darkness" sequence. Sissman was an admirer of the painter Edward Hopper, and in "American Light: A Hopper Retrospective" he detailed with loving, unsparing accuracy the cityscape of one Hopper painting and the marvellous way that, in another one, "a shaft of sun / Peoples the vacuum with American light." This is also the gift, and the promise, of Sissman's art as it comes to focus, still unsparingly, on the hospital where he is a patient:

> If Hell abides on earth this must be it;
> This too-bright-lit-at-all-hours-of-the-day-
> And-night recovery room, where nurses flit

> In stroboscopic steps between the beds
> All cheek by jowl that hold recoverers
> Suspended in the grog of half-damped pain
> And tubularities of light-blue light.

A very different kind of "hard American light" from the one saluted in the Hopper poem is faced just as truthfully.

Reading these last poems, one's reservations about Sissman's work—its tendency sometimes to go on and on, its relative absence of tonal variety, its quiz-kid clever-boy stuff—pale into insignificance. Sissman loved to use other poets' lines and phrases, deploying them in a manner that very much called attention to itself. The habit must have given him so much pleasure that he never grew out of it; but in his final poems, especially in "Tras Os Montes," one hears the man speaking with visionary power through a literary medium become transparent. Whereas in "Dying: an Introduction" he had emerged from the doctor's office and pronouncement into a November day that felt as green as spring, now, in the final section of "Homage to Clotho"

> Home, and the lees of autumn scuttle up
> To my halt feet: fat, sportive maple leaves
> Struck into ochre by the frost and stripped
> From their umbilic chords to skate across
> The black-top drive and fetch up on my shoes
> As if including me in their great fall,
> Windy with rumors of the coming ice.

Not like spring; and the man plans to hide out once more, climb the stairs, seek a place to "recompose" himself in

> A world of voices and surprises, for
> As long as Clotho draws my filament—
> To my now flagging wonder and applause—
> From indefatigable spinnerets,
> Until her sister widows, having set
> The norms for length and texture of each strand
> And sharpened their gross shears, come cut it off
> And send me to befriend the winter leaves.

After the end of 1974 he was unable to write any more poetry; he died in 1976. The cause of wit and perhaps of courage in others, his poetry and his example deserve the most generous attention.

Times Literary Supplement, July 28, 1978

R. P. Blackmur and the
Criticism of Poetry

It is now almost forty years since Richard P. Blackmur's first extended critical piece, a two-part analysis of T. S. Eliot's poetry and criticism, appeared in the earliest issues of *Hound and Horn*. Blackmur died in 1965, but his reputation as the most brilliant and difficult of the New Critics had been thoroughly established twenty years before: in *The Armed Vision* (1948) Stanley Hyman gave him a place of honor at the end of the book, along with William Empson, I. A. Richards, and Kenneth Burke, mainly on the grounds that Blackmur had so scrupulously equipped himself to explicate the obscurities of modern poetry. To anyone in the universities who began to discover literature in the forties and fifties, his name was evocative of a rich and mysterious critical sensibility to be admired discreetly from afar; and as the essays he published became more densely hieratic, getting through them on first try was a test of soul—it was no simple matter to locate oneself with confidence "Between the Numen and the Moha." Experienced readers would often deplore a "later Blackmur" who indulged in verbal fuzziness or played literary confidence games, and since more than one critic has made sport of Blackmur's style, it may be well at the outset to take account of the strongest of these attacks, a review of *Language as Gesture* by Hugh Kenner.[1] Kenner's own formidable and idiosyncratic way with words does not make him any more charitable in dealing with Blackmur's. The latter's verbal and epigrammatic

---

1. Hugh Kenner, "Inside the Featherbed," *Gnomon* (New York: McDowell, Obolensky, 1958), 242–48. For a similar point of view, see John Wain, *Essays on Literature and Ideas* (London: Macmillan, 1963). Intelligent and sympathetic praise of Blackmur can be found in Joseph Frank, *The Widening Gyre* (New Brunswick, N.J.: Rutgers University Press, 1963), 229–50, and in Richard Foster, *The New Romantics* (Bloomington: Indiana University Press, 1962), 82–106.

criticism works well on poets like cummings, Wallace Stevens, and Emily Dickinson, who achieve their effects largely by manipulating closed systems of interacting words, and Blackmur receives a grade of "pretty good" for his Hart Crane and Marianne Moore essays. But Kenner implies that there are other poets for whom such a criticism is not efficacious (he probably has in mind Yeats and Pound, perhaps Eliot); at any rate, increasingly with the years, Blackmur's "linguistic playfulness has run wild." Kenner has hard (and playful) words for this vice: "habitual doodling with other men's idioms . . . in the hope that something critically significant will occur"; "intolerably kittenish"; a "pseudo-wisdom" which toys idly with quotations and "makes large gestures of being utterly free in the possession of their contents"; "loose trumpery counterfeits of the profundities of the poets themselves"; and most strikingly, "his hair-trigger pen, tickled by some homonym or cadence, is free to twitch out dozens of words at a spurt." In a word, Kenner is contemptuous of the "poetry" of a criticism that achieves its effects through words interacting in a closed system, and is exactly to that degree irresponsible and irrelevant to words on the page out there.

As usual, Kenner penetrates to the heart of the matter, the only real "issue" of Blackmur's writing, or at least the issue to which all the rest can be reduced. It will not do to say, in defense of Blackmur, that, yes of course there are excesses, but in the main . . . for in fact there is nothing particularly excessive about the few short quotations Kenner makes; even out of context they could have been written by nobody but Blackmur. Kenner caps his case by instancing as an example of dozens of words twitching out at a spurt, a section from the final essay in *Language as Gesture*, "Lord Tennyson's Scissors," a retrospective look at the modern poets. Kenner quotes without comment, except to call a "record incantation" the following Blackmurian comment on two lines of "The Dry Salvages":

> Here is the salt of death and of truth and of savor, the salt in our souls of that which is not ours, moving there. The salt is on the wild and thorny rose grappling in the granite at the sea's edge, grappling and in bloom, almost ever-blooming; and it is the rose which was before, and may yet be after, the rose of the Court of Love, or the rose of the Virgin. It is the rose out of the garden which includes the rose in the garden. There is in Eliot's line (alien but known to our line that we read) also all the roses that have been in his life, as in the next line is all the fog . . .

At that point Kenner turns away, confident we will shake our heads over all this incantatory fog. But let us hear it out, restoring the two Eliot lines Blackmur takes for his text,

> The salt is on the briar rose,
> The fog is in the fir trees.

and then continuing on from where Kenner ceases to quote:

> The fog is another salt as the fir trees are another rose. It is all there is in fog that lowers, covers, silences, imperils, menaces, and caresses; but in it, as it is in them; there is the slowed apparition, coming up under an island, of evergreen struggling, tenacious life. The two together make an image, and in their pairing reveal, by self-symbol declare, by verse and position unite, two halves of a tragic gesture.
>
> > The salt is on the briar rose,
> > The fog is in the fir trees.
>
> I do not see that any other illustration is needed of how behavior gets into the words of the full mind, and how, a little beyond the time that it is there, it sings.[2]

Confronted only by Kenner's selection, which ends with the least convincing of Blackmur's sentences, and lacking perhaps an immediate sense of just where the lines (not even quoted by Kenner) occur in "The Dry Salvages," it is easy to raise eyebrows at the incantation, without holding any firm convictions about how one ought to behave in relation to the words in question. Should one murmur them tonelessly as a pure participant in an imaginative assertion? Or, as Helen Gardner does, speak of them as "a return to mythical expression" by means of "two images of smell or taste, immediate and pervasive, haunting and formless, images which suggest the eerie menace of the sea felt inland?"[3] Or go on to unfold, using the full resources of words, some of the ways this mythical expression suggests the "eerie men-

---

2. "Lord Tennyson's Scissors" in *Language as Gesture* (New York: Harcourt, Brace, 1952), 422–23. Blackmur's essays are most conveniently located in this volume and in *The Lion and the Honeycomb* (New York: Harcourt, Brace, 1955). See *A Primer of Ignorance* (New York: Harcourt, Brace & World, 1967) also.

3. *The Art of T. S. Eliot* (New York: Dutton, 1950), 13.

ace." This is what Blackmur does in the record incantation, and does it not for the sake of "explaining" gnomic utterances in *Four Quartets*, but as a marvelous example of what poetry does to behavior:

> Poetry is as near as words can get us to our behavior; near enough so that the words sing, for it is when words sing that they give that absolute moving attention which is beyond their prose powers. It is behavior, getting into our words, that sings.

The lines from Eliot's poem are settled on for being both intractable, untranslatable into "what they really mean," yet also impressively yielding, cooperative with a reader who attempts to give expression to his sense of them. It all depends on the kind of a reader-critic who encounters them; Blackmur's awareness of this delicate situation is put forth most fully in his essay "A Burden for Critics," which pleads that criticism "take up some of its possibilities that have been in abeyance, or in corruption, for some time." The relation between criticism and poetry is then developed:

> Poetry is one of the things we do to our ignorance; criticism makes us conscious of what we have done, and sometimes makes us conscious of what can be done next, or done again. That consciousness is the way we feel the critic's burden. . . . He knows that the institution of literature, so far as it is alive, is made again at every instant. It is made afresh as part of the process of being known afresh; what is permanent is what is always fresh, and it can be fresh only in performance—that is, in reading and seeing and hearing what is actually in it at this place and this time. . . . Or put another way, the critic brings to consciousness the means of performance.

Bringing to consciousness the means of performance, demonstrating how behavior gets into the words of poetry and sings, these are "possibilities" for criticism that Blackmur spent his life in vindicating. The poetry he devoted himself to was modern poetry, as perhaps that literature whose means of performance most needed to be brought to consciousness, known afresh at each instant; and to know it afresh Blackmur found that he had, ever more increasingly, to sing. To do that to words was why he came: his work as a whole is truly, in a way Hugh Kenner did not mean, a record incantation of immense personal contribution. A look at certain features of that work will remind us what possibilities of criticism today are still in abeyance.

In his early essay on Marianne Moore's poetry, Blackmur gave a name to
the kind of illustrative operation—the "incantation"—performed most
grandly on the Eliot lines considered above. It is true that the operations
contained in early essays on poets such as cummings, Stevens, D. H. Lawrence, Marianne Moore, Hart Crane, and the Eliot of "Ash Wednesday," are
relatively modest in their behavior and observably anchored to specific lines
or words, thus acceptable to readers like Kenner, who deplore the later flights
as "doodling." But Blackmur's following description of the critical procedure includes both sorts of operations: "What we make is a fiction to school
the urgency of reading; no more, for actually we must return to the verse itself in its own language and to that felt appreciation of it to which criticism
affords only overt clues." There is a nice ambiguity about this description,
which its author would not object to our laying out. A "fiction" schools the
urgency of reading by training that urgency, directing it, suggesting a possible course for it to take. This assumes what most critics assume—that there
is some urgency (inchoate and untutored it may well be) attending our reading of, say, a poem by Moore. But a critical fiction may go further than this,
as Blackmur's in fact does; if the fiction is powerful and compelling enough
it may actually teach us urgency, may at certain moments and in regard to
certain passages or poems convince us of the inert inattention of our previous reading by spurring us to life, to new regard. For a relatively minor example of such a spur, consider Blackmur's "fiction" about the opening of
Moore's poem "The Steeple-Jack":

> Dürer would have seen a reason for living
> in a town like this, with eight stranded whales
> to look at; with the sweet sea air coming into your house
> on a fine day, from water etched
> with waves as formal as the scales
> on a fish.

Here the incongruity works so well as perhaps to be imperceptible. The
reader beholds the sea as it is for the poem, but also as it never was to a
modern (or a sailor's) eye, with the strength and light of all he can remember of Dürer's water-etchings, formal and "right" as the scales on a
fish. It is the same formal effect, the Dürer vision, that sets the continuing
tone, as the moon sets the tide (with the sun's help), for the whole poem,

bringing us in the end an emotion as clean, as ordered, as startling as the landscape which yields it.

And he then quotes without comment the closing lines of the poem. After we have read these words, nothing in "The Steeple-Jack" has been explained, cleared up, or, most crudely, "interpreted" for us. We have probably read the poem a few times at most; our familiarity with it—in any inward sense—is problematic, and we may well ask whether, in reading it, we engage with an emotion as clean, as ordered, as startling as the landscape which yields it? The answer is probably: well, not exactly, or I hadn't thought of it quite *that* way. But insofar as we say something like this about the poem or about the next one by Moore that Blackmur takes up, the urgency of our reading has, however slightly, been schooled.

This kind of criticism has the further virtue that it actually practices what every critic or teacher today can preach with his eyes shut and then promptly behave as if he didn't believe for a minute: that literary criticism exists to send readers back to poems with awakened interest and curiosity, rather than to carve poems up into neatly explained portions. Early in the Marianne Moore essay, Blackmur admits to having "laid out" much of the material of a particular poem, but since the laying out was done in terms of a "lowered consciousness"—that of the critic's—the poem is uninjured. Dissection need not be murder if it's the right kind of dissection:

> Analysis cannot touch but only translate for preliminary purposes the poem the return to which every sign demands. What we do is simply to set up clues which we can name and handle and exchange whereby we can make available all that territory of the poem which we cannot name or handle but only envisage. We emphasize the technique, as the artist did in fact, in order to come at the substance which the technique employed.

Reading the Steeple-Jack poem again after noting Blackmur's remarks is an effort to "come at the substance" in a fresh way, and his tactful respect for the poem encourages us to do this: the remarks only envisage, not handle, the thing itself. By the same token he is not interested in sitting hard on the poem in order to point out effects we may have missed. An observation about one of Moore's subtle uses of rhyme is immediately backed off from, in this manner: "It is a question whether devices of this order integrally affect the poem in which they occur. If they do affect it, it must be in a manner that can neither be named nor understood, suffusing the texture unascertainably. . . . It is part of the poem's weather." This refusal to name, "understand," or handle a particular sound-effect should not be confused with diffidence or obscurantist tactics. Any critic can work up a particular poem and discover some effect that the common reader has missed, then go on to claim that "our" experience of the poem is an experience that perhaps only he has had, or would like to think he has had. Blackmur's invocation of the poem's "weather" is in part a refusal to elbow the reader about, more positively an invitation to us to see for ourselves what the weather of a particular poem is like.

The weather of poems is only one of Blackmur's many tropes for indicating what our words cannot handle but only envisage, and by his changing of the metaphor he suggests how impervious this weather remains to critical chartings of it. Perhaps the most eloquent and revealing of these metaphors is that of language as gesture—"that meaningfulness which is moving, in every sense of that word: what moves the words and what moves us." When form and substance are united as gesture

> the words sound with music, make images which are visual, seem solid like sculpture and spacious like architecture, repeat themselves like the movements in a dance, call for a kind of mummery in the voice when read, and turn upon themselves like nothing but the written word. Yet it is the fury in the words which we understand, and not the words themselves.

Providing a refrain for the essay, that last sentence looks like a formulation calculated to drive an analytical philosopher wild; yet some such distinction between the fury in the words and the words themselves is crucial to any appreciation of the true poem. To understand merely "the words themselves" in Blackmur's distinction means to envisage no territory beyond what our critical language of paraphrase and interpretation can chart; to feel that this language is pretty much exhaustive of what is there in the poem; to read and translate the poem into other terms without feeling much violence has been done. In practice, we can see that Blackmur worked with this distinction in his earliest essays when he criticized cummings for using words as counters, for associating "flower" and "moon" in ways which provoke a "thrill" but deprive the words of anything beyond superficial associative value and deaden them into "ideas": "By seldom saying *what* flower, by seldom relating immitigably the abstract word to a specific experience, the content of the word vanishes; it has no inner mystery, only an impenetrable surface." By contrast with this "absence of known content" in cummings, Blackmur speaks with approval of Wallace Stevens's ambiguity as

> that of a substance so dense with being, that it resists paraphrase and can be truly perceived only in the form of words in which it was given. It is the difference between poetry which depends on the poet and poetry which depends on itself. Reading Cummings you either guess or supply the substance yourself. Reading Mr. Stevens you have only to know the meanings of the words and to submit to the conditions of the poem.

Submitting to the conditions of the poem is the recognition of language as gesture, of poetry that seems to depend on itself rather than on the poet, of natural song as opposed to a willed imitation of song.

But Blackmur gives us no trustworthy magic hammer with which to tap the poem and see if it has substance, if the words move among themselves and thus move us. Either we hear something or we don't. So when I read for the twentieth time the poem that begins

> I think continually of those who were truly great.
> Who, from the womb, remembered the soul's history
> Through corridors of light where the hours are suns,
> Endless and singing. Whose lovely ambition
> Was that their lips, still touched with fire,
> Should tell of the Spirit, clothed from head to foot in song.
> And who hoarded from the Spring branches
> The desires falling across their bodies like blossoms.

I hear, yet once more, Stephen Spender in the guise of a singer. The lines look to be full of images and exciting goings-on—suns and fire and lips and desires and the Spirit—yet nothing moves, the words are counters, easily understood, without substance or fury. It is all too easy to translate the poem into what Spender is "saying," at which point we may admire the solemn sentiment. By contrast, in the poem of substance we also understand something:

> Deer walk upon our mountains, and the quail
> Whistle about us their spontaneous cries;
> Sweet berries ripen in the wilderness
> And, in the isolation of the sky,
> At evening, casual flocks of pigeons make

> Ambiguous undulations as they sink,
> Downward to darkness, on extended wing.

But exactly what do we understand? To paraphrase Randall Jarrell paraphrasing St. Augustine, we *know* what these lines are about so long as you don't ask us to say, and for this reason we refuse to be placed in the position of trying to tell someone else what the "ambiguous undulations" of the pigeons "means," saying instead—there they *are*, look at them, listen to them again; let them school the urgency of your response. Though it may seem odd to speak of the fury in such quiet words, they are surely the ones which move with each other and move us.

As students often complain, it is highly subjective. Emerson's pledge in "The American Scholar"—"So is there no fact, no event, in our private history, which shall not, sooner or later, lose its adhesive, inert form, and astonish us by soaring from our body into the empyrean,"—has its counterpart in Blackmur's unending search for the fury in the words of poetry, a fury that in another context he speaks of as "symbol":

> What writing drags into being and holds there while the writing lasts may be called the experience of the actual; what writing creates—what goes on after the writing has stopped—may sometimes be called symbol. It is symbol when it stands, not for what has been said or stated, but for what has not been said and could not be said, for what has been delivered by the writing into what seems an autonomous world of its own. Symbol is the most exact possible meaning, almost tautologically exact, for what stirred the words to move and what the moving words made. Symbol stands for nothing previously known, but for what is "here" made known and what is about to be made known. If symbol stands for anything else than itself continuing, it stands for that within me the reader which enables me to recognize it and to illuminate it with my own experience at the same moment that what it means illuminates further corridors in my sense of myself.

Here the responsible aesthetician might throw up his hands: "*If* symbol stands for anything else," indeed! Of course it does stand for something else within the disposition of Blackmur's case; it must be a term wide enough to cover "what stirred the words to move" (the preconscious; "surds" of being; the chthonic realm) and "what the moving words made" (behavior singing in the words; language brought to full gesture) and "that within me the reader which enables me to recognize it . . ." (subjectivity; Emersonian soul).[4] Insofar as the moving words are articulation at its highest, just so far must they reach beneath consciousness to bring up the material of poetry, then thrust back, through the articulation, into our Keatsian mansion of many apartments and open the doors to new chambers. Blackmur's critical effort in behalf of this symbolic imagination and its expression of wordless realms was a lifetime's gloss on the closing lines from Wallace Stevens's "To the One of Fictive Music": "Unreal, give back to us what once you gave, / The imagination that we spurned and crave."

ii

If it is fair to say that Blackmur's interest in any given arrangement of words in a poem is exactly proportionate to the depth of those wordless realms it evokes, then the peculiar importance of Irving Babbitt to him becomes clear. Stanley Hyman has pointed out how much of Babbitt Blackmur was able to use by "taking Babbitt's 'moral' concepts—discipline, proportion, moderation—and making them aesthetic criteria of literary form rather than ethical criteria of literary content, while adding to them the extra dimension of the chthonic."[5] The result is "humanism plus symbolic imagination." What Hyman's perception leaves out, in its workmanlike interest of naming and tracing influences on Blackmur, is the high style with which Blackmur turns Irving Babbitt into a poetic, indeed Shakespearian, hero. In his essay "Humanism and Symbolic Imagination: Notes on Re-Reading Irving Babbitt," Blackmur devotes some time to building up a sense of where Babbitt thought he stood, what center and centrality of position he occupied. Blackmur calls this humanism "heroic to the classic extreme; it tempts the gods. For to perfect the human role is fatally to surpass it, and leaves only the possibility of tragedy." He then proceeds, in the following extraordinary paragraph, to elucidate that possibility:

> The tragedy of Irving Babbitt for himself may well have been his isolation—the utter desolateness of the center. For us the tragedy appears as

---

4. As put most finely by Emerson in the famous lines: "I am the owner of the sphere, / Of the seven stars and the solar year, / Of Caesar's hand, and Plato's brain / Of Lord Christ's heart, and Shakespeare's strain."

5. Stanley Edgar Hyman, *The Armed Vision* (New York: Knopf, 1948), 251–52.

the damnation, the attendant mutilation, of every foray, every footstep of his faculties outside the center. He was sound motionless, in position; in motion, in the restless, driven effort to gather the world of experience home to his position, he was ruined. To summon the tragic sense to the consideration of a critical mind is perhaps to stain our appreciation with raw colors, but if we do not think of the absolute activities of the mind as tragic we have only a flat affair, a thing merely to reject. It is the special vividness, the life-giving quality of the tragic sense that it gives perspective, background, both to the emotion achieved and to the actuality consequently uncovered.

One imagines Babbitt reading this about himself with some distaste, perhaps wondering what "tragedy . . . for himself" Blackmur has saddled him with and why he needed to do so at all. But the "us" referred to in "For us the tragedy appears "is equally the product of Blackmur's symbolic imagination. To how many people besides Blackmur has the career of Irving Babbitt appeared as a tragedy, indeed (and unfortunately) appeared as anything to be much concerned with? The reason why Blackmur will not take Babbitt simply on Babbitt's own terms—as solidly placed humanist—is that these terms leave no room for the symbolic imagination. And so Blackmur defends and exercises this imagination by invoking it in relation to Babbitt, by presenting the humanist as tragic hero in words that move and sing as they build to annunciation: ". . . in motion, in the restless, driven effort to gather the world of experience home to his position, he was ruined." In other words, Blackmur's aim is to create a supreme fiction called "Irving Babbitt" which will school the urgency of our reading Babbitt, and make us confront afresh that intransigent figure. By implication, and by the example of his own work, Blackmur's own critical effort is no less immune to some later critic's consideration that brings to it "the life-giving quality of the tragic sense." Blackmur sees his own work as, unlike Babbitt's, dynamic and flexible; a coming-out to experience, to literature; an acceptance of the invitation to engage with words behaving, no matter what doctrine or position is behind those words. In this subjective, dramatic manner lies its power and also its risk, since avoidance of the "restless driven attempt" to bring all experience home to a center is but avoidance of one kind of ruin. We have seen evidence that Blackmur's own dynamic flexibility (as he would see it) may be called "doodling" and "kittenish" by the next critical voice heard in the dialectic. At any rate, Blackmur needed and used Irving Babbitt to school the urgency of his own criticism; needed a hero, preferably a tragic one, against whom, again by implication, he could set forth his own correspondingly heroic endeavor.

iii

> It was as if he taught music, and taught it magnificently, but only in the written score. He was right, everlastingly about everything which may occur before the playing begins.

This epitaph from the essay on Babbitt takes us back to where we began: with the critic's necessity of bringing to consciousness the means of performance. The analogies with music that Blackmur is so fond of making tell us much about his conception of the critical task. Babbitt's humanism was a prejudgment of experience, a "barrier between the mind and the sensibility in which it lodged, between the score of the music and its performance." In Blackmur's own case the score becomes words on the page, while the performance is his own attempt to respond freely to those words and to sing them well, with most sensitive expression. In this respect one takes seriously his insistence in the Hart Crane essay that poetry is not architecture but a linear art—an act of succession resembling song. And one can also imagine his skepticism about recent critical fashions that neglect the poem as it develops in time, the better to know it as a bit of literary timeless space. Furthermore, an emphasis on performance of the score makes for a sense of the poem's dynamic "naturing" rather than its static nature. In demonstrating how cummings's words often became ideas merely, without depth or substance, Blackmur allowed himself a more than usually sharp footnote directed at "those who regard poetry only as a medium of communication." For them it is undoubtedly best to have what is communicated remain as abstract as possible; for himself on the other hand, poetry must be regarded "not at all as communication but as expression, as statement; as presentation of experience, and the emphasis will be on what is known concretely. The question is not what one shares with the poet, but what one knows in the poem."

For Babbitt, literature was a form of knowledge that provided him with ideas to ballast and prove his criticism of culture. Blackmur's effort, once more in contrast, is a dynamic attempt to come out to all literature, regardless of what it is saying, and engage with it. Thus "what one knows in the poem" will be a quite different matter, closer to our "knowledge" of song.

No doubt the ideal virtues of skepticism and irony, as saluted in his essay

"A Critic's Job of Work," will be useful in freeing that critic for song, but those virtues are founded on a deeper admission: that of the bedrock of ignorance—of how absolute is the gap which exists between the moving poem and our attempts to move our words in performing it. In a scornful dismissal of Basic English, Blackmur once exclaimed, "What, should we get rid of our ignorance, of the very substance of our lives, merely in order to understand one another?" For all his inveterate politeness, a similar spirit informs his attitude toward claims for understanding poetry either by extraction of content, or by subtler games of critical connection-making that treat images as though they were static content rather than momentary utterance. Like Wallace Stevens in his poems, Blackmur is always "trying to put down those tremendous statements, those statements heard in dreams." The passages from modern poems that move him most are made of such statements, though they are far from what we usually mean by the term "statement"; for example,

> A woman drew her long black hair out tight
> And fiddled whisper music on those strings
> And bats with baby faces in the violet light
> Whistled, and beat their wings
> And crawled head downward down a blackened wall
> And upside down in air were towers
> Tolling reminiscent bells, that kept the hours
> And voices singing out of empty cisterns and exhausted wells.

about which Blackmur says:

> The exegetes tell us, and it is true, that we are in the Chapel Perilous and the Perilous Cemetery is no doubt near at hand, and it may be as one of the exegetes say that we hear something like the voice of John the Baptist in the last line. But for myself, I muse and merge and ache and find myself feeling with the very sense of my thought greetings and cries from all the senses there are.

What one knows concretely in the poem is at such moments indistinguishable from that ignorance which is the very substance of our lives. Blackmur's term for it in this late pamphlet is "our sensual metaphysics," but whatever it is called, I would argue that it forms the ultimate burden for any critic of literature, perhaps most especially so when the literature is lyric poetry and when it is just close enough to us in time as to make us overconfident about how well we "know" it. The burden has been taken up and carried into the practice of a surprisingly small number of recent American critics; one thinks of Randall Jarrell's fine evocations of the feel of certain poems and poets, or, ironically enough, of Hugh Kenner's summoning-up of a poem's weather.[6] There is a necessary element of virtuosity in any attempt to suggest, by a rival creation of one's own, the power and fascination of the poem one has read; and doubtless if everybody tried to imitate Blackmur, there would be a lot of embarrassing, irrelevant writing to push aside. But we could just as doubtlessly survive it, and it might even prove less deadly than the present spectacle of endless critical articles and books which tell us in plain, simple and undistinctive words what went on in such a poem by so-and-so. In a sense we are always asking that the critic just for a moment do the poem one better and school the urgency of our own response, "the gesture of our own uncreated selves" of which Blackmur speaks. We can be trusted to know when criticism behaves as if the man who wrote it embodied such a gesture, and we will be grateful for the effort of creative articulation that gave the gesture words that speak to us.

6. As an example of creative criticism, take the following sentences about "Gerontion" from Kenner's book on Eliot:

The old man with neither past nor present, reduced to a Voice, employs that Voice, fills up the time of the poem with the echoes and intermodulations of that Voice, draws sustenance from the Voice and existence itself from the Voice for as long as he can animate the silence. . . . It is a great grotesque conception, greatly achieved, everywhere evading the deadness of pastiche, everywhere embodying the deadness of retrospect, the hollowness of personality which can express itself so admirably, and still express nothing but the bits of purely verbal intensity with which it has filled itself out of books.—*The Invisible Poet* (New York: McDowell, Obolensky, 1959), 122–23.

Massachusetts Review, Autumn 1967

NOVELS AND NOVELISTS

THIS section devotes itself to twentieth-century English and American novelists. "Lawrence and Lewis" was written soon after I'd published a book on Wyndham Lewis, who had displaced D. H. Lawrence in my head as a major interest. My calling them "the two most significant English novelists of our century" was certainly a stretch, but is still arguable even if few would agree about (at least) Lewis's eminence. "Ford Once More" attempts—once more, since I have written about him previously—to take his measure, the occasion being Max Saunders's impressive two-volume biography. Another biography, Kenneth Lynn's of Ernest Hemingway, gave me the chance to say something about Hemingway's literary style. "Classic Chandler" was the result of rereading Raymond Chandler's novels after the Library of America brought them out in two volumes.

The essay on Anthony Burgess's novels is the earliest published piece in this collection (1966). My justification for reprinting it is that, except for *A Clockwork Orange*, which people have heard about rather than read, Burgess's novels are pretty much forgotten. My judgment is that the increasingly "experimental" ones he wrote after 1966 until his death in 1993 were destined for oblivion, but that the ones up to 1966 are still very much worth reading. I would single out his extraordinary futurist one, *The Wanting Seed*, along with *Inside Mr. Enderby*, the first and by far the best of what would be four novels about the hapless, flatulent poet. *The Worm and the Ring* also deserves more attention than I gave it in the essay. Gore Vidal called Burgess, along with Iris Murdoch and William

Golding, the best English novelist of his (Vidal's) time. Certainly Burgess is up there with the best of his contemporaries.

Including five brief reviews of novels (under the rubric "First Impressions") breaks my rule of not reprinting perhaps the most ephemeral of journalistic forms. But these novels are ones that have borne out my initial admiration and become more rather than less alive over the course of years. So I have retrieved the reviews.

Lawrence and Lewis

Wᴴᴏ has forgotten F. R. Leavis's famous pronouncement in *D. H. Lawrence: Novelist:* "If you took Joyce for a major creative writer, then, like Mr. Eliot, you had no use for Lawrence, and if you judged Lawrence a great writer, then you could hardly take a sustained interest in Joyce." Somehow, happily enough, one managed to forget it in practice; but if the name of Wyndham Lewis were substituted for Joyce—and Leavis might permit the substitution—the suggestion would not seem as immediately outrageous. Historically, the only significant comparisons of Lawrence with Lewis were made over thirty years ago by critics with the sharpest of axes to grind—T. S. Eliot, and Leavis in response to him. The terms were as follows: in *After Strange Gods* Eliot had pointed to a "ridiculous" element in Lawrence—his lack of a sense of humor, his possession of a "certain snobbery," and, in a highly inflammatory phrase, his "incapacity for what we ordinarily call thinking." At this point Eliot cited the "brilliant exposure by Wyndham Lewis in *Paleface* as a conclusive criticism of this incapacity." Leavis, concerned to insist that on the contrary Lawrence had a supreme intelligence, rich sense of humor, and all other admirable qualities, leaped at the chance to expose the man whom Eliot had chosen as exposer: while not denying Lewis talent, Leavis managed to make it look suspect: "He [Lewis] is capable of making 'brilliant' connections"—as if they weren't really brilliant at all, or as if to make a "brilliant" connection were a bit flashy and reprehensible. But it is really Lewis who is incapable of thinking, the air of solid argument in his books is just bluff, and the only side of Lawrence he exposed is the primitivistic yearning Lawrence was capable of detecting and analyzing in himself, without outside help. And since Lewis's treatment of sex "is hard-boiled, cynical and external," he is a poor witness to call as alternative to Lawrence's supposed "sexual morbidity"—which Eliot had stressed. Best of all, Leavis could turn the tables on Eliot by allowing Lawrence himself to expose Lewis with some words written in a review of Edward Dahlberg's *Bottom Dogs:* "Wyndham Lewis gives a display of the utterly repulsive effect people have on him, but he retreats into the intellect to make his display. It is a question of manners and manners. The effect is the same. It is the same exclamation: They stink! My God, they stink!" This placing of Lewis by Lawrence was sufficient, in Leavis's mind, to establish his favorite writer as "the representative of health and sanity" while Lewis took his place—along with countless other modern writers—with those who do dirt upon life, as the now familiar phrase has it.

I am convinced that this account travesties both writers, smoothing out every Lawrentian kink in the interests of clear-eyed affirmation of life, while it takes a part of Lewis, unjustly magnifies it onto the whole, and makes him sound like a ludicrous and nastily fastidious aesthete ("My God, they stink!"). As any reader goes deeply into Lawrence or Lewis he will see the unsatisfactoriness of Leavis's account; what he may also see, and what I should like to point the way toward briefly, are some ways of taking the two writers together as voices who, despite their remarks about one another, had profound things in common as critics and as novelists.

They were born within three years of each other, and neither of them to the English manner. The earliest work of each (short stories by Lewis, poems by D. H. L.) appeared in the *English Review* under the eye of Ford Madox Hueffer. Pound's championing of Lewis is well known, but Lawrence didn't escape him either, as can be noted from his immortal tag "Detestable person but needs watching." It turned out rather soon that both Lawrence and Lewis needed watching; further, that they were willing to turn themselves into fair enough specimens of detestable persons if it were necessary in order to get across a message about England. The message was that English humor, as expressed through the beloved English grin, was no longer enough, was bad equipment for life in the twentieth century. Lewis made it explicit in the epilogue to his first novel, *Tarr,* where the second in a list of points proposed is "that the Englishman should become ashamed of his Grin as he is at present ashamed of solemnity. That he should cease to be ashamed of his 'feelings': then he would automatically become less proud of his Grin." If it looked in *Tarr* that the author himself were grinning, readers were advised to look closer and "perceive that it is a very logical and deliberate grimace." The deliberate grimace became more noticeable during the 1920s as Lewis cast himself into a series of increasingly antagonistic and histrionic roles (that of The Enemy being the most striking one) when it transpired that the grinner was without a self and could be manipulated as a puppet for revolutionary purposes. As for Lawrence, his whole career must be seen as a protest on behalf of the feelings—of the "passional self"—against whatever form of cultural or personal repression (the "grin" being one of them) the modern Englishman suffered under. And though an Enemy-like self with its own distinctive grimace frequently appears in his essays and reviews, it speaks out most powerfully through the characters of Rupert Birkin in *Women in Love* and Richard Lovat Somers in *Kangaroo.*

It would not have done for these self-styled detestable persons merely to adopt a gloomy and cavilling tone as they responded to English traits, since complacency—"the grin"—could be truly subverted only by a really revolutionary laughter, a harsher and wilder kind of play. Leavis, reviewing *Phoenix,* singles out this play as one of Lawrence's distinctive virtues as a critic: "His critical poise is manifested in . . . a lively ironic humour—a humour that for all its clear-sighted and mocking vivacity is quite without animus." And Leavis finds the ironic humor "free from egotism" as well. Certainly if egotism and animus are taken to be disfiguring qualities for a critic to possess, then the Lawrence of *Studies in Classic American Literature* and the occasional essays and reviews in *Phoenix* is guilty of such possession. But it's arguable that the best modern critics of literature and society, partly when they engaged in defending or attacking some aspect of the contemporary scene, were all equipped with enough egotism and animus to keep them going in a lively manner: think of Leavis himself on Bloomsbury, Auden-Spender, Christian Discrimination; or think of Pound, Eliot, Lawrence, or Wyndham Lewis on one of their own favorite stalking-horses. All these writers are notable for their ironic humor and mocking vivacity; and it could be maintained that of the five, Lewis's particular thrusts and sallies are most thoroughly and consistently amusing.

Two examples from his criticism of Lawrence may suggest what I mean: the first occurs in *Paleface* where Lewis is busying himself (in a section titled "Love? What Ho! Smelling Strangeness") with the strangeness smelled and admired by Lawrence in *Mornings in Mexico.* The subject is Lawrence's notion of "virtue" in woman:

What is *virtue* in woman? Mr. Lawrence becomes very Western at once, under the shadow of a kind of suffragist chivalry, at the mere thought of "Woman."

In woman [virtue] is the putting forth of all herself in a delicate, marvellous, sensitiveness, which draws forth the wonder to herself, etc. (To "draw the wonder to herself" is to be a witch, surely? So virtue and wickedness would get a little mixed up.)

What would the Indian think if he heard his squaw being written about in that strain?—"delicate, marvellous sensitiveness." He would probably say "Chuck it, Archie!" in Hopi. At least he would be considerably surprised and probably squint very hard, under his "dark" brows, at Mr. Lawrence.

The brilliance of comic creation lies not only in Lewis's pretense that, really, we most look at this matter from the Indian's point of view, but in the rich aptness of the phrase provided him to express that view—"Chuck it, Archie!" (in Hopi, of course). The point is not that Lawrence has been triumphantly exposed for all time and the falsity of his primitivistic yearning demonstrated, simply that it is good to imagine the squaw's mate answering back in such resplendent terms. Lewis's own "critical poise" is manifested in the independent comic life taken on by his creation—as it is in the following anecdote, again directed at Lawrentian doctrine:

Only a few years ago (1940) in New York an English writer of my acquaintance went about for a while with an American woman-intellectual. He told me how one day "Lady Chatterley's Lover" had been mentioned. He expressed contempt or indifference for it. Thereupon his lovely friend burst into tears. It was almost as if he had spoken disparagingly of her person; or had high-hatted the sexual impulse, while visiting the Venusberg.

This was the kind of atmosphere heavy with emotion one had to contend with from the start. When lecturing at Oxford once I ventured a few criticisms of Lawrence's "dark unconscious." Indeed the room was full of them. At the end of my address I was darkly heckled for half-an-hour by woman after woman.

The moral of this cautionary tale seems to be that you had better not high-hat and mock the dark unconscious, or it will rise up and darkly heckle you or worse. Who is mainly exposed here, Lawrence or Lewis? The question isn't relevant to the detached pleasure we take in a deadpan comic creation that is also "criticism." It is exactly the kind of thing Lawrence did so well, if not as coolly, with regard to Ben Franklin or Whitman in the *Studies* book, or in his reviews of H. G. Wells or Galsworthy.

Further than this, as a critic of Lawrence's work, Lewis was unable to go. At one moment he will refer to him as "that novelist of genius"; at another, and in the same book, *Rude Assignment,* he confesses to being sick of Lawrence's "invalid dreams," his "arty voodooism." *Paleface,* as well as quoting and commenting on passages from *Mornings in Mexico,* refers briefly to *Sons and Lovers* and to *Women in Love* but only to describe the first as "an eloquent wallowing mass of Mother-love and Sex-idolatry" and the latter as "again the same thick, sentimental, luscious stew." The language is inflammatory rather than helpful. In 1931 Lewis reviewed Middleton Murry's *Son of Woman,* and describing Murry's literary criticism as "a sort of sickly and blasphemous clowning," spent most of the review laying out the book's thesis. But Lewis made it clear that he preferred Lawrence the poet to Lawrence the prophet—even as he calls him "except in patches, a very bad writer." As for Lawrence's remark about Lewis, the question of from exactly what reading "They stink! My God, they stink!" came is not easy to answer. Lawrence had perhaps read *Tarr* and the *Wild Body* stories, although they seem rather too genial work to display "the utterly repulsive effect" people had on Lewis. On the other hand, that sort of display is often found in *The Childermass* and especially in *The Apes of God,* the latter published the year Lawrence died—though he may well have seen the section from it Eliot published in *The Criterion.* What Lawrence could not have foreseen, since he died in 1930, was that Lewis would go on in the next twenty-five years to write his finest novels, most of which deal fully and intensely—and not as the vehicle of repulsion merely—with the satirist's sense of other people, with the relation of the intellect to "life."

As novelists, even more than as critics, what holds the two writers together is a violence of thought, a persistent effort to imagine themselves (through the protagonists of their novels) as lonely heroes: embattled figures out of step with fashion and its wares. And since, in a phrase of Lewis's, woman is "eternally the enemy of the Absolute" it is appropriate that Lawrentian and Lewisian heroes come up hard against women who won't quite yield to their heroic male versions of themselves. For example, there is a moment in *Kangaroo* when Richard Lovat Somers tells his wife how he wants to haul down the flag of "perfect love" from their marriage-ship and put in its place "this crowned phoenix rising from the nest in flames. I want to set fire to our bark *Harriet and Lovat,* and out of the ashes construct the frigate, *Hermes,* which name still contains the same reference, *her* and *me,* but which has a higher total significance." To which long speech Harriet simply replies "You're mad!" and leaves Somers holding the flag, or the bird. Lewis's most memorable treatment of an analogous situation occurs in the late novel *Self Condemned* where the refusal of his perfectionist hero, René Harding, to climb down from his commitment to life in Momaco (Canada) as against England eventually results in his wife, Hester, throwing herself under a truck. After her death René entertains the following reflection:

> It had been a fearful estrangement between them when she made a return to England a supreme issue, a life or death issue. She still, in death, spoke of England. But all he spoke to her about was forgiveness. Could he ever be forgiven? No, forgiveness was of course impossible . . .

Both *Kangaroo* and *Self Condemned* are books about an exile, filled with despair—and alternate enthusiasm—about the land to which exile has taken the hero, while they regard England with a mixture of loathing and nostalgia. They are also books about the modern century, about history, about an old imperfect Europe-England put behind for temporary immersion in some raw new world; they convey as well their authors' dissatisfaction with more ordinary styles of novel-writing, or at least with certain contemporary "well-made" ones. Neither Lewis nor Lawrence manages or even seeks to avoid a constant, sometimes lurching and awkward, often poignant but always unmistakable appeal to the reader over the head of whatever "story" the novel is getting on with: so Lewis lectures us on how badly the modern state is run, or on how invigorating was American radio comedy during World War II, while Lawrence talks on about what marriage should or shouldn't be, or recalls (in the "Nightmare" chapter) the personal indignities he suffered in England during World War I.

Nothing of course is "proved" by juxtaposing two novels written thirty years apart. And *Kangaroo* is very far from Lawrence's best work; perhaps *Women in Love,* with its perfectionist hero, Rupert Birkin, would be a better choice for comparison. But this matters less than the fact that coming away from the experience of reading Lewis and Lawrence, of dealing with the intense, complicated, nagging, ironic presence of, in each case, an author not the least shy of putting in personal appearances in his pages, makes us see how partial, how far from the last word were the words each writer used to type and simplify the other. Lawrence, we are assured, is a partisan of the body, of the dark unconscious: yet *Kangaroo* and *Women in Love* are filled with argument, hesitations, qualifications, but always talk and more talk about matters said to be beyond language. Lewis, we are as confidently assured, is the clever wordy satirist who retreats into his intellect from which point he can peer out and assure us of the repulsiveness of other people: yet *Self Condemned* (or it might be *The Revenge for Love*, or *The Vulgar Streak*) sounds like this at the moment when René confronts the body of his dead wife,

> The Hester he saw at present was a living and moving one, one that he had loved, a witty, at times malicious one: but one who had become as much part of his physical being as if they had been born twins . . . Once or twice he thought he must get back to England, and if he should ask her forgiveness *there*, then the sweet face would smile as if to say, "You have returned! We could not *both* return! But you found your way back. That proves that there really was love in you and me."

Perhaps no comment is needed beyond uttering once more Lawrence's dictum about trusting the tale rather than the artist, especially when one artist must have perceived in the other a presence alien and disquieting.

Not for a moment would one want to have unsaid what they said about each other. We are the richer even for moments as trivially amusing as this one in a letter written by Lewis to Naomi Mitchison while he was on holiday in Morocco:

> as you see I am there still, upon the edge of the Spanish Sahara, baked by breaths from the Sudan, chilled by winds from the Atlantic luckily, too, and gathering much material for an essay on Barbary—you know, I expect, *Berbering* is probably just *Barbary*, and I am amazed that Lawrence (D. H.—not the Colonel) did not find it out. I have been to places, and broken bread with people, calculated to lay him out in a foaming ecstasy . . .

But by this time—it was 1931—Lawrence was beyond reach of the thrust; and the same year, reviewing Murry's book, Lewis insisted that he had no inclination to judge, "so near to the death of Mr. Lawrence, at a time when many people must be mourning sincerely the vanishing of such a gifted, and, it would seem, attractive man." It would seem, though undoubtedly it never quite seemed so to Lewis. But the gesture was a decent one. Now, almost forty years later, with the atmosphere cleared of recriminations—Leavisian or Eliotic—we need and should insist on having both Lawrence and Lewis, one against the other, yes, but also together against others: as invaluable critics of literature and society, and as two of the most significant English novelists of our century. To rewrite the sentence, then: if one reads either of them, one would naturally and necessarily take the most sustained interest in the other.

Agenda, Autumn–Winter 1969–1970

Ford Once More

> But master, mammoth mumbler, tell me why
> the bales of your left-over novels buy
> less than a bandage for your gouty foot.

ROBERT LOWELL'S question to the novelist (in his poem "Ford Madox Ford") has never quite been answered, but Max Saunders's massive two-volume biography tells Ford's story as definitively as any "definitive" biography is likely to. There is no point in complaining about its length or in asking whether Ford, man and writer, is worth fourteen hundred pages on his life and work. Almost no one is likely to read Mr. Saunders from covers to covers; but then, who besides professional Ford scholars has read through, let alone remembers details of, the eighty-some volumes that constitute his contribution to literature: novels, memoirs, biographies, poems, political and social argument, children's books—you name it. This reader's attempt over the past few months to put himself more fully in the Fordian picture is representatively imperfect: in front of me on the desk are various volumes at various stages of incompletion—from *The Rash Act* to *The English Novel* to *New York Essays* to *Henry James* to *The New Humpty-Dumpty* to *England and the English*. What opinions, oh reader who admires *The Good Soldier*, do you have about any of the above titles? Some years back, Auberon, son of Evelyn, Waugh declared, reviewing what he called smartly "an idiotic little book" of mine in which I had praised Wyndham Lewis' novels, that my writing on Lewis was "incomprehensible," since "none of us has read him." Ford, whose cumulative output exceeded even Lewis's, presents, to Auberon and I suspect to others, a similar challenge—or threat. Sondra Stang's now out-of-print *Ford Madox Ford Reader* (1986) was a gallant but hopeless attempt

---

Ford Madox Ford: A Dual Life, by Max Saunders. Vol. 1, *The World before the War;* vol. 2, *The After-War World.* New York: Oxford University Press, 1996.

to represent the writer by excerpting bits from unfamiliar novels and other prose works; but the "mammoth mumbler" remained, in vast stretches of his writings, still inaudible.

There have been a number of biographies of Ford, beginning with Arthur Mizener's attempt to separate fact from fiction in Ford's statements and claims. More recently, Alan Judd produced a highly readable and deft one-volume account that presented the life gracefully but didn't have much new to say about the art. Saunders has much to say about every aspect of Ford, and interrupts his narrative of the career in order to provide lengthy critical excursions into major and not-so-major books: fifty-eight tightly packed pages on *The Good Soldier;* eighty-four on *Parade's End;* thirty pages on Ford's autobiographical writings. These excursions are always intelligent, strongly and minutely argued, and quite difficult to read or at least to read well, since that necessitates having the books in question very much to the front of your mind. For most readers only *The Good Soldier* is likely to be available in such a way. Saunders is also a passionate advocate, losing no chance to defend Ford by explaining how others have misunderstood and misinterpreted him. He also finds much of interest, even of artistic success, in the "unread" novels Ford turned out: *Mr. Apollo, A Call,* and *Ladies Whose Bright Eyes,* from the prewar Ford Madox Hueffer years; *The Rash Act, Henry or Hugh,* and *Vive Le Roy* (his final novel) from the postwar years in which Hueffer became Ford. With the best of effort and good will, I am unable to share his enthusiasm, while recognizing—as one once enthusiastic about unread Wyndham Lewis novels—how a biographer and critic may be carried by his subject into responses that others, more detached, simply can't share.

The biography is subtitled "A Dual Life," and it would be less than useful to catalog the many ways and contexts in which Saunders explores Ford's dualities, beginning with the inescapable fact that in 1919, with a raft of books, two "wives" (his first and only real one, Elsie Martindale, refused to divorce him so he could marry Violet Hunt), and with shattering service in the Great War behind him, he changed his last name, by deed poll, from Hueffer to Ford. The second "half" of his life has its own symmetry: two more "wives," Stella Bowen and Janice Biala, plus affairs and romances; another raft of books; increasing time spent away from England, first in France, then in America; gradual metamorphosis into the persona he liked to call "an old man mad about writing." That "mad" has of course a dual sense signifying Ford's deeply held conviction that to write, or at least to read, imaginative literature was the greatest, perhaps the only great thing to do in one's life. But there is also the sense, felt by some of his friends and not a few of his enemies, that Ford was something like "mad," unable to distinguish between truth and falsehood, fiction and reality. Of course mixing up these categories, "deconstructing" them, is exactly what Ford thought was the impressionist writer's task. His 1924 memoir of Conrad he termed a novel; his books of sociological impressionism all aspired to and partly achieved the condition of fiction, of poetry; and his bona fide novels often frustrate and madden the reader through their devious, extravagant ways of *not* getting on with "story," of not behaving as if fiction were an imitation of an action with a beginning, middle, and end. English fiction, rather than exhibiting form and technique in the service of art, was composed largely of what Ford called "nuvvles," fat books full of plots and characters—written by Fielding, Thackeray, Dickens, the Brontës, George Eliot—for most of which Ford had no enthusiasm at all.

Saunders goes to great pains, especially by way of arguing with his predecessor Mizener—who took Ford to task for distorting and subverting what really happened—that Ford's way of transforming literal truth (granted, a slippery notion) into something more congenial to his imagination, was a playful and complicated kind of wit. But when all is said and done, what does one do with, say, the claims made by sentences like these from a letter Ford wrote to Herbert Read in 1920:

> You are unjust, rather, to Conrad. . . . He has done an immense deal for the Nuvvle in England—not so much as I, no doubt, but then that was not my job, and he is of the generation before mine. I learned all I know of Literature from Conrad—and England has learned all it knows of Literature from me. . . . I do not mean to say that Conrad did not learn a great deal from me when we got going; I daresay he learned more actual stuff of me than I of him. . . . But, but for him, I should have been a continuation of *Dante Gabriel Rossetti*—and think of the loss that would have been to you young things . . . and think what English literature would be without Conrad and James. . . . There would be nothing.

(The ellipses, by the way, are Ford's own, one of his shiftier habits.) Consider what these sentences "say": that Conrad has done an immense deal for English fiction, though not so much as Ford; that Ford learned everything he knew about Literature from him (though Conrad really learned more "actual stuff" from Ford); that without Conrad and James—and surely, it is implied, Ford Madox Ford—English literature would be nothing. So much for whatever Great Tradition you thought was there. I enjoyed this letter and its unapologetic clearing of the decks, but thought again of lines from Robert Lowell's poem: "Fiction, I'm selling short / the lies that made the great your equals." I presume that Saunders would say about this letter (he doesn't discuss it) that it is another example of how literary claims, like Ford's claims or beliefs in politics or religion, present attitudes that are impressionist: "illuminative exaggerations, unrealistic renderings of unrealistic positions." But they don't inevitably illuminate the subject; rather the subject becomes, yet once more, the indefatigable, irrepressible performance that is Ford Madox Ford, an important element in that performance being braggadocio. Allen Tate put it perfectly when he wrote that Ford's best biographer, when he came along (and now Mr. Saunders has come along), "will understand at the outset that Ford himself must be approached as a character in a novel, and that a novel by Ford."

I can't recall any biography of a writer in which so much space is devoted, so intensely, to rendering a critical description and judgment of individual works. Martin Stannard's two-volume biography of Waugh has much relevant and sensitive commentary on the books, but nothing comparable to Saunders's. By way of suggesting its scale, the eighty-four pages in the second volume devoted to Ford's tetralogy, *Parade's End*, at seven hundred words on a large page, add up to roughly sixty thousand words, the size of a substantial critical monograph. Nor is Saunders's discussion conducted through leisurely chronological retelling of what happens in the four novels; instead the discussion is topical, grouped under three large heads—Impressionism and Authority, Psychology, and Writing—each head then subdivided into categories like Political Views, Confession, Values, The Father, Metaphor, and many others. Questions of "doubling," of paranoia, of male intimacy, are explored in relation to the tetralogy, with a fullness that is, to say the least, challenging. For example, the section on paranoia contains the following sentence: "The real 'problem' in discussing Ford in relation to paranoia turns on six judgements," after which Saunders spells out each of the six. This may suggest something of the architectonic nature of the discussion, also why any reader except the most undaunted might well at least breathe a sigh before plunging on.

Saunders is especially illuminating with respect to the tetralogy's final volume, *The Last Post* (he refers to it by its English title, *Last Post*), certainly the least read of the four novels, in part because, in his Bodley Head edition of some years back, Graham Greene controversially chose to omit it. (Ford seems to have been of two minds about whether he wanted it as part of the whole work.) *The Last Post* is a very hard novel, also a surprising one in that the saga's hero, Christopher Tietjens, the war having concluded (the previous volume, *A Man Could Stand Up*—ends with Armistice Day) is absent from the book until its very end. Instead we get a series of monologues from his brother Mark, who is dying; from Mark's French wife, Mary Léonie; from Christopher's wife and nemesis, Sylvia; from his mistress and love, Valentine Wannop; and others. It takes unremitting attention, even more so than do *No More Parades* and *A Man Could Stand Up,* which are largely conducted within Christopher's head, to know where at any moment you are in *The Last Post.* Saunders quotes Dorothy Parker, whom I had no idea had written about Ford, as saying that his style in *The Last Post* "becomes so tortuous that he writes almost as if he were parodying himself," and that the long interior monologues constitute "grave hardships for the reader." Quite right, though Parker finally found the book worth its difficulties and responded to its "vastly stirring quality." Saunders speaks most originally about *The Last Post* in relation to its predecessors, noting that it looks more like a romance—a word that reverberates through Ford's career, his major co-product with Conrad being their unreadable novel *Romance*—and unlike the "ironic modernism of Joyce, Eliot, and Wyndham Lewis." This temperamental and formal difference may explain, or corroborate, the sense that, though he doesn't share Pound's simplified politics, it is with Pound that Ford shares most important affinities. (Pound's early study of the troubadours was of course titled *The Spirit of Romance.*)

Reviewing *The Last Post* when it was published, the novelist L. P. Hartley shrewdly called Ford "as mannered a writer as Meredith" and added that, like Meredith, "he rejoices in his manner." As one whose struggles with Meredith are remembered unhappily (ah, those graduate school days of pushing through *The Egoist!*) but who has just reread *Parade's End,* mainly with satisfaction, I'm sure Hartley puts the emphasis where it should be put. Ford remarked someplace that no Englishman ever finishes a sentence; thus the ellipsis is of crucial importance in his writing, fiction or not, and is instrumental in creating a highly mannered page. This is the case especially in *No More Parades* and *A Man Could Stand Up*—where Tietjens's consciousness

is so much at the center of things, roaming and swooping, concluding and
not concluding. Hartley's description of *The Last Post* suits the tetralogy as a
whole: "It moves with the *tempi* of life, sometimes tediously slow, sometimes
at break-neck speed. It is full of complicated issues, of pure and base motives,
of noble endeavours and unhappy outcomes, all bewilderingly mixed—all
viewed partially and fleetingly from a hundred angles. It has the richness and
the confusion and the profusion of life." By coincidence I have recently read,
with an expanded sense of what a marvelous work it is, Waugh's war trilogy,
Sword of Honour. That Ford and Waugh, those two analysts of, in Saunders's
language, "social posing and posturing," should have had nothing to do with
one another—especially that Waugh, who lived until 1966, never mentioned, perhaps out of perversity or concealment, what must have been his
debt to Ford—is strange indeed.

Compared to *Parade's End,* Ford's other masterwork, *The Good Soldier,*
has had more than its share of attention and admiration. It is, among other
things, a wonderful book to read and (yes) study with students, as an example of what astonishing things a novel can be made to do. But as Roger
Sale once put it, in his excellent essay "Ford's Coming of Age," "the fancy narration of *The Good Soldier* blinds many to the fact that it is shabby little
shocker."[1] Sale meant to provoke but in doing so put his finger on something
important, and limiting, about the novel: that with whatever combination
of sympathy or contempt you regard its narrator, Dowell, the book is full of
poison, self-pity, disgust, sexual horror. Sale thinks that the superiority of
Parade's End (I concur in the judgment) has everything to do with where it
came in Ford's career: that Stella Bowen, Ford's "wife" in the early twenties
when he began *Some Do Not,* rather than Violet Hunt, whom he was trying
to get out of his system when he wrote *The Good Soldier,* was the presence
that made all the difference. Perhaps so; but at any rate the sense of "life"
Hartley, Sale, and others find in *Parade's End* is altogether more generous
and capacious than anything that shows up in *The Good Soldier:* the tetralogy is a morally and humanly more attractive piece of work, even—to hesi-
tatingly invoke the Lawrentian ideal—a "bright book of life."[2]

---

1. To be found, along with other interesting essays, in *The Presence of Ford Madox Ford,* ed.
Sondra Stang (Philadelphia: University of Pennsylvania Press, 1981).

2. Anthony Powell wrote, on rereading *The Good Soldier,* "Once more I found it deplor-
able. I can understand Graham Greene's passion for [it], indeed all Ford, because he is full of
Graham's sort of baggage, RC problems, everyone lapped in self-pity. . . . The story is narrated

Ford's novels before *The Good Soldier,* only sampled by me, have their appeal to certain kinds of readers: *The Fifth Queen* trilogy, of which I got through volume 1, is impressive as historical recreation of spectacle in Tudor England, but to appreciate it you need to enjoy historical novels. *A Call,* by consent his most Jamesian performance, published three years before his casual little book of anecdotes (calling itself "a critical essay" about the Master), has its London atmosphere down pat, but otherwise its unreality is patent. Arnold Bennett, who knew something about reality, having written *The Old Wives' Tale,* said that *A Call* was "profoundly and hopelessly untrue to life," but that as an "original kind of fairy tale" it was just about perfect. (Ford's first publication, in 1893, was *The Brown Owl,* a fairy tale for children.) Still, it's not easy, and perhaps not wise, to trade in the novel for the fairy tale. Ford's final novels from the 1930s— *The Rash Act, Henry for Hugh,* and *Vive Le Roy*—feel similarly unreal. They receive words of praise from Saunders (Mizener was, by contrast, much more critically severe on them), but it's hard to take them seriously when we're constantly running up against writing like this, from the opening of chapter 2 of *The Rash Act:*

> Hugh Monckton Allard Smith had strolled across the floor of the little *dancing* to where Henry Martin had sat beside the silent depressed *poule.* Hugh Monckton, who had been rolling a cigarette as he walked, looked down on them from his considerable height, and, still rolling, had remarked nonchalantly to Henry Martin:

> "Met you somewhere, haven't I? Know your face. Because it's damn like my own." He added: "Would you pay for my drinks? I find I've left my notecase at home."

Can it be that this is by the lover of Flaubert, compatriot of Conrad, proselytizer for *progression d'effet,* the time shift—for Style as the only thing that makes writing interesting? It sounds rather as if P. G. Wodehouse were at the controls, except that Wodehouse is a good deal more amusing.

For me, Ford's books of biographical impressions and reminiscences of

---

by an American wholly unlike any American one ever met, about a good old English squire and cavalry officer, the background completely cardboard, who sleeps with every woman he meets. The last is believable enough, at same time immensely heavy weather made about it all. Finally he commits suicide in orgy of Ford's Teutonic sentimentality" (*Journals, 1990–1992* [London: Heinemann, 1997], 54).

himself in relation to other writers are much more interesting, indeed delightful than, with a very few exceptions, his novels. *Memories and Impressions* (on the pre-Raphaelites); *Thus to Revisit* (on English writers from the
early part of this century); the splendid memoir of Conrad; *Return to Yesterday* and *It Was the Nightingale* (his two novelistic visits to his own past); *Portraits from Life*—these can be reread, skipping judiciously here and there, by
way of discovering, as one always discovers, some memorable formulation.
This time through *Thus to Revisit*, for example, I found the following, just to
name three:

> [On Conrad's *The Secret Agent:*] Other writers would render a London
> that is just London. Mr. Conrad gives us the Eternal City that floats in the
> minds of an immense company of men. . . . It is, this place, triumphantly
> A City—but a city, rather of the human soul than any place in topography.
> Similarly the Anarchists of *the Secret Agent* are Anarchists of Nowhere.

> [On Henry James:] He liked to appear as a sort of Mr. Pickwick—with the
> rather superficial benevolences, and the mannerisms of which he was per-
> fectly aware. But below that protective mask was undoubtedly a plane of
> nervous cruelty. I have heard him be—to simple and quite unpretentious
> people—more diabolically blighting than it was quite decent for a man to
> be—for he was always an artist in expression."

> [On his own poetry:] "When I read my own verse I know that I have *tried*
> to write like a brandified sentimentalist. And I have succeeded every time."

There are of course countless more of such scattered throughout these
books as well as *The March of Literature,* the immense survey of writing from
Confucius to the present, that was published in 1938, a year before Ford died.
Saunders calls it a "captivating demonstration of what it means to read" and
quotes Margaret Cole, in a letter to Stella Bowen written after Ford was dead,
saying about the book "I have not for years read anything that so really
breathed the spirit of literature as a thing that lived & went on through every
sort of language & through every sort of age." *The March of Literature* (now
available in paperback, courtesy of Dalkey Archive) was written partly at the
Clarksville house of Allen Tate and Caroline Gordon, aptly titled Benfolly,
where Ford and Janice Biala spent time in the summer of 1937 (Ford was beginning and concluding his academic career as a professor at Olivet College
in Michigan). Biala noted that it was "awful" that summer at Benfolly, that

"in every room in the house there's a typewriter and at every typewriter there sits a genius." The host himself, Tate, put it this way:

> My wife Caroline Gordon, with one idiotic servant, ran the precariously balanced *ménage*. Ford could eat French food only, but Ida, with the occasional assistance of her mother Electra, the washerwoman, could not even cook Tennessee, much less French. Ford was unhappy in the 95°F, but every morning he paced the columned gallery—which had nothing but the earth to support it, and dictated to Mrs. Tworkov several pages of *The March of Literature*.

It should also be remembered that Robert Lowell, who dropped in on the Tates and stayed for three months, had pitched his tent someplace on the lawn, which doubtless added to the daily festivities.

I have said virtually nothing here—and Max Saunders says a great deal, always to the point—about Ford and women, especially the two he lived with in the last two decades of his life, Stella Bowen and Janice Biala, both of whom appear as something close to heroines, certainly most admirable and attractive human beings. Biala, interviewed by Sondra Stang in 1979 for the collection Stang was putting together, said this when asked if Ford's life was a sad one (Mizener titled his biography, alluding to *The Good Soldier, The Saddest Story*):

> I don't think Ford had a sad life. I think of his great vitality (I think of all the books he wrote, how *much* he lived), his gaiety, his confidence, his optimism, his wild sense of humor. Ford did what he pleased all his life. . . .Those last days in Deauville, I had in a local doctor. He was a little mean-looking man, and after the first visit, Ford having been not a very good patient, he said: "It is obvious that Monsieur has always done whatever he wanted in his life." He said it spitefully and I could see *he'd* never done anything he wanted to do in his life. But how right he was.

And in response to the perception on the part of some contemporaries and critics that Ford's life looked to be a "disordered" one, Biala said it all in a single sentence: "A man who never missed a day's work in his life can't be said to have a disordered life."

Hudson Review, Autumn 1998

The Trouble with Ernest

K<small>ENNETH</small> L<small>YNN</small>, author of the latest and best biography of Ernest Heming-way, is Arthur Lovejoy Professor of History at Johns Hopkins University. His field is American civilization, and he has published—among other works—a book on Mark Twain and an excellent, sympathetically critical biography of William Dean Howells. Latterly his criticism has become more polemical and programmatically unillusioned. A recent collection of essays and re-views, *The Air-Line to Seattle,* chastised the American professariat for what Mr. Lynn termed its capitulation to the "genteel tradition" (but now with a strong leftist bias) George Santayana had analyzed years ago. Not only did Lynn set himself against various critical and historical versions of American literature and culture, he also pushed for major reseeings of writers such as Emerson, the Twain of *Huckleberry Finn,* and, most radically, Hemingway. In the course of reviewing an unsatisfactory book on the last-named (Lynn was already at work on his own biography), he insisted that, contrary to pop-ular legend, Hemingway was in fact a mama's boy, fearfully and destructively inhibited, "wounded" in a way quite other than had been assumed by the band of critics who—and with Hemingway's own encouragement of the myth—took his wounding at Fossalte di Piave in 1918 to be the source of later traumas, in his life and in his fiction.

The new biography is built on Mr. Lynn's conviction, developed and justified at length in the book's early stages, that Grace Hall Hemingway was (in Lynn's good phrase) "the dark queen of Hemingway's inner world," and that she reigned there for all his life. To simplify what Lynn goes into in ex-tensive detail, it was Grace Hemingway's passion—and that is the word for it—to treat Ernest and his sister Marcelline as if they were twins, dressing them in lookalike outfits, the first of which consisted of "crocheted bonnets,

---

Hemingway, by Kenneth S. Lynn. New York: Simon & Schuster, 1987.

three-quarter length coats and ruffled dimity skirts that brushed their ankles." Photos taken of Ernest when he was three-and-a-half years old and his sister almost five show them (in the mother's words) "always dressed alike, like two little girls"; at other times she dressed them as "two sturdy little chaps in overhauls." Grace also paid great attention to the hairstyles of—again in her words—"my two Dutch dollies," sometimes decreeing that long hair was in, sometimes the opposite. Indeed Lynn suggests that it was the arbitrariness and changeability of Grace's sartorial whims that confused the children, and in Hemingway's case hurt him in a major way.

If one is tempted—and I was immediately tempted—to scoff at this line of argument as making too much out of how some mothers dressed their children back then, a reading of Hemingway's posthumous, editorially stapled-together novel *The Garden of Eden* gives Lynn's case strength. For the puzzling and insistent fuss made in that book about confusion of sexual identity—especially in much tiresome gushing about the wife having her hair cut short, and dyed, so that she will be "like" the husband—makes sense (if it can be called that) only by seeing how deep the matter ran in Hemingway's psyche. Lynn gives us a way to view this matter and to understand why Hemingway's hatred for Grace—"that bitch," as he loved to refer to her—needed to be worked at full-time, took up enormous psychic energy. Not of course that it was "just" hate. He loved the fact that his mother was proud of him for having been wounded in action (he was in an ambulance unit of the Red Cross) and wrote to her that "when a mother brings a son into the world she must know that some day the son will die, and the mother of a man that has died for his country should be the proudest woman in the world and the happiest." This absolute capitulation to Gold-Star Mom boosterism is merely the other, saccharine side of his nastiness toward her. Like all tough babies, Hemingway was consistently sentimental and cruel by turns, even at once; Lynn's biography misses no opportunity to detail instances of such behavior.

At one point in the book, just before taking up Hemingway's years in Paris, Lynn steps back to give us the following summary of how he imagines his subject's inner life to have been shaped:

To be a boy but to be treated like a girl. To feel impelled to prove your masculinity through flat denials of your anxieties (*Fraid a nothing* had been your motto as a child) and bold lies about your exploits. To be forced to practice the most severe economy in your attempts to "render" your life artistically, because your capital of self-understanding was too small to permit you to be expansive and your fear of self-exposure too powerful. To make a virtue of necessity by packing troubled feelings below the surface of your stories like dynamite beneath a bridge.

One could object to this account for the way it turns the writer wholly into the passive agent of his sexual or familial curse, the famous Hemingway style reduced to nothing more than the result of being "forced" to practice economy in the writing of sentences and paragraphs. The brilliant discovery we had thought he made, about how by leaving things *out* of the writing it could be made the more suggestive and troubling, now becomes nothing more than the consequences of minimal self-understanding—this man didn't know himself well enough to let things hang out.

"Freudian" understandings or explanations of how writers got to produce the art they produced—after which the art itself can be dismissed, or at least put in its place—should be treated with impatience, or worse. What makes Lynn's dealings with Hemingway something other and better than such non-esthetic procedures, is that he cares about Hemingway's art (especially his early stories and first two novels) but also sees how very odd is that art, how little it invites us to see it as the result of thoughtful, "objective" planning. If all writers could be said to be in the grip of their gift—or their beast—Hemingway was in its grip more than most; he is less likely to be distorted by an approach such as Lynn's, since the distortions, the twists in his art, are so apparent and inescapable.

At the same time, there are at least two American writers whose work yields richer satisfactions and pleasures than Hemingway's and whose biographers, committed to elaborate psychological explanations of their subjects, manage to tell us very little by way of locating and describing the literary value of their work. I am thinking of Leon Edel on Henry James and Lawrance Thompson on Robert Frost. Both biographers relentlessly wielded a theory about how their subjects came to arrive at their respective inner landscapes; both biographers were helpless before the novels or poems that somehow emerged from that landscape. (Edel contented himself with telling plots and identifying this or that "real-life" character source; Thompson quoted a poem and found it illustrated one or another "dark" tendency in the poet's makeup.) It almost seems that the very intentness with which these biographers fix on a scheme that explains everything, debars them from anything like flexible, critical attention to the poem or novel in question; they are so busy showing how the example confirms their theory that they have no time to listen to what and how it speaks. Kenneth Lynn is a much better critic than either Edel or Thompson; but Hemingway, while not the equal of James or Frost as a writer, was surely—at least in his early stories and novels—a stylist of great delicacy ("a very considerable artist in prose-fiction," wrote Wyndham Lewis, before proceeding to make fun of that artist's fondness for his "Dumb-ox" heroes). Hemingway's style still presents a challenge to criticism and is why one keeps returning to him in the classroom, where passages can be read aloud and pondered. In the light of this challenge, let us consider Lynn's treatment of three of Hemingway's very best stories from *In Our Time:* "Indian Camp," "Soldier's Home," and "Big Two-Hearted River."

In the first of these, the boy Nick goes with his father and his Uncle George to an Indian shanty where Nick's father, a doctor, performs a Caesarean section on an Indian woman (he performs it with a jackknife and then sews up the incision with gut leaders for sutures); meanwhile her husband, as she screams, slits his own throat from ear to ear with a razor. Afterwards, rowing home in their boat, Nick questions his father about death and whether many men and women kill themselves. Lynn says that beyond the obvious "autobiographical emotion" in the boy's feelings of closeness with his father and dislike of his uncle's sarcasm (there was a real Uncle George Hemingway), the story's major inspiration comes from emotions generated by the circumstances of Hemingway's recent fatherhood. Living in Toronto, and a reporter on the *Star,* he had returned to town from a news assignment to find a telegram saying that his wife, in labor, had been taken to the hospital; at this news he became distraught with fear and a sense of helplessness (though in fact the birth went smoothly enough). Lynn argues that the terrified-to-death Indian in the story is a "symbolic equivalent of Hemingway":

> When the Indian slits his throat, he acts out the thought of suicide to which Hemingway had made reference in his letter to Gertrude Stein and Alice Toklas after Hadley and the baby came home from the hospital. The probability that in describing the awful fate of the Indian Hemingway achieved catharsis is evident in the story's final moments of peace.

And he adds that, of course, we can't help thinking of how the real-life counterparts of both Nick and his father would one day do away with themselves.

All this may well be so, but is it—especially the developed parallel between Hemingway and the Indian husband—what we really care about in "Indian Camp"? Lynn rightly calls the story "a miracle of verbal compression," but his analysis does little to suggest how that miracle is shaped, concerned as it rather is with such matters as "symbolic equivalents." The story concludes with two magical paragraphs in which Hemingway's touch has never been surer:

> They were seated in the boat, Nick in the stern, his father rowing. The sun was coming up over the hills. A bass jumped, making a circle in the water. Nick trailed his hand in the water. It felt warm in the sharp chill of the morning.
> In the early morning on the lake sitting in the stern of the boat with his father rowing, he felt quite sure that he would never die.

Here is the style at its purest and most compelling, and nothing Lynn says about the parallels or "the probability . . . that Hemingway achieved catharsis" can touch it. To be sure, his commentary avoids the crudities of ham-fisted interpretations of "Indian Camp," like Philip Young's ("an initiation . . . an event which is violent or evil, or both") or Judith Fetterley's ("a story of initiation . . . a lesson in the meaning of growing up male in America").[1] But a really relevant comment on the style would have to speak about the beautiful sequence of the father rowing, the sun coming up over the hills, the jumping bass, the boy trailing his hand in the water and feeling it warm in the morning's sharp chill. Hemingway would have approved of Frost's assertion that poetry was "performance and prowess and feats of association," since, in a passage like the one above, he was so good at those things. And he might also have sympathized with Frost's question: "Why don't critics talk about those things?" Lynn does, but not enough; he may believe that such notations are the reader's business, or he may have other—in his opinion, more important—fish to fry.

"Soldier's Home" presents, in Lynn's words, "a face-to-face conflict between mother and son, on a battlefield that was normally off-limits to the fictive imagination." The conflict occurs over fried eggs with bacon and a stack of buckwheat cakes, cooked for the come-home soldier, Harold Krebs,

---

1. Philip Young, *Ernest Hemingway: A Reconsideration* (University Park: Pennsylvania State University Press, 1966), 31; Judith Fetterley, *The Resisting Reader* (Bloomington: Indiana University Press, 1978), 46.

by a mother who has designs on him, wants him to think about earning his living, reminds him that there can be "no idle hands in His Kingdom." Krebs denies that he's in that Kingdom, and when his mother asks him whether he doesn't love her, says no, he doesn't love anybody. He then tries to apologize, and after the mother tells him that "I held you next to my heart when you were a tiny baby," Krebs (Hemingway writes) "felt sick and vaguely nauseated." Since she has made him "lie," he determines to head out soon for Kansas City. Lynn rightly calls this finale "excruciatingly painful," but also insists that "the utterly unrelenting, utterly unqualified characterization of Mrs. Krebs as a monster" reveals Hemingway to be in thralldom to his real mother: "Only a man who was truly free could have seen that she had done her best to be a good mother, that she had not meant to harm her son and that she, too, had been tossed about by psychological impulses she did not understand." Is there not something odd about this suddenly generous attitude on the biographer's part toward Grace Hemingway? After all, it is Lynn who has spent so much devoted energy demonstrating how she warped her son's character; now the son is blamed for lack of understanding, and Hemingway's fictional characterization of Mrs. Krebs as a "monster" is seen to reflect at least as much discredit on the writer as on the poor mother. If I'm going to agree that Hemingway was not "truly free," I need to be told what writer was or is. At any rate, and Lynn would I think agree, a "freer" writer, dispensing more even-handed justice, could not have achieved the partial, simplifying, but absolutely memorable force of "Soldier's Home."

Finally, "Big Two-Hearted River"—which Lynn is concerned to rehabilitate by first demolishing the notion that Nick Adams goes fishing in order to block out his memories of being wounded in the war. That notion, encouraged by Hemingway in a letter of 1948 to Malcolm Cowley ("I was hurt bad all the way through and I was really spooked at the end"), Lynn sees as a cover for the real hurt occasioned by Grace, who in 1920 had told him off in a scorching (and quite eloquent) letter expelling him from their summer place.

Why then, in the story, is Nick so preoccupied with holding off upsetting memories? Lynn speculates as follows:

> Perhaps . . . the "other needs" Nick feels he has put behind him include a need to please his mother, while his talk of his tent as his home may represent a reaction to being thrown out of his parents' summer cottage. Perhaps, too, the burned-over country and the grasshoppers that have turned

black from living in it constitute tacit reminders to him of his mother's penchant for burning things. And finally, the activity of his mind that keeps threatening to overwhelm his contentment could be rage.

In life, surely, these "could" be, but in Hemingway's art there are no coulds or perhaps. Lynn seems to agree when in the next paragraph he admits "First and last, Nick remains an enigma," then goes on to castigate critics who account for him by adducing—with his creator in mind—the First World War as culprit.

But does talking about Hemingway's mother put us in any closer touch with the rhythms and sensations so marvelously present in "Big Two-Hearted River"? Here is Nick, having settled into his camp, cooking his dinner:

> The beans and spaghetti warmed. Nick stirred them and mixed them together. They began to bubble, making little bubbles that rose with difficulty to the surface. There was a good smell. Nick got out a bottle of tomato catchup and cut four slices of bread. The little bubbles were coming faster now. Nick sat down beside the fire and lifted the frying pan off. He poured about half the contents out into the tin plate. It spread slowly on the plate. Nick knew it was too hot. He poured on some tomato catchup. He knew the beans and spaghetti were still too hot . . . He was very hungry. Across the river in the swamp, in the almost dark he saw a mist rising. He looked at the tent once more. All right. He took a full spoonful from the plate.
> "Chrise," Nick said, "Geezus Chrise," he said happily.

This fine moment is poised on the edge of the stylistically ludicrous ("He liked to open cans," runs a neighboring sentence). But so much of Hemingway's writing is poised there—the crafty, "dumb" sentences, the minimal verbs, the repetitions that appeal to our ears while suspending our urge to find "meanings" in them. Hemingway's low-mimetic, "noble" style is but an inch away from the bathetic: think of how similar is the prose in his travesty, *The Torrents of Spring,* to "pure" moments in the stories like the one above. (Yogi Johnson or Scripps O'Neill from *Torrents* could surely rise to the degree of articulateness Nick reaches with his happy "Geezus Chrise.")

"No one who looks *at* it, will want to look *behind* it," said Wyndham Lewis about Joyce's *Ulysses.* But from the beginning, those who have looked at Hemingway's sentences felt they needed to look behind them for a significance not found on their surface; it all began with Edmund Wilson finding that Hemingway's "naivete of language" served "actually to convey profound emotion and complex states of mind." But what is the force of "actually," and why should we presume that behind the simple language lies profundity and complexity, or even states of mind?[2] Are we justified in moving from Hemingway's troubled psyche in order to endow his characters and his fiction with a similar set of feelings? Or is it all the magnificent stunt of an illusionist, casting his spell over us for as long as the story takes to tell? Despite his acumen and conviction, I don't think Lynn deals enough with such matters, since—committed to his "strong" interpretation of what lies behind or underneath Hemingway's writing—he neglects to look sufficiently *at* that writing.

In spending so much time discussing (niggling at?) Lynn's reading of some of Hemingway's best work, I have of necessity left most things in the biography untouched. My partial excuse here will be that Frederick Crews has treated the book at great length—and accorded it the highest praise (in "Pressure Under Grace," *New York Review of Books,* August 13, l987). But among its aspects I found particularly illuminating were the pages on *The Sun Also Rises* and *A Farewell to Arms,* especially the earlier novel, which Grace Hemingway called "one of the filthiest books of the year" and whose publication, she opined, was "a doubtful honor." (There's nothing like having your mom in your corner!) Lynn gives a brilliant account, by far the best I've read, of Hemingway's relations with Scott Fitzgerald, and there are original, sharply turned, revisionary readings of famous stories like "The Short Happy Life of Francis Macomber" and "The Snows of Kilimanjaro."

Of course any biographer's problem with Hemingway is that after 1930 everything begins to go downhill: the novels get worse, the stories dry up, the behavior becomes more horrendous. Then there is the prodigious drinking to be chronicled, testified to, for example, in Hemingway's "regular Sunday hangover letter" (to his editor, Max Perkins, in 1940) which fills out the scorecard for the previous night's journey from absinthe to red wine to vodka to having "battened it down with whiskeys and soda until 3 a.m." Concurrent with the drinking, there were the physical injuries, accidents, and general bodily deterioration. The unpleasant story of it all is told here with thoroughness and some compassion. I think it fair to say that for all the

---

2. The most (and almost the only) astute criticism of Hemingway's style is to be found in James Guetti's *Word-Music* (New Brunswick, N.J.: Rutgers University Press, 1980), 139–49.

heavy interpretive artillery directed at Hemingway's psyche, Lynn does not end up, as have some biographers, more or less hating his subject. At one point he quotes Norman Mailer's assertion about Hemingway that "what he accomplished was heroic, for it is possible that he carried a weight of anxiety with him which would have suffocated any man smaller than himself." Lynn's book allows us to follow the accomplishment in detail, indeed see it clearly for the first time.

Hudson Review, Spring 1988

Classic Chandler

DREISER, Cather, Wharton, Dos Passos, Faulkner, Steinbeck, Richard Wright, Flannery O'Connor, most recently Nathanael West: the list of twentieth-century American fictionists whose work has been published in *The Library of America* is unsurprising. But that two volumes in the *Library* should be devoted to the work of Raymond Chandler is rather more so. This surprise at Chandler getting into the club so soon or at all (obviously, the absence of Hemingway and Fitzgerald involves rights to reprint) has everything to do with the fact that he is the first writer of thrillers, the first "mystery" novelist to be selected. But there are further indications that Chandler's reputation has never stood higher than at present: a biography by an English journalist, Tom Hiney, and a reissue of a 1962 collection of letters and essays testify to interest in him on more than one front. Nor is the interest of an antiquarian sort: the assumption behind these books is that there are people out there who still want to read about—even to read—Chandler.

Tom Hiney's biography is well written, sensible, and sympathetic to Chandler and his work, though it doesn't justify itself as an improvement on the pioneering Chandlerian Frank MacShane's biography of two decades back (MacShane also edited Chandler's letters). The main events of the life are capably rehearsed: Chandler's birth in Chicago; his move to England with his mother, after she and his alcoholic father separated; schooling at Dulwich College in London; brief identity as an impressionistic young poet and prose writer who published in English magazines; return to the United States and service in the Canadian Expeditionary Forces during World

Stories and Early Novels and *Later Novels and Other Writings,* by Raymond Chandler, with notes by Frank McShane. New York: Library of America, 1995. *Raymond Chandler: A Biography,* by Tom Hiney. New York: Atlantic Monthly Press, 1997. *Raymond Chandler Speaking,* edited by Dorothy Gardiner and Katherine Sorley Walker. Berkeley: University of California Press, 1997.

War I; life in Southern California, the death of his mother, and his marriage soon thereafter to Cecile "Cissy" Pascal, already twice-married and significantly older than her new husband. In the 1920s Chandler worked as an auditor for an oil company, with some success; he had affairs with other women, none of them serious or prolonged. His eventual firing in 1932 on grounds of absenteeism and alcoholism precipitated his decision to become a writer, indeed the kind of thriller writer who didn't yet exist (not even Dashiell Hammett, whose career was winding down). He published a number of "pulp" fictions in the crime magazine *Black Mask*, later "cannibalizing" them in his novels. When Chandler was fifty, his first novel, *The Big Sleep*, was brought out by Knopf, followed by *Farewell, My Lovely* a year later. Although these novels were *succès d'estime*, their good reviews didn't make them big sellers, and it wasn't until 1943, Hiney points out, when his fourth novel, *The Lady in the Lake*, appeared, that his career took off. It did so not because of that novel but because, a few weeks previously, Knopf had sold the paperback rights of *The Big Sleep* to Avon. The twenty-five-cent edition sold 300,000 copies, with a further 150,000 in a special armed-services edition. Four months later Knopf gave Pocket Books the rights to *Farewell, My Lovely:* result, one million copies sold. Chandler had arrived.

There followed, in the 1940s, his fling with Hollywood, a relatively productive one compared to those of some writers who tried it. His collaboration with Billy Wilder on the screenplay for James M. Cain's *Double Indemnity* almost insured the superb movie that resulted (more than helped along by Fred MacMurray, Barbara Stanwyck, and Edward G. Robinson.) Although he also worked on less distinguished products, such as *And Now Tomorrow* and *The Unseen* (unseen by me since my thirteenth year), and though the final version of *Strangers on a Train*, in which he collaborated with Hitchcock, didn't satisfy him ("no guts . . . no characters, no dialogue"), he made a substantial amount of money—$40,000 for eight weeks' work on *Strangers*. At that point the total earnings from American royalties on his novels—of which only sixty-eight thousand of the three and a half million copies sold had been in hardback—totaled $56,000.

Perhaps even more important in adding luster to the Chandler image were the movies Hollywood made, with varying amounts of fidelity and artistic success, from his own novels. In 1944 Edward Dmytryk directed *Murder, My Sweet* (title changed from *Farewell, My Lovely*) with an unthreatening but wholly agreeable Dick Powell as Philip Marlowe, a lot of good Californian interiors, and much fog, exterior to and inside Marlowe's drugged and battered head.[1] *The Big Sleep* followed in 1946, with Bogart as the detective, following up on his performance as Sam Spade in *The Maltese Falcon*. The "sexy" antics added to the production, between Bogart and his real-life sweetheart, Lauren Bacall, aren't much fun (was Lauren Bacall ever much fun?), but the pacing is admirable and there is Elisha Cook Jr.'s memorable portrait of the doomed little man, Harry Jones. Neither *The Brasher Doubloon* (*The High Window*), with improbable George Montgomery as Marlowe, nor *The Lady in the Lake,* also made in 1947, with the also improbable Robert Montgomery and the famous (boring) "camera-eye" technique, added anything worth seeing of note to Chandler on film.

My introduction to him, whose name at the time I barely associated with them, was effected through the movies of his first two books, and it wasn't until a decade later that, as a graduate student, I read the novels—partly by way of demonstrating I was no dryasdust Eng lit pedant. For the first time I experienced Chandler's style, the way he liked to put sentences together into a paragraph. When early in the film of *The Big Sleep*, Marlowe heads for Geiger's bookshop on the pretext of locating some rare book, we see Bogart in a splendid trench coat striding through the pouring L.A. rain. But the prose that opens chapter six of the novel shows something else, something more:

> Rain filled the gutters and splashed knee-high off the sidewalk. Big cops in slickers that shone like gun barrels had a lot of fun carrying giggling girls across the bad places. The rain drummed hard on the roof of the car and the burbank top began to leak. A pool of water formed on the floorboards for me to keep my feet in. It was too early in the fall for that kind of rain. I struggled into a trench coat and made a dash for the nearest drugstore and bought myself a pint of whiskey. Back in the car I used enough of it to keep warm and interested. I was long overparked, but the cops were too busy carrying girls and blowing whistles to bother about that.

The writer is having a good time, even as his hero's situation ranges from uncomfortable to "warm and interested." Those "big cops" turn into Mack Sennett figures of fun; the leaky car whose roof with its "burbank top" (a

---

1. *Murder, My Sweet* was nominated for an Academy Award in 1944 but lost out, because of censorship fears, to *Going My Way,* with Bing Crosby and Barry Fitzgerald as those loveable Irish priests. Commented Chandler, "My belief is Hollywood will never find itself until it has the guts to tell the Catholics to go to hell."

nostalgia item?) is there by way of hatching the mildly sardonic reference to the convenient water buildup, "for me to keep my feet in." An unobvious way to talk about what whiskey does for you—keeps you warm and interested— and the final friendly return to the cops, still doing their thing, add up to a paragraph that is, first and last, highly entertaining. (An earlier version of the paragraph occurs in Chandler's pulp story, "Killer in the Rain.")

Here and elsewhere Marlowe is the beneficiary of Chandler's genial performing skills, in a way that distinguishes him from Hammett's private eye in *The Dain Curse*, who notes from his car window, "Rain and darkness shut out the scenery. . . . It was a rotten ride, wet, noisy, and bumpy. It ended in as dark, wet, and muddy a spot as any we had gone through." Hammett strings sentences together with a minimum of tone and reflexive commentary; so when in *The Maltese Falcon* Sam Spade returned home after finding his partner, Archer, murdered, he reached for a tall bottle of Bacardi, "poured a drink and drank it standing. He put bottle and glass on the table, sat on the side of the bed facing them, and rolled a cigarette. He had drunk his third glass of Bacardi and was lighting his fifth cigarette when . . ." Just the facts, please: if Spade feels any more "warm and interested" than before he got out the Bacardi, we won't know about it. Hammett is dedicated to keeping things extremely cool indeed; Chandler, by contrast, humorously warms them up.

More than once, in his letters and prose statements that make modest attempts at theoretical claims, Chandler let it be known that for him the beginning—and maybe the end—of writing fiction was verbal play: "All I wanted when I began was to play with a fascinating new language, and trying, without anybody noticing it, to see what it would do as a means of expression which might remain on the level of unintellectual thinking and yet acquire the power to say things which are usually only said with a literary air." Hemingway had done this, and starting out in the thirties to write his own sentences, Chandler owed an immense debt to him. Although he spent energy scoffing at modernist critics who "fawned" on T. S. Eliot, he would have liked Eliot's insistence, apropos of *The Waste Land*, that it was in the main "a piece of rhythmical grumbling." That definition would have seemed truer to Chandler than saying the poem was about the decline of Western civilization. He insisted that Marlowe, and by implication himself, had no "social conscience," although he had "a personal conscience, which is an entirely different matter."

He took every opportunity in his correspondence to disabuse people of the notion that subject matter was central to his fictional operation. Charles Morton, an editor at the *Atlantic*, to whom some of Chandler's liveliest letters were posted, was once invited by him to commission a piece titled "The Insignificance of Significance," "in which I will demonstrate in my usual whorehouse style that it doesn't matter a damn what a novel is about, that the only fiction of any moment in any age is that which does magic with words . . . and that the only writers left who have anything to say are those who write about practically nothing and monkey around with odd ways of doing it." This sense of belatedness and the aggressiveness here and elsewhere conceal, not too subtly, an uneasiness on Chandler's part about the subject matter—detectives, crooks, cops, graft, sleaze, Los Angeles—he had stuck himself with. After all, he was a man who had been given the benefit, at Dulwich College, of what he more than once refers to as "a classical education" and who had written some "sensitive" if not very convincing poems. He wanted to be praised by "highbrows," even as he was contemptuous of them; that Edmund Wilson, in his dismissal of the detective novel ("Who Cares Who Killed Roger Ackroyd?"), singled out Chandler as an exception to the form's triviality, only provoked in reply the following shot: "The problem of what is significant literature I leave to fat bores like Edmund Wilson—a man of many distinctions—among which personally I revered most highly . . . that of having made fornication as dull as a railroad time table." (He is referring, not without justice, to Wilson's *Memoirs of Hecate County.*)

Chandler is engaging as a writer partly because he was so open about his aim to write about "practically nothing" but "monkey around with odd ways of doing it." What is there to say about a practically anonymous office building in L.A. called the Fulwider Building? Quite a bit when you monkey around with it:

A single drop light burned far back, beyond an open, once gilt elevator. There was a tarnished and well-missed spittoon on a gnawed rubber mat. A case of false teeth hung on the mustard colored wall like a fuse box in a screen porch . . . Painless dentists, shyster detective agencies, small sick businesses that had crawled there to die. . . . A nasty building. (*The Big Sleep*)

And here is Marlowe on a nasty section of L.A. he calls Bunker Hill:

> Bunker Hill is old town, lost town, shabby town, crook town. Once, very long ago, it was the choice residential district of the city, and there are still standing a few of the jigsaw Gothic mansions. . . . They are all rooming houses now, their parquetry floors are scratched and worn through the once glossy finish and the wide sweeping staircases are dark with time and with cheap varnish laid on over generations of dirt. In the tall rooms haggard landladies bicker with shifty tenants. On the wide cool front porches, reaching their cracked shoes into the sun, and staring at nothing, sit the old men with faces like lost battles. (*The High Window*)

The writing makes decay, the down and out, into something fresh.

Chandler liked to drop loud hints about his work that he was afraid critics and readers would overlook: "Why is it that the Americans—of all people the quickest to reverse their moods—do not see the strong element of burlesque in my kind of writing? Or is it just the intellectuals who miss that?" When in *The Little Sister*, Marlowe says "yes" to something the sister, Orfamay Quest, has asked him, he says it "in a voice that sounded like Orson Welles with his mouth full of crackers." It's hard to miss that, as it is to ignore the element of farce or burlesque in a "violent" moment when Marlowe is struggling, in *The Big Sleep*, with Carmen Sternwood, Joe Brody, and Brody's girl friend, "Blonde Agnes": "The blonde spat at me and threw herself on my leg and tried to bite that. I cracked her on the head with the gun, not very hard, and tried to stand up. She rolled down my legs and wrapped her arms around them. I fell back on the davenport."

That comfy thirties object, the davenport, which shows up in all the novels, is perfect for the Keystone Cops routine at the end of which Marlowe finds himself laughing unaccountably. (No doubt he's amused by Chandler's writing.) Everyone has his favorite Marlowe trope, many of them dutifully racist ("Cute as a Filipino on Saturday night") or fetched from far, as in the rainy night where "you can grow a beard waiting for a taxi." At times the comparison is deliberately over the line, even to the diminishing of sinister moments, as when in *The Big Sleep* Marlowe listens outside the office to the killer, Lash Canino (well played in the movie by one Bob Steele), speaking to his about-to-be victim, Harry Jones: "The purring voice was now as false as an usherette's eyelashes and as slippery as a watermelon seed." Surely this goes too far, and surely that's the point: the element of burlesque, even in grim scenes, can't help asserting itself.

Rereading Chandler, I came across things I'd somehow missed previously, but that stood out when the novels' affinity with burlesque is stressed. For example, I wonder how many readers of *Farewell, My Lovely* remember that, when Marlowe is summoned for a chat with the sinister Jules Amthor, leading to his doped-up incarceration in Dr. Sonderborg's "rest home," he is taken to Amthor by an Indian of memorable proportions. Chapter 20 begins succinctly: "The Indian smelled," and goes on to detail the extent of that smell and the panache of the Indian's sartorial habit: "A tie dangled outside his buttoned jacket, a black tie which had been tied with a pair of pliers in a knot the size of a pea." Almost immediately Marlowe and the Indian get into a verbal tussle, as the latter orders him to "Come quick, come now":

> "Come where?" I said.
> "Huh, Me Second Planting. Me Hollywood Indian."
> "Have a chair, Mr. Planting,"
> He snorted and his nostrils got very wide. They had been wide enough for mouseholes to start with.
> "Name Second Planting. Name no Mister Planting."
> "What can I do for you?"

After Second Planting replies in a "sonorous boom" with "Indian" talk— "Great white father say come quick"—Marlowe tells him to cut out the pig Latin, to which he replies, eloquently, "Nuts," and Marlowe adds, "We sneered at each other across the desk for a moment. He sneered better than I did."

None of this, of course, is necessary in any terms of plot, character, theme, but is there purely for itself. This is no Native American but a true Hollywood Indian, just as Alex Morny and his bodyguard Eddie Prue, in *The High Window*, are out of Central Casting: "All these boys have been to picture shows and know how night club bosses are supposed to act." In fact, Alex Morny's nightclub looks exactly like a Hollywood stage set with the "cop on the gate, the shine on the door, the cigarette and check girls, the fat greasy sensual Jew with the tall stately bored showgirl, the well-dressed, drunk and horribly rude director cursing the barman . . ."—and so on. In circumstances like these, as framed by Marlowe/Chandler's witty imagination, the air can't really get too sinister. It's been the habit to condescend to Dick Powell's Marlowe in comparison with Bogart's, but in fact Powell, who seems to be having a fine time in the role (and isn't distracted by high jinks with Bacall) is true to much of the comedy in Chandler's work.

Although the selection of prose *Raymond Chandler Speaking* contains a number of his letters, it is far from a substitute for Frank MacShane's generous selection. Time and again I found myself assenting to Chandler's literary judgments, such as that Graham Greene lacked a sense of humor: "I am reading *The Heart of the Matter,* a chapter at a time. It has everything in it that makes literature except verve, wit, gusto, music and magic; a cool and elegant set-piece, embalmed by Whispering Glades." He contrasts it with the "life" felt in even the worst chapters of Dickens or Thackeray. He draws a bead on Elizabeth Bowen's *The Heat of the Day,* where she "is falling into the sad error of thinking that the involution of the language necessarily conceals a subtlety of thought. It doesn't; it conceals a vacuum"—precisely my response to that cobwebby novel. He admired the not-enough-admired-these-days Somerset Maugham, as the "complete professional," and thought Maugham's *Ashenden* was "far ahead of any spy story ever written." In the same letter he provided a list of some of his favorite "classic" books, a list interesting for its not-so-predictable character: "*Carmen* as Merimée wrote it, *Herodias, Un Coeur Simple, The Captain's Doll, The Spoils of Poynton, Madame Bovary, The Wings of the Dove* . . . these are all perfect." His incisive remarks on somewhat forgotten novelists like James Gould Cozzens and John Marquand show that he had a taste for more than "classic" books; and his singling out of especially good novels by aspiring crime writers—like Julian Symons's *The 31st of February*—show a caring eye and ear.

Chandler's last years, after his beloved Cissy died in 1954, make for sad reading. *The Long Goodbye,* his longest and most full-of-feeling novel, was published in 1952, after which he wrote almost nothing, except the final, short *Playback.* He spent a lot of time in London, cared for by what he called "a shuttle service" of five or more women of whom Natasha Spender was chief. The trouble was, as Tom Hiney remarks, that he tended to fall in love with them (not all at once), and such motives sat awkwardly with the periodic depressions and excessive drinking marking these years. (Soon after Cissy's death he attempted an alcoholic suicide, but, probably on purpose, botched it.) But as far as I know, he never wavered in his belief that it was a great thing to be a writer, and he didn't understand when another novelist complained about how painful the actual writing was. To his English publisher, Hamish Hamilton, he declared, "A writer who hates the actual writing is as impossible as a lawyer who hates the law or a doctor who hates medicine. . . . The actual writing is what you live for. . . . How can you hate the magic which makes a paragraph or a sentence or a line of dialogue or a description something in the nature of a new creation?" The sentiment has never been more convincingly expressed.

It may be less than essential to discriminate among and rank the novels. Chandler thought when he was writing *The Little Sister* that *Farewell, My Lovely* was probably his best book, but he could also see ways in which the unfinished *Little Sister* was superior. There are those who promote *The Long Goodbye* to the top of the list; and I find the lake scenes in the San Bernardino hills in *The Lady in the Lake* especially appealing (they were wholly omitted from the turgid 1947 film). The early pulp stories seem to me of interest mainly to the Chandler scholar; but essays like "The Simple Art of Murder," "Writers in Hollywood," and "Notes on the Mystery Story"—all contained in the *Library,* volume two—are invaluable, sophisticated reflections on the art of the detective story and his own art. The screenplay he did with Billy Wilder for the excellent *Double Indemnity* (also in volume two) is a thing of beauty.

The aforementioned Julian Symons, who more than once wrote appreciatively about Chandler, nevertheless, in his survey of thriller writing, *Bloody Murder,* places him firmly below Hammett as an artist. Hammett was tougher, says Symons, and Chandler, in trying to create—in his Marlowe— "a man of honour" (Chandler's words), fell into softness and idealization and made up a detective the likes of which were never met on sea or land. Maybe so, but think of the things Chandler's books contain—atmosphere, humor, leisurely exploration of surface, farcical bits like the Indian—that Hammett's mainly lack. My own preference is unequivocally for Chandler, recognizing the ingenuity and hard work—and genius—he put into his literary career. He wrote: "What greater prestige can a man like me (not too greatly gifted, but very understanding) have than to have taken a cheap, shoddy, and utterly lost kind of writing, and have made of it something that intellectuals claw each other about?" We are moved to reply, what indeed?

Hudson Review, Spring 1998

The Early Novels of Anthony Burgess

ANTHONY BURGESS published his first novel in 1956, his most recent one in the present year, a fact which becomes of interest only when it is added that in the intervening period he published thirteen additional novels.[1] No doubt the figure is already dated, for there are no signs of slowing down; in a recent apologetic valedictory to reviewing theater for *The Spectator* he confessed ruefully to not having written a novel in six months or more. One raises an eyebrow at all this plenty, yet only one of the novels marks itself off as a casual, slight creation, nor does the astonishing rate of production signal slapdash composition. The five novels selected for consideration here represent a judgment of his best "early" and "later" work; no doubt any admirer will have his particular favorite to add to the list. Burgess is a comic writer, a term broad and common enough to cover supposed refinements of it, such as satire, grotesque, or farce. None of the labels substantially promotes understanding of his work, nor does the knowledge that he, like all British comic novelists, is "the funniest . . . since Evelyn Waugh." If comparisons are desired, one would begin with the guess that the contemporary novelist Burgess most admires is Nabokov; beyond that one goes to Joyce, to Dickens, and ultimately to Shakespeare as the literary examples most insistently behind his work. In *Nothing Like the Sun,* his novel about Shakespeare, the hero sees himself as a "word man," and his author is not likely to quarrel with the term as a description of himself. But then, like Nabokov or Joyce or Dickens or Shakespeare, he is more than just a word man: the brilliant exploration of a verbal surface will lead to the discovery of truths about life, of in-

---

1. Depending on how you count. His first three published novels, counted individually here, form a trilogy. Aside from titles mentioned in this essay, there are *A Vision of Battlements,* written in 1949; two novels—*One Hand Clapping* and *Inside Mr. Enderby*—published under the pseudonym Joseph Kell; and *Tremor of Intent* (1966).

ward revelation. Or will it, does it in fact, lead to such truths in the unfolding of Burgess's best work? The question is an interesting one to entertain, though only after we have first been moved and delighted by the books themselves and the continuing presence of their author.

I

Burgess is at his most direct and perhaps most simply appealing in his early novels about life in Malaya just before independence; published last year as a trilogy, *The Long Day Wanes,* the books are given continuity through the presence of Victor Crabbe, an embattled liberal schoolmaster for whom things get progressively worse. Crabbe is one of us: reasonable, guilt-ridden, alternately shabby and decent in his relations with others. In a word, colorless, though he looks colorless only when put next to the characters that surround him, grotesques such as Nabby Adams, an enormous police official whose life is devoted to the ensuring, each day, of his proximity to about two-dozen bottles of Tiger beer (*Time for a Tiger* is the first volume of the trilogy). Or, emerging from the words themselves, Crabbe's boss Talbot, married to a young and adulterous wife, but truly wedded to his stomach:

> "My dear fellow, you ought to eat. That's the trouble with my wife. Thin as a rake, because she won't bother to order anything. She says she's not hungry. I'm always hungry. The climate has different effects on different people. I always have my lunch out. There's a little Chinese place where they give you a really tasty and filling soup, packed with chicken and abalone and vegetables, with plenty of toast and butter, and then I always have a couple of baked crabs."
>
> "Yes," said Crabbe.
>
> "With rice and chili sauce. And then a pancake or so, rather soggy, but I don't dislike them that way, with jam and a kind of whipped cream they serve in a tea-cup. Anne, what is there to eat?"

Crabbe's mild "yes" is a typical Fred Allen response to the antics performed by assorted characters throughout the trilogy. But we are asked to take Crabbe, unlike Fred Allen, seriously as a person. He is presented as a recognizably psychological figure, available for easy identification with on the part of any ordinary reader; his death terminates the trilogy and should evoke some feelings on our part. But the feelings do not appear. We accept

Crabbe's fate, whatever it is, without much interest, because we are being so royally entertained elsewhere. Robert Garis has demonstrated brilliantly how the art of entertainment, as it appears in Dickens's novels, is typically a "loud and distinct" one, apprehended firmly and easily by the reader.[2] In what Garis terms Dickens's "theatrical" art, the reader is happy to watch the artist-showman at his performance, and does not expect to receive complex insights into characters who have to be "taken seriously" as we take Anna Karenina or Dorothea Brooke seriously. The satisfied reader of Dickens delights in the showman's ability energetically to command a large and various number of acts by an inexhaustibly creative language. Burgess's comedy, particularly in his early novels, if not as loud and distinct (or expansive and assured) as Dickens's, is as purely verbal in its workings; for example, all we need or want to know of the glutton Talbot is that he is gluttonous and that his poems are filled with highly nutritious images: we are satisfied to watch the pancakes and whipped cream roll by. Or to delight with Nabby Adams in his acquiring, without payment, eight large unopened bottles of Tiger beer, and in his anticipation of the "hymeneal gouging-off of the bottle-top, the kiss of the brown bitter yeasty flow, the euphoria far beyond the release of detumescence." The novel-reader's desire to find out what happens next does not assert itself, for the narrator is in no hurry to press on toward exciting revelations. He contemplates instead, with the satisfaction of Nabby Adams viewing the bottles of Tiger, his own agile high-humored creations.

One of the most original and satisfying elements of Burgess's theatricality is a persistent literary allusiveness that teases us to make something out of it and then mocks our efforts. *The Long Day Wanes* invokes Tennyson's "Ulysses"; but is Victor Crabbe an "idle king" who eventually drowns in the "deep [that] moans round with many voices"? Only a solemn explicator would be interested in displaying that connection, for the theatrical novelist is less interested in creating symbolic expressions of a complex truth about man than in making play with the words of writers who have expressed such truths. Although the trilogy is filled with allusions to *The Waste Land*, their interest does not lie in suggesting that Victor Crabbe fears death by water (he does), but in the purely amusing way they are woven into the narrative and

2. Robert Garis, *The Dickens Theatre* (Oxford: Clarendon Press, 1965). Part I—"The Dickens Problem"—is filled with valuable observation about particular artistic styles and about literature in general.

made to seem at once absurdly confected and perfectly natural: "This music crept by Syed Omar in Police Headquarters, sitting puzzled while others were going out to lunch." As Crabbe's wife reads *The Waste Land* to Nabby Adams and his Malayan sidekick, Nabby remarks:

> "He's got that wrong about the pack of cards, Mrs. Crabbe. There isn't no card called The Man With Three Staves. That card what he means is just an ordinary three, like as it may be the three of clubs."
> And when they came to the dark thunder-speaking finale of the poem, Alladad Khan had nodded gravely.
> "Datta. Dayadhvam. Damyata.
> Shantih. Shantih. Shantih."
> "He says he understands that bit, Mrs. Crabbe. He says that's what the thunder says."

This "contributes" nothing to the novel except as one more of the witty satisfactions that occur throughout the trilogy. The long day has indeed waned, and the play made with Eliot or Joyce shows us just how late in the game we are, how far from the epic worlds of our modern legendary authors. Far enough it seems so that we can be entertained by a contemporary's familiar use of them.

These isolated examples of entertainment have little to do with the presentation of the hero, Crabbe, who is brought eventually (like all Burgess's heroes) to some sort of reckoning. Typically, the reckoning involves a sexual humiliation; in this novel, Crabbe learns a shocking fact about his first love, then slips into the water while trying to board a launch. We view this event through the impassive gaze of a Malayan doctor who lets him drown, deciding that "human lives were not his professional concern." There is no other significant comment on the scene. Although it is perfectly well to say that Crabbe is essentially a device for holding together loosely related characters and episodes, he is also allowed an inner life we must take seriously—his psychological anxieties are given full expression. When it comes to ending the trilogy, the author doesn't seem to know how seriously he wants to take that life, so it is easier to show up the Malayan doctor's sophistry (if it is that) than to assign significance, however minor, to Crabbe's end. It may seem pedantic to accuse Burgess of trying to have it both ways, since *The Long Day Wanes* is a comedy of humors in which, with the exception of Crabbe's story, the narration is external and detached. But the problem is there, and it becomes more complicated when the theatrical novelist does his tricks through a first-person narrator.

This narrator appears as J. W. Denham in what is surely Burgess's most engaging novel, *The Right to an Answer* (1960). A civil servant in the Far East, home on holiday in England for much of the book, Denham is over forty, has bad teeth and a cushy job, and can smell the TV-corruption of England in the late fifties. England is a mess because people have too much freedom, and Denham claims to have learned from Hobbes that you can't have both freedom and stability. By the end of the novel he does not pronounce on matters with the arrogant certainty of the opening pages, but it would be wrong to conclude, therefore, that Burgess has written a moral novel with a dramatic change of view. How much, really, can a narrator learn who early in the book talks this way about Sunday dinner at his sister's:

> There was a smell of old dog in the hall, an earthy rebuke at least to the blurry misty pictures of dream-dogs on the walls. The honest black telephone shone coyly from behind flowery curtains—Beryl's homemade booth for long comfy talkie-talkies with women friends, if she had any. I noticed a poker-work poem of slack form and uplifting content: "In a world of froth and bubble two things stand like stone: kindness in another's trouble, courage in your own." Beryl's unimpaired high-school humour was indicated by a framed macaronic paradigm: "je me larf, tu te grin, il se giggle; nous nous crackons, vous vous splittez, ils se bustent." Beryl herself could be heard singing in the kitchen at the end of the hall— an emasculated version of "Greensleeves"—and the fumes of heavy greens gushed out under the noise of the masher.

And on and on. Crackling with wordy Nabokovian irritation, the writing individuates Beryl so firmly that there is no temptation to see her as a representative of England's corruption. If this is satire, it is satire that, as Eliot would say, creates the object that it contemplates. Beryl's house is as unforgettably there as the love-nest Lolita's mother designs for Humbert. In neither case are we interested in using the descriptions to censure the ladies in some moral way; by the same token, any claims the narrator makes about his own moral progress will have to compete with his continuous and self-contained verbal brilliance.

At one point in the novel, Denham, playing the inept narrator, apologizes for the lack of action in his tale: ". . . you have had merely J. W. Denham on leave, eating, drinking, unjustifiably censorious, meeting people, especially Mr. Raj, recounting, at the tail of the eye, almost out of earshot, the adultery of small uninteresting people." Mr. Raj is an eager sociologist from Colombo who comes to Denham's hometown to investigate the manners and to court an Englishwoman. His most notable capabilities, however, are pugilistic and culinary: in Ted Arden's Shakespearean pub, Mr. Raj disposes of a vocal racist, and Ted muses as follows: "'Queer bugger that is. It Jack Brownlow, quick as a flash, right in the goolies. . . . I didn't let on when e did it so quick like. E did it real gentleman like."' Eventually Mr. Raj moves in with Denham and his father, to cook Sunday afternoon curries that are too rich and deep for tears:

> We fell to. My father spooned in curry and panted. He frequently tried to stagger to the kitchen for fresh glasses of cold water, but Mr. Raj said, "No, no. I will get. This is my privilege, Mr. Denhams both." To my father all this was a new world; he ate with Renaissance child's eyes of wonder. "I'd no idea," he gasped. "Never thought." He was like a youth having his first sexual experience.

But all these pleasant events are shattered abruptly as Denham resumes his job in the East and leaves his father in the hands of Mr. Raj, who proceeds to kill him with the kindness of curry. This is one of a series of violent acts, including assault, rape, murder, and the suicide of Mr. Raj, that cause Denham to reexamine his earlier superiority to "the mess." Although after Mr. Raj's suicide Denham moralizes that these are "just silly vulgar people uncovering the high explosive that lies hidden underneath stability," he is allowed a meditation in the concluding chapter that places him in a different relation to these people. Denham disgustedly contemplates his body in the mirror, then moves to his equally unsatisfactory spirit:

> It was the eyes I didn't like, the unloving mouth, and the holier-than-thou set of the nostrils. . . . The mess was there, the instability, but I wondered now if that sin against stability was really the big sin. What I did realize quite dearly was the little I'd helped, the blundering or not-wishing-to-be-involved plump moneyed man of leave inveighing against sins he wasn't in the position even to begin to commit. For surely that sneered-at suburban life was more stable than this shadow life of buying and selling in a country where no involvement was possible, the television evening, with

the family round, better than the sordid dalliance that soothed me after work? . . . If poor bloody innocent little Winterbottom had died, and striving Mr. Raj . . . surely it was something that they invoked the word Love? Even the word was better than this emptiness, this standing on the periphery and sneering.

This seems to offer us a secure vantage point from which to review the events with understanding. But are we convinced by it? What indeed would it mean to be "convinced" by it? Doesn't the analysis unjustly simplify Denham's earlier behavior, since that behavior has been presented to us through a style which delights? How can we accept "sneering" or "standing on the periphery" as adequate labels for the description of Beryl's house quoted earlier? Or, from the same chapter, is the following menu a sneer at the English Sunday meal?

> The meal was pretentious—a kind of beetroot soup with greasy *croûtons;* pork underdone with loud vulgar cabbage, potato croquettes, tinned peas in tiny jam-tart cases, watery gooseberry sauce; trifle made with a resinous wine, so jammy that all my teeth lit up at once—a ghastly discord on two organ manuals.

One quickly grows fond of those encased peas, that loud cabbage; the food, through these words, becomes not just awful but fascinatingly awful. Here, as in general, the imaginative vitality of Denham/Burgess's prose elbows aside the moralist who later repents of his hypercritical satiric self.

Denham's relationship to "the mess, the instability" represents a novelistic questioning of the satirist's relationship to life, to the materials of fiction. *The Right to an Answer* is unique in Burgess's work for the way it shows an aggressively comic and satiric intelligence taking us in through a casual first-person style of reporting. At the same time, or perhaps as a result of such aggressive dealing, the "I" repents of it, apologizes to us for putting himself outside the reek of the human. I am really no better than they are, probably not as good, he winningly admits. But if the apology is an engaging gesture of humility, it has things both ways only through a noticeable straining in the very prose of the book. When the narrator refers harshly, in the above passage, to "the sordid dalliance that soothed me after work," just how seriously can we take something which is referred to by a demonstrably witty intelligence as "sordid dalliance"? And does Burgess himself know how seriously he wants to take it? The attempt by a marvelous entertainer to discover a truth about life, to engage in moral reappraisal of himself, results in an uncomfortable sleight-of-hand effect that isn't quite quick enough to escape our notice. And the question remains: how much can the dark comedian afford to enlighten, with sincere reflection, the chaotic scene he has so wittily imagined?

II

This question, asked by the critic, is of course one the artist is under no obligation to answer. Burgess goes on to publish three novels (*Devil of a State, The Worm and the Ring, The Doctor Is Sick*) which in their individually interesting ways avoid the issue, and which, for all their excellent goings-on, are not as solidly entertaining as *The Long Day Wanes* or as humanly ambitious as *The Right to an Answer*. It is the three novels that appear in 1962–63 which present a truly experimental attempt to unite brilliance of entertainment with a seriousness toward human beings—more accurately, toward humanity. *A Clockwork Orange, The Wanting Seed, and Honey for the Bears* are (at least the first and last) Burgess's most popular books, and they ask to be considered together. All of them concern the individual and the modern state; all of them are felt to have a connection with the quality of life in the 1960s, but they approach life obliquely by creating fantasies or fables which appeal to us in odd and disturbing ways. As always with Burgess's work, and now to a splendidly bizarre degree, the creativity is a matter of style, of words combined in strange new shapes. Through the admiration these shapes raise, rather than through communication of specifiable political, philosophical, or religious ideas about man or the state, is to be found the distinction of these novels; for this reason it is of limited use to invoke names like Huxley or Orwell as other novelists of imagined futurist societies.

A Clockwork Orange, most patently experimental of the novels, is written in a language created by combining Russian words with teenage argot into a hip croon that sounds both ecstatic and vaguely obscene. The hero, Alex, a teenage thug, takes his breakfast and morning paper this way:

> And there was a bolshy big article on Modern Youth (meaning me, so I gave the old bow, grinning like bezoomny) by some very clever bald chelloveck. I read this with care, my brothers, slurping away at the old chai, cup after

tass after chasha, crunching my lomticks of black toast dipped in jammi-wam and eggiweg. This learned veck said the usual veshches, about no parental discipline, as he called it, and the shortage of real horrorshow teachers who would lambast bloody beggary out of their innocent poops and make them go boohoohoo for mercy. All this was gloopy and made me smeck, but it was nice to go on knowing one was making the news all the time, O my brothers.

Although the American paperback edition provides a glossary, one doesn't need it to get along very well after the first few pages. In fact such translation is a mistake, for it short-circuits the unmistakable rhythms of speech by which the sentences almost insensibly assume meaning. Moreover, though the book is filled with the most awful violence—what in our glossary or newspaper would be called murder, assault, rape, perversion—it comes to us through an idiom that, while it does not deny the connection between what happens in the second chapter and what the newspaper calls a "brutal rape," nevertheless makes what happens an object of aesthetic interest in a way no rape can or should be. Life—a dreadful life to be sure—is insistently and joyously deflected into the rhythms of a personal style within which one eats lomticks, not pieces, of toast.

The novel is short and sharply plotted: Alex is betrayed by his fellow "droogs," imprisoned for murder, then by a lobotomizing technique is cured of his urges to violence; whereas music, Beethoven in particular, had in-spired him to heights of blood-lusts, he now just feels sick. Caught between the rival partics for state power, he tries suicide, but lives to recover his orig-inal identity, as listening to the scherzo of the Beethoven Ninth he sees him-self "carving the whole litso of the creeching world with my cut-throat britva." The book concludes on this happy note, for oddly enough it *is* a happy note; we share the hero's sense of high relief and possibility, quite a trick for the novelist to have brought off. And without questioning it we have acceded to the book's "message," as radical and intransigent as the style through which it is expressed:

> More, badness is of the self, the one, the you or me on our oddy knock-ies, and that self is made by old Bog or God and is his great pride and ra-dosty. But the not-self cannot have the bad, meaning they of the govern-ment and the judges and the schools cannot allow the bad because they cannot allow the self. And is not our modern history, my brothers, the

story of brave malenky selves fighting these big machines. I am serious with you, brothers, over this. But what I do I do because I like to do.

Doing what you do because you like to do it is what the Burgess hero—Crabbe, Denham, others—has done and has been punished for doing by his creator. But the hero of *A Clockwork Orange* is rewarded and endorsed in a way more recognizably human characters in a more "realistic" atmosphere could not possibly be. In the world of creative fantasy we can admire hero and event as they are shaped by language; our response is akin to the old-fashioned "admiration" proper to the heroic poem. By the same token the defense of self, no matter how twisted it may be, and the condemnation of the state, no matter how benevolent it pretends to be, is absolute. Such a simple and radical meaning is not morally complex, but it must be taken as a serious aspect of fantasy. Within its odd but carefully observed limits the book is entirely consistent, successful, and even pleasing, Burgess's most eye and ear-catching performance.

Published a few months later, *The Wanting Seed* pleased critics a good deal less, the general feeling being that Burgess had overreached himself and produced a hodgepodge book. It is true that nothing is alien to its virtuoso atmosphere: elemental poetry, broad jokes, science fiction, and political philosophy consort together, couched throughout in a highly pedantic and jaw-breaking vocabulary ("corniculate," "vexillae," "fritinancy," "parachronic"). But in this most Joycean of Burgess's novels, that virtuoso atmosphere is precisely what appeals. The novel takes the population explosion as fictional opportunity and imagines a society presided over by a Ministry of Infertility, which encourages homosexuality ("It's Sapiens to be Homo" is their motto) and forbids any woman to bear more than one child. As in *A Clockwork Orange*, the lawless individual is at odds with a "benevolent" state; the heroine, Beatrice-Joanna, married to Tristram Foxe, a history teacher, is having an affair with Tristram's brother, a government official. Beatrice-Joanna's rebellion consists in her refusal to accept the death of her son and her rejection of the doctor's sensible advice: "Think of this in national terms, in global terms. One mouth less to feed. One more half-kilo of phosphorus pentoxide to nourish the earth. In a sense, you know, Mrs. Foxe, you'll be getting your son back again." Emerging from the clinic, she walks down the great London street (once Brighton but now a part of Greater London) to the sea and perceives it with a special poetry granted her:

If only, she felt crazily, poor Roger's body could have been thrown into these tigrine waters, swept out to be gnawed by fish, rather than changed coldly to chemicals and silently fed to the earth. She had a mad intuitive notion that the earth was dying, that the sea would soon be the final repository of life. "Vast sea gifted with delirium, panther skin and mantle pierced with thousands of idols of the sun—" She had read that somewhere, a translation from one of the auxiliary languages of Europe. The sea drunk with its own blue flesh, a hydra, biting its tail.

Then looking up at the Government Building, she sees the figure of a bearded man: "A cynosure to ships, man of the sea, Pelagius. But Beatrice-Joanna could remember a time when he had been Augustine. And, so it was said, he had been at other times the King, the Prime Minister, a popular bearded guitarist, Eliot (a long-dead singer of infertility), the Minister of Pisciculture, captain of the Hertfordshire Men's Sacred Game eleven, and most often and satisfactorily—the great unknown, the magical Anonymous." A hodgepodge of style perhaps, but no more so than *Ulysses:* at one moment the scientific knowingness of a Buck Mulligan, then the moody broodings of Stephen Dedalus, followed by an inventive Bloomlike list. What holds the various styles together is a linguistic virtuoso who moves his characters up and down the map of England: to complain as one reviewer did that the hero and heroine were mechanical contrivances is not to the point, since more "character," more recognizably human dimension, would destroy the fable.

For proof of this, consider the block of chapters describing Tristram's attempt to join his wife in the north of England (he has just escaped from jail and she, pregnant, has fled to her brother-in-law, an old-fashioned Roman Catholic, to have what turns out to be twins). As the state moves from a Pelagian phase to an Augustinian one, a great famine impels man toward cannibalism, fertility rites, the genesis of drama, and from homo- to heterosexual love. Tristram observes these effects as he moves from Brighton to Wigan, but we have heard reports of them already, courtesy of Anthony Burgess the announcer:

> In Stoke-on-Trent the carcass of a woman (later identified as Maria Bennett, spinster, aged twenty-eight) grinned up suddenly—several good clean cuttings off her—from under a bank of snow. In Gillingham, Kent, Greater London, a shady back-street eating-shop opened, grilling nightly,

and members of both police forces seemed to patronize it. In certain un-regenerate places on the Suffolk coast there were rumours of big crackling Christmas dinners. . . . The New Year commenced with stories of timid anthropophagy. . . . Then the metropolis flashed its own sudden canines: a man called Amis suffered savage amputation of an arm off Kingsway; S.R. Coke, journalist, was boiled in an old copper near Shepherd's Bush; Miss Joan Waine, a teacher, was fried in segments.

Some might consider this (especially the reference to imagined fates of An-gries) a debilitating cleverness, fatal to Burgess's art; to me it seems admirably indigenous to his ruthlessly literary sensibility. But in any case, it must be agreed that an attempt to give a hero traveling through such a scene much "dimension" would result in an awkward and uncertain book. *The Wanting Seed* is neither: its inventiveness is large enough that we are content to follow the fortunes of heroine and hero without desiring some further "inward" reach of understanding. What is to be understood—taken in—is put before us in the theatrical manner spoken of earlier. Even the closing paragraphs of the book, coming as they do after the longest of journeys and bringing to-gether the Tristram Foxes and their twins, united on the promenade at Brighton, are less a moving tribute to a particular man or woman than they are a general and now mythicized embodiment of love, of possibility:

> She clung to him, the huge air, the life-giving sea, man's future history in the depths, the present towered town, the bearded man at the pinnacle, all shut out from the warmth of his presence, the closeness of his embrace. He became sea, sun, tower. The twins gurgled. There were still no words.

And as if to formalize and make shimmery this closing atmosphere, the nar-rator dons prophetic robes and plays a late Shakespearean sage or Joycean lyricist, in language stolen from Valéry:

> The wind rises . . . we must try to live. The immense air opens and closes my book. The wave, pulverized, dares to gush and spatter from the rocks. Fly away, dazzled, blinded pages. Break, waves. Break with joyful waters.

This looks more vulnerable in quotation than it feels in the act of finishing the novel, although one understands how such writing might give rise to dis-trust or skepticism about its narrative poise. Burgess knows the extravagant overreaching that attaches to grand incantations, and as a rule his fictions do not make them. But *The Wanting Seed,* like *A Clockwork Orange,* has its affinities with the heroic poem: "faring forward" is saluted by the Bard when he ends his tale with an imitative gesture meant just as seriously as the cannibalistic jokes inspected earlier. In creative fantasy or fable, no suggestion that its figures are merely human is in order: Alex prepares to resume his career as a hoodlum; Beatrice-Joanna and Tristram prepare for—what? The fact is we are not interested in these "characters" but only in the action in which they have figured. A reader of *The Wanting Seed* must vouch to the extent that, like it or not, it is very much a linguistic action.

By contrast, *Honey for the Bears* would seem to be a return to the real world—the Soviet Union in 1963—where Paul Hussey, an English antique dealer, and his American wife, Belinda, are engaged in smuggling in and selling twenty-dozen drilon dresses, the loot for which will be turned over to the widow of a dead friend. A mysterious rash sends Belinda to the hospital, where she falls under the influence of a female Dr. Lazurkina, who analyzes Paul as a homosexual ("gomosexual"; there is no "h" in Russian) and spirits Belinda off to the Crimea for what promises to be a long talk. Paul makes his own liaison with a bearded young Russian struggling to be hip and properly disenchanted about the modern state: "'Russia or America,' said Alexei Prutkov, 'what's the difference? It's all the State. There's only one State. What we have to do is get together in these little groups and start to live.'" But after an unsuccessful attempt by Paul to seduce Alexei's mistress, and a drunken party where Paul suggests the guests strip "stark ballock naked," he is thrown out of Alexei's group with the accusation "What you like, dig, is your own sex, and that's what's so filthy and disgusting." Other humiliations and confusions follow (teeth knocked out, thrown into prison) until Paul leaves Russia, this time smuggling out (as his wife) the son of a Russian composer in disgrace named Opiskin, whose works Paul's dead friend Robert had loved.

It makes little difference whether we call this "plot" (inadequately summarized here) brilliant or absurd, so long as the detailing of it removes all suspicion that Burgess has abandoned us to Real Life in the Soviet Union today. *Honey for the Bears* is just as fantastic or fabulous as its two predecessors; characters (possibly excepting the hero) are viewed externally as ever, and their dimensions (and our sympathies) are thus severely limited. Stylistically the book moves at whirlwind pace with events and thoughts rapidly telescoped through Paul Hussey's mind; for example, on the first page we have this response to an unknown aged master in a wheelchair:

> The face was trenched and riven, as by a killing life of metaphysical debauchery. That was it, decided Paul: a head that philosophy had unsexed, some final Shavian achievement. He had seen a head like it on television newsreels; an old proud eagle squatting in Whitehall among students, Banning the Bomb. But these oyster-coloured eyes surveyed with disdain the scruffy redbrick layabouts who nearly filled the Cultural Saloon, the nose twitched at them.

Paul's own "unsexing" is to come, when by the end of the book he admits that he no longer knows what he is, sexually. And so the novel invites us, as did the earlier *Right to an Answer,* to relate the satiric intelligence accorded Paul in the passage above, to something he learns in Russia; more generally, to feel a unifying of the style of entertainment with the content of truth.

In the best single piece of writing about Burgess ("The Epicene," *New Statesman,* April 15, 1963), Christopher Ricks argues that this can be done, insofar as the book makes an analogy between sexual and political behavior. Politically, the book presents America and Russia as equally monolithic and insufficient states, and opts instead for what Ricks calls a "Third Force." So, by analogy, homo- and heterosexuality need not be exclusive choices; without singing hymns to bisexuality, it can at least be entertained and admitted to be perhaps more fun, more attractive to the individual who would be free. Ricks points out correctly that this is a subversive message, but that it is transmitted in an "inventive and gay" manner that takes the fear out of it. And he goes on to claim that the book is more humane and "says more" than Burgess's earlier minglings of black violence with comic lightness. It would be pleasant to take *Honey for the Bears* as evidence of this kind of novelistic breakthrough, especially since at the moment it is the most recent full-fledged novel Burgess has given us. But it is much more problematic than Ricks suggests, whether the "message" about sex and about politics is convincingly worked into the texture of the novel. There are difficulties in knowing just how to take Paul's sexual humiliations with his wife and Alexei's mistress—they are indeed fiascos but do not recommend themselves to us as, in book-jacket language, "outrageously funny" or "wildly comic." They are no more comic than Paul's difficulty in keeping his false teeth in place. On the other hand, the narrator makes no attempt to extend Paul sympathetic understanding. We are free, if we choose, to connect heterosexual failure with Paul's memories of "poor, dead Robert," though these memories are sentimental moonings we assume the narrator doesn't fully share. But even this is an assumption. Burgess treats Paul any way the spirit moves him: now harshly, now pathetically, now as a witty, perceptive satirical eye—all depending on the exigencies of a moment. When we try to say what these moments add up to, the trouble begins. What they claim to add up to is concentrated in two passages late in the novel: in the first of these, Paul relates a dream to his cell-mates about how there was a little man who lived between two greatly opposing tsardoms. They bully the little man by giving him a wife who accuses him of not being a real man, an adequate protector. Like Belinda, the wife walks out. The second passage makes the Paul-as-England identification explicit: "I'm going back to an antique-shop, but somebody's got to conserve the good of the past, before your Americanism and America's Russianism make plastic of the world. . . . You'll learn about freedom from us yet." Even as he says it, he feels a "doubt," as does surely the reader. For England (Ricks's political "Third Force"?) is simply not *there* in the novel, any more than is Paul Hussey's inner life, which, we are told, has undergone some sort of change. Once more, the imagination of comic disorder proves stronger than the fable's attempt to make thoughtful sense out of it.

This is not cause for alarm, nor a gloomy note on which to conclude. When Ricks says, in the essay mentioned above, that Burgess has yet to write a really "first-rate comic novel," we may feel the standards are high indeed after reading through a group of novels distinguished by their abundant qualities of imaginative energy, creative invention, complicated wit, and verbal delight. Since *Honey for the Bears*, Anthony Burgess has given us a number of books somewhat off-the-center of his literary vision: juvenilia, a fascinating novelistic sport about Shakespeare, books on language and on Joyce. In a recent *Times Literary Supplement* article titled "The Manicheans," he mused aloud on why the novel has not made more use of religious experience, and he specified further: "I do not mean the tribulations of priests among the poor, or deanery gossip, or pre-ordination doubts; I mean rather the imaginative analysis of themes like sainthood, sin, the eschatological sanctions of behaviour, even that dangerous beatific vision."

One of the best ways to analyze sin is to become a comic novelist; there is every reason to suspect that the remaining themes will occupy Burgess in the novels to come. At any rate we can be grateful for the books we have. After Nabokov there is no other, but that is because, in part, Nabokov sees the world through imaginatively obsessed narrator-madmen who impose their strange shapes on reality. Burgess, despite the variety of narrators and situations in his fiction, speaks to us as one of us: a fallen man with the usual amount of ambition, irritation, guilt, decency, and common sense. Given such ordinary qualities or modest sins, how can things go as wrong as they do for the heroes of these painful books? That they go not just wrong, but marvelously wrong, is the result of the one quality Burgess does not share with the rest of us or with his heroes—the art of the novelist.

Massachusetts Review, Summer 1966

First Impressions

John Updike: *Rabbit Is Rich*

For this third novel in what we may perhaps now refer to as the Rabbit trilogy, John Updike has chosen two perfectly appropriate epigraphs. The first is from *Babbitt*, some words from George Babbitt's portrait of the Ideal Citizen: "At night he lights up a good cigar, and climbs into the little old 'bus. . . . He mows the lawn, or sneaks in some practice putting, and then he's ready for dinner"; the second is three lines from Wallace Stevens's poem "A Rabbit as King of the Ghosts." Updike's brilliant and touching new novel has the local richness and comic bite of Sinclair Lewis's best one; while his portrait of Rabbit Angstrom, age forty-six and a fair candidate for king of the ghosts, contains expressions of lyric feeling as full and deep as anything in the writer's previous work. More than either *Rabbit, Run* (1960) or *Rabbit Redux* (1971), the new book moves easily, and convincingly in the main, from vulgar talk about physical matters—particularly various parts of women's bodies—to a rather elegant and sad poetry of the spirit, particularly the spirits of the dead who surround and haunt our protagonist:

> The dead, Jesus. They were multiplying, and they look up begging you to join them, promising it is all right, it is very soft down here. Pop, Mom, old man Springer, Jill, the baby called Becky for her little time, Tothero. Even John Wayne, the other day. The obituary page every day shows another stalk of a harvest endlessly rich, the faces of old teachers, customers, local celebrities like himself flashing for a moment and then going down. For the first time since childhood Rabbit is happy, simply, to be alive.

In the first of the Rabbit books, Harry Angstrom is known not only by his nickname but also as "Mr. Death" by his lover, Ruth, who makes a memorable reappearance in *Rabbit Is Rich*. His son Nelson blames him (in *Rabbit*

Redux) for the death of the girl Jill when Rabbit's house mysteriously catches fire. The obsession with death is a religious one: *Rabbit, Run* is full of fairly dense theological meditation, its whole metaphor of running (as in the beautifully done nighttime flight in the car from Pennsylvania to West Virginia and back) a desperate poetic response to the constrictions of domesticity, of aging one day at a time with one thing at the end of it all. And the hero's absorption, sexual and political, with the outlaws Jill and Skeeter, doomed embodiments of those who would keep running, has a religious intensity enough to have put some readers off *Rabbit Redux*.

Updike's resourcefulness reveals itself in the wonderfully executed opening pages of his new novel, set in late June of 1979, when America was running out of gas. But Rabbit is rich, and why? Why, because he's the owner of his dead father-in-law's flourishing operation, Springer Motors, now hooked into the people who bring you Toyotas:

> But they won't catch him, not yet because there isn't a piece of junk on the road gets better mileage than his Toyotas, with lower service costs. . . . People are going wild, their dollars are going rotten, they shell out like there's no tomorrow. He tells them, when they buy a Toyota, they're turning their dollars into yen.

As for Rabbit's personal proclivities for lighting out into another territory when pressed too closely, he has nicely come to terms with the metaphorical wildness of "running" by turning himself into just another runner: "I've begun this jogging thing and it feels great. I want to lose thirty pounds." Though such running resolves itself mainly into a trot around the block after supper, at least it gets him out of the house, away from his wife, Janice, and her mother. So at the beginning of the novel words like "rich," "run," "energy," and others show their potential for playful expansion—as do old cultural friends like "Lost in Space" or "You Asked for It, You've Got It."

Rabbit not only rhymes with Babbitt, they are the same age (forty-six) and they love their cars. Updike has previously been eloquent about the terrible beauty of 1950s cars, and now it is extinct American convertibles that take on some of that power: "They were gallant old boats . . . all that stretched tin and aerodynamical razzmatazz, headed down Main Street straight for a harvest moon with the accelerator floored." Yet when Nelson, whom Rabbit has grudgingly taken on at the lot, buys a few convertibles to sell while Rabbit is on vacation, sullying the purity of the Toyota franchise, the father is furious and there ensues one of the book's finest scenes of conflict, ending, as it always does where Nelson is involved, with collision: "The pale green fender collapses enough to explode in the headlight; the lens rim flies free. Oh what a feeling." Everything involving cars, Toyota sales, gas stations is effortlessly and lovingly presented, as is anything on the highway generally. There are fine drives out to a place called Galilee in search of a girl who might possibly be his daughter, lost in space until now; there is a beautifully remembered childhood trip to the Jersey shore, the long wasted day on "poky roads," as "town after town numbingly demonstrated to him that his life was a paltry thing, his specialness an illusion."

Rabbit then is rich, not running out of gas. He makes love, with much satisfaction, to his wife, Janice, who has fallen asleep, and upon reflection produces such engaging good sense as "Ought to try fucking her some night when we're both awake." He hangs around with "their" group at the club, plays golf with the men, lusts after Cindy Murkett, but is also presented as more sensitive than they are (and surely than Janice is), not amused by certain kinds of sexual humor, extremely acute in detecting behavior that he calls "asshole." He can do all this of course because, as previously, Updike creates him in the present tense rather than telling us about him. With one or two exceptions, everything that comes to us comes through Rabbit's senses, highly tuned so as to register "the wooden gobbling sound the cup makes when a long putt falls," the richness of a morning in the Poconos, or the memory of Johnny Frye's Chophouse, a onetime restaurant for German *Fressers* "who had eaten themselves pretty well into the grave by now, taking with them tons of porkchops and sauerkraut and a river of Sunflower Beer." Rabbit sees through the fads and pieties of life in the 1970s: why are all these people having their beloved crepes for lunch? Because "people now want to feel they're eating less, and a crepe sounded like hardly a snack whereas if they called it a pancake they would have scared everybody away but kids and two-ton Katrinkas." And when his wife speaks at one point of "achieving closure with somebody," Rabbit accuses her of having watched too many talk shows on television.

There is a certain slipperiness in the convenience with which present-tense narrative confirms the worth of its hero, especially when, as with Updike, the writing is so continuously packed with perception and satiric force. This is also why the question of to what extent Updike "is" his protagonist can't profitably be pursued. He "is" Rabbit insofar as his interests as a novelist don't lie in a critical and dramatic treatment of his hero's moral life; he is not interested in exploring Jamesian-Conradian complexities and ambiguities of character and judgment, and surely not in showing his car salesman hero to be really a slob. Instead what it's like to be Harry Angstrom, to think and talk and feel a certain way, is all that counts, and even more than in the earlier books since he has now become king of the ghosts:

> The day is still golden outside, old gold now in Harry's lengthening life. He has seen summer come and go until its fading is one in his heart with its coming, though he cannot yet name the weeds that flower each in its turn in the season's tide, or the insects that also in ordained sequence appear, eat, and perish. He knows that in June school ends and the playgrounds open, and the grass needs cutting again and again if one is a man, and if one is a child games can be played outdoors while the supper dishes tinkle in the mellow parental kitchens.

These responses to the time of year, the time of day, are delicately orchestrated, for an ex-basketball star with a big gut and a penchant for saying "Fuck them all." Perhaps too delicately, if you are bothered by Updike writing over Rabbit's shoulder; yet the character is ennobled by it, made safe from moral scrutiny, from any possibly adverse judgment. The answer then to the concluding question from *Rabbit Redux*—"O.K.?"—is still, finally, yes.

Writing about *Rabbit, Run* after it appeared, Norman Mailer excoriated its style ("atrocious," "stale garlic") but urged its author to go deeper into what he called "the literature of sex," a subject on which he thought Updike showed promise. This, Updike proceeded over the years to do, and near the end of *Rabbit Is Rich* there is a couple swap (not without its comic edge) in which Rabbit eventually if somewhat nervously plays a Mellors to the secret places of his Lady Chatterley for a night. (Rabbit of course suffers from the Lawrentian disease of "sex in the head," though as some wag commented, where else should it be?) There is an effort to turn this sex into a revived "sense of miracle," a reminder to Rabbit "that he was here on earth on a sacred assignment," and his partner tells him that thinking that way makes him "radiant. And sad." However you feet about radiance (and I feel the way Rabbit does about closure), the book never escapes sadness for long, right down to its "happy" ending, which I dare you to read without a shiver.

What stays with one, beyond any generalized wisdom about things, is truth of particularity: of rain beating on the garden of bean leaves decimated by Japanese beetles; of an early morning in the Poconos when it seems to Harry there must be a good way to live, and this is it; of a return home to his refrigerator, which now contains only wheat germ, yogurt, and Chinese vegetables (Nelson and his girlfriend are in residence), not the food for a hungry Rabbit. The book entertains ultimate thoughts about transience: "In middle age you were carrying the world . . . and yet it seems more out of control than ever, the self that you had as a boy all scattered and distributed like those pieces of bread in the miracle"; it also entertains them about toothpaste ("He wonders whatever happened to Ipana") or about Rotary Club ("How can you respect the world when you see it's being run by a bunch of kids turned old?"). If Rabbit could make certain common causes with his ancestor Babbitt, we might also allow him the company of Leopold Bloom and of Moses Herzog, for each of whom their authors would go to the stake. Updike's insistence here once more is in caring for what he cares about no matter how "wrong" it may look to all sorts of deep readers or academics who wouldn't dream of taking him seriously, in the same league as Pynchon, say, or Borges, or Italo Calvino. But that anyone can finish *Rabbit Is Rich* and not seriously be ensnared once more by the illusion that the novel is the one bright book of life, I find hard to believe.

New Republic, September 30, 1981

J. F. Powers: *Wheat That Springeth Green*

Forty years ago, when a writer named Peter Taylor published his first book, a collection of stories, it was reviewed in *Commonweal* by a writer named J. F. Powers, whose own first book of stories had been published the previous year. Powers liked the way Taylor refused to tell tales as they had been told before: "He refuses, moreover, to exploit his material to the limit, to manufacture characters, drama, suspense—in short, he won't traffic in what is known as a 'strong story line.' He refuses to be electric. He knows that life itself has a very weak story line." The disdain expressed here is directed at writers who turn it on—who, unlike Taylor, manufacture and exploit "life" in the interests of a presumed artistic success that is, in fact, a failure of realism.

Yet in the two longest and most ambitious pieces from Powers's first collection, *Prince of Darkness* ("Lions, Harts, Leaping Does" and the title story), he himself had, if not "trafficked" in a strong story line, at least built narratives that ended strongly in revelations, in "epiphanies," as in the work of his master, Joyce. At the close of "Lions, Harts . . ." the dying Father Didymus closes his eyes as the snowflakes whirl at the window of his sickroom and enter "darkly falling" into his failing consciousness. And in "Prince of Darkness," the fleshy, materialistic Father Burner, burning for a pastorate of his own, opens the archbishop's letter to find that he has been assigned to a new parish, but as an assistant to the priest in charge. It is fair to say that the best stories—some of them clerical, others not—in *Prince of Darkness*, and in *The Presence of Grace*, which followed it nine years later, operated through a practiced, well-shaped narrative voice whose command of its materials was authoritative, as opposed to life's "weak story line."

Powers's early stories were admired by readers who looked to discover in fiction the metaphoric, "poetic" qualities of lyric verse—qualities that were present in the work of writers like Katherine Anne Porter and Eudora Welty. Like them, and like his young contemporary Flannery O'Connor, Powers had a genius for capturing some of the ways people talked; much of the pleasure in reading him had to do with the pure satisfactions of American speech accurately rendered. But Powers was also a midwesterner whose first favorite writer was Sinclair Lewis, who loved Sherwood Anderson's "Triumph of the Egg," and whose distinctive subject was the American Catholic clergy.

Powers would say, in an interview in 1964, that he wrote about priests "for reasons of irony, comedy, and philosophy," and that these were compelling reasons because priests "officially are committed to both worlds in the way most people officially are not." Its commitment to sacred as well as spiritual reality meant that the priesthood was an especially good place to observe what Powers called the "intramural dogfights between ascetics and time servers." The typical protagonist in a Powers story has made some sort of choice or compromise between the two worlds; and it is usually an unsatisfactory compromise, since—like the rest of us only more so—priests are the victim of their position.

Such a victim was the hero of Powers's award-winning first novel of 1962, *Morte D'Urban*. In that book, he became more expansive—after all, he was writing a novel—and brought an exploratory-creative manner to his study of the get-ahead priest. Throughout the novel Father Urban is both the object and the vehicle of Powers's satire, as he strives to improve the Clementine order and bring about useful accommodations between the Church and the world. But by the end of the book something has happened to make this time server care less about whether or not he represents a "first class outfit." He has become physically weaker but (Powers seems to suggest) spiritually stronger.

The tone of *Morte D'Urban* was more relaxed than the earlier stories, even wayward. A reader couldn't always see exactly how one chapter followed from its predecessor. Weaken the story line, Powers seemed to be reminding himself, in order to see how much "life" can be let into a novel. In shorter works such as "Keystone" and "Farewell" (from his third collection, *Look How the Fish Live*, which appeared in 1975), a similarly reflective and leisurely spirit kept the narrative from becoming too streamlined. These stories gave the impression that when Powers began them, their endings were not already in sight, waiting to happen on the horizon. The surprising, wonderfully casual ending of "Farewell" provides a nice instance of concluding by not exactly concluding: we're told that the bishop, his car having been sideswiped by a truck, "was in the hospital for a while, doing fairly well for a man of his age, he understood, until he took a turn for the worse."

Two stories from *Look How the Fish Live*, "Bill" and "Priestly Fellowship," now turn up rewritten and expanded. They are episodes in Powers's extremely funny and satisfying new novel, a long twenty-six years after *Morte D'Urban*. *Wheat That Springeth Green* takes its hero, Father Joe Hackett, from a youthful portrait of the priest as young rascal, through his experiences at seminary and as a curate celebrating his first mass, and into his life as the pastor of St. Francis and Clare in suburban Inglenook, out there someplace in Powers's Minnesota. As with his earlier novel, the structure is episodic, the episodes mainly organized to exploit serious matters for comic purposes.

These matters include Joe's sexual awakening (really the first time Powers has dealt with such material, and very successfully); his strivings as a seminary student to become more contemplative by discomforting the flesh with a hair shirt; his principled refusal as a rookie priest to participate in the taking up of a special collection at his first mass. Compared with most of his fellow seminarians, the young Joe Hackett is an "ascetic," unpopular and unbending in the stands he takes on spiritual matters. Powers treats him with an irony that is affectionate and offhand. In fact, the narrative style of the early episodes—and most sustainedly so in the two hundred or so pages about Joe's life as a priest (the second and by far the longest of the book's three sections)—is a more racy, idiomatic, and intimate one than that of

Morte D'Urban. Part of Powers's design, in the earlier novel, was to make us uncertain just how to respond to Father Urban's success as a publicist for the Clementine order and to his prideful irritation at being closeted with intellectual and social inferiors at the Clementine rural retreat. Is Urban a snob, unpriest-like in his pride? Or does he have a right to be furious? Powers never tells us, and his sentences maintain a cool distance from Urban, whose character is more observed than delighted in, more inspected than used as a vehicle through which his creator could perform.

Performance, however, is very much the stuff of *Wheat That Springeth Green.* Powers has said that in writing fiction he thought mainly about giving his readers an experience, that he was a performer, "a little monkey with a cup." The new novel makes its appeal through the variety and charm of its particular performances, to which strong story lines and thematic emphases take a back seat. In one of the best of such sequences we follow Joe on a pilgrimage to a mall where "[he]e alone, with his knowledge of batters (encyclopedic), his stuff (world of), his control (phenomenal), had made the Twins a constant threat down the years." Those parenthetical insertions make the sequence delightful. Or there is the following explicit comparison between the priesthood and the sport: "As was true of many players, some the best, the history and mystique of the Church evidently meant little to Lefty, as the history and mystique of the Church evidently did to many priests, some of the best." Anyone, we feel, who can think this way, in such an aptly cadenced pattern of wit, should keep on doing what he's doing and not reform his character. Powers provides his hero with so many splendid formulations that, verbally at least, he can't be improved on.

There is no need, in the case of a writer whose output over forty years has been as small as J. F. Powers's, to rank his books in relation to one another. But his new novel seems to me the best book he has written. He would perhaps approve of Pope's couplet, "Let the strict Life of graver Mortals be / A long, exact, and serious Comedy." Joe Hackett puts the idea in a different idiom but comes up with something just as true: "Sure, birth was a big deal—after death, the biggest deal—but what was there to say about either of them, after a point?" *Wheat That Springeth Green* says a lot of what there is to be said about the life in between those big deals.

New Republic, September 26, 1988

Kingsley Amis: *The Old Devils*

THIRTY-THREE years ago Kingsley Amis published *Lucky Jim,* the most auspicious debut of an English comic novelist since Evelyn Waugh's *Decline and Fall* in 1928. The book was so funny and so successful that Amis's subsequent novels—like Norman Mailer's after *The Naked and the Dead*—were faulted for not living up to its high standard. In fact, the fifteen novels that followed *Jim* were richly entertaining in quite distinct ways, as they experimented with genres like the spy, ghost, or mystery story, the futuristic fantasy, and the black comedy (*Ending Up*—an instance of such comedy, its subject old age—was his most assured success after *Jim*). Recently, with *Jake's Thing* and *Stanley and the Women,* Amis has engaged in a sending-up of assorted pieties and ideologies, from psychoanalysis to internationalism to feminism to contemporary "improvements" in landscape, cityscape, pubscape.

Now, with the age theme to the fore and with women and men suffering equally under its stroke, comes *The Old Devils,* winner of England's Booker Prize for 1986. Amis's most ambitious and one of his longest books, this is neither a send-up nor an exercise in some established genre. It sets forth, with full realistic detail, a large cast of characters at least six of whom are rendered in depth as well as on the surface. *The Old Devils* is also Amis's most inclusive novel, encompassing kinds of feeling and tone that move from sardonic gloom to lyric tenderness.

The devils in question are a group of Welsh married couples in their sixties (Amis was born in 1922), whose firmly established daily routines on the parts of both sexes consist in talking a lot while consuming enormous, indeed unbelievable, quantities of drink. These routines are complicated by the return from England of Alun and Rhiannon Weaver, members of the group from decades past and implicated with several of them, through affairs of the heart, the body or both. To nobody's surprise, Alun—a successful literary publicist of things Welsh, who has sold out whatever real literary talent he possessed—takes up with vigor his career as seducer of two of the wives, while Rhiannon is thrown into sentimental and extremely poignant relations with two of the husbands, still lovers of her in their different ways. Divided into ten parts, each of them focusing on one or more of the characters, the novel proceeds through ironic comedy to the point where Alun, the subversive scapegoat, or *pharmakos* (as the critic Northrop Frye would call him), is rejected. Sudden death by a stroke claims him (he chokes on his whisky and water), and the society resumes its "normal" functioning, even with a change or two for the better.

Alun Weaver is a particularly vivid example of a recurrent type in Amis's fiction, the rogue male who is often though not always a womanizer, usually though not always a heavy drinker, but invariably endowed by his creator with plentiful verbal resources. When such a hero stays at the center of the narrative (as in *Jake's Thing* or *Stanley and the Women*) in either first or third person, he dominates it to such an extent that other characters can't compete with him. They may be more virtuous, but the rogue is more interesting (or, depending on your perspective, more repellent), since we know so much of his consciousness and participate so closely in his performance. Readers appalled by the misogyny vigorously expressed in *Stanley and the Women* were suffering partly because they couldn't get outside the first-person narrator's consciousness, which covered everything like a tent. In *The Old Devils* Amis has solved his problem of narrowness by a more dramatic kind of presentation in which the aggressive speech and sentiments of the rogue are responded to, with different degrees of approval and disapproval, by the other old devils.

In the Glendower—a tavern-and-grill place owned jointly by one of the foremost old devils, Charlie Norris, and his brother Victor—Alun has the following exchange with a waiter:

> "What is the vintage port?" asked Alun.
> "Port is a fortified wine from Portugal, " said the waiter, having perhaps misheard slightly, "and vintage port is made from—"
> "I didn't ask for a bloody lecture on vinification, you horrible little man." Alun laughed a certain amount as he spoke. "Tell me the shipper and the year and then go back to your hole and pull the lid over it."

Alun's response, aggressively inventive to the edge of viciousness, provokes mixed feelings in us, and these feelings are shared by his companions. In a similar moment, after Alun abuses a boring minor devil named Garth Pumphrey, once a veterinarian, Charlie says to Peter Thomas, the fattest and nicest of the oldsters: "Not very nice, that just now, was it? . . . In fact not at all nice. It's odd, that was exactly what you've always wanted to say to him, you hoped somebody would one day and then when they do it's nothing like the treat you'd been banking on. Bloody . . . bloody little cowshed mountebank was it? M'm. There's trenchant, eh?"

The book's real trenchancy lies, as with any of Amis's novels, in the language, especially as it renders the physical infirmities, the embarrassments and humiliations of getting old. In the first pages, Malcolm Cellan-Davies sits down to eat his breakfast of toast and diabetic honey: "He had not bitten anything with his front teeth since losing a top middle crown on a slice of liver-sausage six years earlier, and the right-hand side of his mouth was a no-go area, what with a hole in the lower lot where stuff was always apt to stick and a funny piece of gum that seemed to have got detached from something and waved disconcertingly about whenever it saw the chance." Reading such prose, one is constantly surprised by something extra, a twist or seeming afterthought signifying an originality of mind that is inseparable from the novelist's originality of language. At age sixty-one Yeats wrote bitterly in "The Tower" of "this absurdity . . . this caricature, / Decrepit age that has been tied to me / As to a dog's tail." Amis fleshes out and domesticates the caricature by showing us Peter's plight, a fat man who can't cut his toenails in the house for fear his wife may discover telltale fragments of them:

> After experimenting with a camp-stool in the garage and falling off it a good deal he had settled on a garden seat under the rather fine flowering cherry. This restricted him to the warmer months, the wearing of an overcoat being of course ruled out by the degree of bending involved. But at least he could let the parings fly free, and fly they bloody well did, especially the ones that came crunching off his big toes, which were massive enough and moved fast enough to have brought down a sparrow on the wing, though so far this had not occurred.

After various felicities, we encounter that final stroke of mastery, the assurance that in fact Peter has not yet unintentionally brought about the fall of a sparrow. The caricature of decrepit age, passively endured by one of its sufferers, has been opportunistically converted into an occasion of imaginative pleasure.

The novel is filled with mordant, but also affectionate and nostalgic, feelings and observations about Wales (Amis taught at Swansea in the early 1950s, and his second novel is set there) expressed in typically Amis sentences like the following about a deconsecrated church: "This one had been converted not into a pornographic cinema but, less inoffensively some might have thought, into an arts centre." Best to read carefully, so as not to join the "some" who assume that an arts center is clearly better than the offensive cinema. But along with the expected clevernesses, there are welcome surprises, not to be counted on in an Amis novel, like a woman (Gwen, married to Malcolm) being convincing about how awful men are when they pretend to listen to women: "Tell us what you think, love—no go on, I really want to hear. And then when you did tell'em, well it was quite a long time before I started noticing the glaze in their eyes. They were being good about you talking." The best surprise of all happens twice, in two dramatic sequences— Rhiannon with Peter, then with Malcolm—that are unashamedly moving in their expression of loss and of memory's tricks. There has been nothing quite like them in Amis's previous fiction (though see his poem to his father, "In Memoriam W.R.A."), and their presence makes the book, for all its skill in caricature, much more than a caricature.

As I read and reread *The Old Devils* (it gets better on a second try), I found myself wishing that Philip Larkin—who called Amis "quite the funniest writer I had ever met"—could have stayed alive to read it, especially since so many moments in it recall specific Larkin poems as well as his general ethos. When Rhiannon and Malcolm visit a shut-up Welsh church on a remote promontory, we think of Larkin's "Church Going"; as we do when they encounter a crowd of bathers that might have stepped out of "To the Sea." At another point, Charlie Norris rewrites a line from "Dockery and Son" into "Life was first boredom, then more boredom, as long as it was going your way, at least." And the novel's title surely recalls Larkin's great poem about age, "The Old Fools." But the kinship is stronger than any matter of specific references: both Amis and Larkin are deeply humorous writers, and never more serious than when humorous. In *The Old Devils* Amis has tried to be seriously humorous about the impossible subject of death, as he was in the little poem that concludes his collected poems: "Death has got something to be said for it; / There's no need to get out of bed for it; / Wherever you may be, / They bring it to you, free."

The close of the novel has a mythy feel about it, a marriage between young people who are viewed with respect, even admiration, by the novelist. There is the sense that life goes on, with the young entertaining hopes as high as those some of the old devils once entertained. Peter's son tells him at his wedding reception that, strangely enough, his relationship with his bride has been nothing less than splendid: "'Absolutely no snags or problems of any kind at any stage right from the start. My God, I've just realised it was love at first sight. Doesn't that sound ridiculous?' 'No,' said Peter." This is undoubtedly the most affirmative "no" Amis has ever had a character utter, and it comes as a fitting end to a book that, along with its eloquent and wonderfully comic presentation of life's awfulnesses, is, very much on life's side.

New York Times Book Review, March 22, 1987

Robert Stone: *Outerbridge Reach*

Robert Stone's fiction has always been preoccupied with the unlovely underside of American life. Eighteen years ago, soon after the conclusion of the Vietnam War, he published his second novel, *Dog Soldiers*, a book that made connections between folly and violence in Southeast Asia and countercultural disorders back home in the Age of Aquarius. *Dog Soldiers* won the National Book Award, and with good reason. It spoke to American disenchantment, it was a compellingly executed tale of action, and the witty brilliance of its prose created a dark comedy of disaster—of attempted heroic gestures that were also, as its unheroic hero, John Converse, observed, "peculiar and stupid."

Nothing in the novels that followed it—*A Flag for Sunrise* (1981) and *Children of Light* (1986)—suggested that Stone had embraced a more "balanced" view of the world; indeed, when talking about his vision of things, balance seemed hardly the word to use. But his latest novel, *Outerbridge Reach*—which, like *Dog Soldiers*, centers on a triangle of husband, wife, and friend who is also betrayer, and which frequently alludes to Vietnam as a gathering focus of troubled memories—also brings a new possibility into the novelist's work: that not to believe in anything, to see through everything, may be a peculiarly stupid way to cheat oneself of life. In *Outerbridge Reach* the Converse figure, much cleaned up, is a handsome fortyish husband and father named Owen Browne. A 1969 graduate of the Naval Academy who served in Vietnam, Browne uses no drugs and drinks very sparingly, reads, keeps himself fit and tries to be a good man around the house. Soon after we meet him, he thinks about the morning he left Penn Station bound for Annapolis and wonders how the Owen Browne of those days might have imagined himself twenty years later: "The image would have been a romantic one, but romantic in the post-war modernist style. Its heroic quality would have been salted in stoicism and ennobled by alienation. As an uncritical reader of Hemingway, he would have imagined his future self suitably disillusioned and world-weary!" The trouble is that Browne has become an unsatisfactory parody of that disillusioned figure, since his work consists of writing advertising copy for Altan Marine, a yacht brokerage firm in Connecticut. (One thinks of lines from Robert Lowell's poem about his father, "Commander Lowell": "'Anchors aweigh,' Daddy boomed in his bathtub. . . . When Lever Brothers offered to pay / him double what the Navy paid.")

The Hylan Corporation, the parent company of Browne's firm, has planned to advertise its boats by having its head man, Matty Hylan, sail one of them around the world by himself in a highly publicized race. When Hylan, a buccaneering entrepreneur, disappears amid evidence of financial disarray, Browne decides that he will enter the race in Hylan's place, even though his solo sailing experience is limited. His wife, Anne (who works for a sailing magazine, is handsome, and tends to drink too much), perceives that her husband has been mourning an unrealized dream and sees the race as an opportunity to move their marriage onto a new track—so she resists her fears that the venture is really a desperate one. For all their self-doubts, both she and Browne are idealists, unwilling to believe that the Melvillean advice Browne later enters into his log of the race—"Be true to the dreams of your youth"—is really a fool's counsel.

Into their orbit comes a documentary filmmaker named Ron Strickland, hired by the Hylan Corporation to make a movie about its entry in the race. Strickland prides himself on his lack of illusions, his way of penetrating to the false heart of every plausible or pretentious human affirmation; his business is to expose ideals as trumpery, to exploit "the difference between what people say they're doing and what's really going on." In what he sees as the all-American marriage of the Brownes, Strickland finds a rich subject for exposure; and since "almost all the attractive women Strickland knew had been to bed with him," Anne Browne is of special interest.

The novel divides almost exactly in half, with its first part patiently inter-weaving the narratives of Browne, Anne, and Strickland, placing these prin-cipals in relation to a number of strongly presented subsidiary characters—particularly Strickland's sometime companion, Pamela, a prostitute ("ho" as she calls herself) and drug user who starred in one of his earlier docu-mentaries: "Her eyes were a caution, warning away the faint of loin, the troubled and the poor." In part two, the race begins and we move back and forth between the tumultuous course of Browne's voyage and the equally vivid and self-destructive course of Anne's affair with Strickland.

The novel's movement is leisurely, but the narrative has shapeliness and great cumulative power. The source of that power—and pleasure—is, of course, Stone's language as it creates a style. On every page something ver-bally interesting happens: the insolent voice of a Hylan executive "suggested gulls over India Wharf"; Strickland's 1963 Porsche has rusty fittings, "but the engine reported like a Prussian soldier on the first turn of the key"; Cap-tain Riggs-Bowen, club secretary of the Southchester Yacht Club (where a publicity party for the race is held) "had a brick-red blood-pressure mask around his eyes, which resembled those of a raptor." Anne's father, who dis-approves of Browne, calls the sea a desert ("Nothing out there but social cripples and the odd Filipino"), while his sixty-year-old secretary, An-toinette Lamattina, looks "as though she thrived on chaste bereavement, fre-quent communion and the occasional excursion to Roseland Ballroom." As with Stone's earlier books, there's an edge to the gritty idiom of description and dialogue that makes us think of Hemingway, certainly, but also of Ray-mond Chandler. In fact, *Outerbridge Reach* is like a thriller in that we're made to care intensely about what happens next and who's going to get hurt.

Stone's novels are always heavily allusive, to previous books and styles as well as to places and their names. This one about the sea contains, among many others, references to *Moby-Dick* and "Billy Budd" (Browne is the Handsome Sailor, thinks Strickland ironically); moments from *Richard III* ("What dreadful noise of waters in mine ears! What ugly sights of death," thinks Browne), as well as *Henry V* and *Romeo and Juliet;* lines from Mar-lowe's *Doctor Faustus*, Henley's *Invictus*, Hart Crane's *The Bridge*, and even John Gillespie Magee's "High Flight" ("I have slipped the surly bonds of earth / And danced the skies on laughter-silvered wings"). The allusion needn't be explicit and isn't inevitably ironic or parodic. When Browne, on the voyage, recovers from what at first looked like a case of tetanus, he cooks himself a cheese omelet with fried ham that tastes "marvelous," "as things did at sea"—and as those canned pork and beans and canned apricots tasted to Nick Adams on the fishing trip in "Big Two-Hearted River." As for the spirit of places, the novel is full of New York City (Stone grew up there, but New York has been largely absent from his books), from Penn Station to Staten Island to the Brooklyn Bridge, as well as more exotic neighboring spots like Atlantic City, Bayonne, Port Newark, the Arthur Kill, and the Outerbridge Reach of the title.

At a key moment early in the book, Browne, on an impulse, takes out the *Parsifal II*, a boat from the Altan repair yard on Staten Island, and comes upon a salvage yard where the hulks of old tugs and ferries rot in ominous peace. (The moment recalls an eerily memorable one in *The Best Years of Our Lives*, when Dana Andrews walks among disused aircraft.) The yard belongs to Anne's father and is an unlikely scene for a quest: "On Browne's left, the hulks lay scattered in a geometry of shadows. The busy sheer and curve of their shapes and the perfect stillness of the water made them appear held fast in some phantom disaster. Across the Kill, bulbous storage tanks, generators and floodlit power lines stretched to the end of darkness. The place was marked on the charts as Outerbridge Reach." My reading of the novel says that the phantom disaster in which Browne later involves himself also involves a discovery—which his wife and Strickland also make—that Outerbridge Reach reaches further and deeper than anyone could have thought. So when, deep in the Southern Hemisphere, he sees an iceberg, it appears to him as a steam tug, "like the ones his father-in-law owned at Outerbridge Reach." And as, in relentless succession, he confronts high winds, freezing rain and the second-rate qualities of his unworthily built boat—"plastic unmaking itself"—Browne understands at last that he is "about to experience the true dimensions of the situation in which he had placed himself."

At any rate, it's impossible to read the final, dazzling hundred pages of the novel without feeling that something terrible has happened for which nobody is to blame. Alone at sea, Browne muses that "it was necessary to experience life correctly but at the same time compose it into something acceptable." (Melville may have had a similar notion when he attached the motto "Keep True to the Dreams of Thy Youth" to his writing desk.) Robert Stone's blend of heroic aspiration and mordantly deflationary irony results in something like tragicomedy—maybe even something like Shakespeare, our best tragic comedian. But whatever you call it, *Outerbridge Reach* seems to me a triumph—a beautifully and painstakingly composed piece of literary art.

New York Times Book Review, February 23, 1992

Philip Roth: *Sabbath's Theater*

Asked in an interview about his relationship to the character of Nathan Zuckerman, also a novelist, Philip Roth replied that it was a matter of impersonation: "Making fake biography, false history, concocting a half-imaginary existence out of the actual drama of my life *is* my life." In Zuckerman's own word for it, the novelist must be, above all else, a "personificator." Over the ten years since *Zuckerman Bound*, Roth has published five books that contrive to make "fake biography, false history" by calling their narratives into question—by confusing the distinctions between art and life, truth and falsity, the real and the imagined. Most recently, in *Operation Shylock*, he invented a second Philip Roth with whom to confront Philip Roth the protagonist; and while subtitling that book "A Confession," he claimed in a final note to the reader that it was all made up, wholly imaginary. Yet the note's closing sentence advised us, "This confession is false." (The foregoing "novel"? The note to the reader?) Now, after all these elaborate, sometimes confusing dialectics, debates and interrogations, comes *Sabbath's Theater*, Roth's longest and, in my judgment, richest, most rewarding novel. As always, similarities will be noted between the book's protagonist and his creator: each was born in New Jersey, has been married to an actress, is now in his sixties. But it should be insisted that Mickey Sabbath, like John Berryman's Henry in *The Dream Songs*, is "essentially an imaginary character," not Philip Roth the novelist or the man.

The bare bones of character and story are as follows: Morris (Mickey) Sabbath, a sixty-four-year-old ex-puppeteer with fingers now crippled by arthritis, has lived for decades in a rural New England village, Madamaska Falls, teaching drama at a local college until forced to resign over a scandal involving a phone-sex tape and a student. Sabbath is married to a recovering alcoholic, Roseanna. (His previous wife, Nikki, the actress, disappeared in 1964, after which Sabbath left New York City for the country.) The great erotic love of his life, his Croatian mistress, Drenka Balich, who along with her husband ran the inn at Madamaska Falls, has recently died of ovarian cancer, leaving Sabbath grief-stricken and desperate. Sabbath grew up on the Jersey Shore with his parents and his older brother, Morty, who was shot down and killed by the Japanese in 1944. Fifty years later, he is haunted by his mother's voice, vividly speaking to him in the way she once did before the shattering death of Morty. News of yet another death, that of a former friend and business backer from Sabbath's days in New York, precipitates his decision to leave Roseanna and drive to the city for the funeral, then arrange for his own death. ("He had to see what it looked like before he did it himself.") Through flashback and fantasy, in a narrative that moves, as its emotional temperature dictates, from third-person comic or dispassionate to extremes of first-person clowning and perverse confession, we are treated to the full range of Sabbath's theater, "where the atmosphere was insinuatingly anti-moral, vaguely menacing, and at the same time, rascally fun."

Readers of Roth will think pretty quickly of *Portnoy's Complaint*, whose sexual theatrics had some of the great jokes and rascally fun of this new novel but none of its menacing sense of last things. The book's epigraph is Prospero's vow, made near the end of *The Tempest*, that "every third thought shall be my grave." Although the aging Sabbath doesn't sound much like Prospero, he has his own brand of death-directed eloquence, funny and profound, as he thinks about the loss of family, friends, lovers, and—not least—his morning erection. He wonders whether any other species wake with hard-ons: "Do whales? Do bats? . . . It takes a lifetime to determine what matters, and by then it's not there anymore." In his younger days, Sabbath evidently spent some time with Shakespeare, Yeats, Joyce, and others; he now reads only books about death. Unlike his creator, he is a failed artist, attempting to turn the energies that once went into his puppets to more outrageous performances in life—performances that carry him, literally, to the edge of the grave.

Ever since *Portnoy*, Roth has been preeminent as a literary stand-up comedian, and some of the routines in *Sabbath's Theater* show him in top form. Preparing to attend the funeral of his friend, Sabbath looks out from the eighteenth floor of an apartment onto the green of Central Park and thinks that perhaps "the time had come to jump":

Mishima. Rothko. Hemingway. Berryman. Koestler. Pavese. Kosinski. Arshile Gorky. Primo Levi. Hart Crane. Walter Benjamin. Peerless bunch. Nothing dishonorable signing on there. Faulkner as good as killed himself with booze. As did (said Roseanna, authority now on the distinguished dead who might be alive had they "shared" at A.A.) Ava Gardner. Blessed Ava. Wasn't much about men could astonish Ava. Elegance and filth, immaculately intertwined. Dead at 62. . . . Ava, Yvonne de Carlo—*those* are role models!

After an obscenity about "the laudable ideologies," he pronounces them "Shallow, shallow, shallow! Enough reading and rereading of *A Room of One's Own*—get yourself *The Collected Works of Ava Gardner*." This stream of thought is of the sort Joyce invented for Leopold Bloom, and Sabbath often makes us think of that resourceful monologuist. But of course Bloom hadn't read Virginia Woolf, didn't know about Ava Gardner or Yvonne de Carlo.

Roth's genius for juxtaposing impressions, feelings, and names that usually don't belong together continually enlivens the narrative. His extraordinarily active style revels in the play of words, as in this partial catalogue of the American idioms Sabbath's mistress, Drenka, gets delightfully wrong: "bear and grin it . . . his days are counted . . . a roof under my head . . . the boy who cried 'Woof!'. . . alive and cooking." One of the cruelest, funniest moments in the book occurs when Sabbath persuades Drenka that her husband, invited by members of the Rotary to address them on the art of hostelry, must speak for at least an hour, and at a very slow pace, as he describes the "nuts and bulbs" of his profession.

But Sabbath's disgust at "the laudable ideologies" gives the book a polemical edge that takes things beyond verbal playfulness. His wife's incessant talk about sharing and identifying makes Sabbath rasp at her, "And is the only way to get off the booze to learn to talk like a second grader?" The question "Why must you be so racially prejudiced against Japanese!" brings the reply, prompted by memories of his dead brother, "Because of what they did to Alec Guinness in *The Bridge on the River Kwai*." His campaign against treating women as persons rather than as sexual objects is instanced by his quoting from Yeats's "For Anne Gregory" ("Only God, my dear, / Could love you for yourself alone / And not your yellow hair"). In his car, listening to Benny Goodman, he sings along with "The Sheik of Araby," whose lyrics "celebrating date rape and denigrating Arabs" he finds irresistible. "For a pure sense of being tumultuously alive, you can't beat the nasty side of existence," he exclaims in a burst of manic affirmation.

There is plenty of nastiness in this book, and certain readers will find it repellent, not funny at all. One of Sabbath's friends, his patience exhausted by Mickey's abusive behavior, calls it "the discredited male polemic's last gasp." There is something to this charge, and the novel is stronger for allowing readers to consider the hero in such terms, if they choose. But it would be a mistake to do so exclusively, for that would involve foreclosing on the sympathies we give to the outrageous Sabbath when, in a section of sixty pages, the heart of the novel and one of the great sequences in American fiction, he returns to the Jersey Shore of his boyhood. After visiting the graveyard where his family lies, then staking out his own gravesite, Sabbath discovers, in a derelict house nearby, a one-hundred-year-old cousin of his father's, named Fish. He finds not only Fish but also—in a chest that once belonged to Sabbath's mother—a box marked "Morty's Things," full of the souvenirs she kept of his dead brother. Contemplating all the "beloveds" on the cemetery tombstones, he had reflected, Bloomlike, that "nobody beloved gets out alive." Now, still alive, Sabbath finds that his conversation with old Fish draws him ironically and painfully toward life as, in a rush of memory, everything comes back.

Sabbath tells Fish (who doesn't remember him) that, yes, his parents have sent him over to see Fish, and the old man responds with "Isn't that remarkable?" The word gives Sabbath "an enormous boost," makes him feel he is dealing "with a man on whom his life has left an impression." They proceed to share commonplaces that turn out to be not commonplace at all: that Fish has been sent a birthday card from his optometrist; that the Atlantic Ocean once uprooted the boardwalk; that everything has changed; that death is terrible. As Fish goes off to cook his lunch, Sabbath steals the box of Morty's things—at the bottom of which, he knows, is the American flag his mother kept—and heads for the ocean. The section concludes in what is surely the finest passage in the novel, right down to a line from Yeats's late sonnet "Meru," a poem Sabbath came across earlier in a student's notebook:

> The boardwalk was gone. Goodbye, boardwalk. The ocean had finally carried it away. The Atlantic is a powerful ocean. Death is a terrible thing. That's a doctor I never heard of. Remarkable. Yes, that's the word for it. It was all remarkable. Goodbye, remarkable. Egypt and Greece goodbye, and goodbye, Rome!

The accumulated force of this seemingly unremarkable writing can be felt only by one who has read the fifty—or the four hundred—pages that precede it. In its exclamatory poignancy, it takes its place with comparable moments at the end of *Zuckerman Unbound* (the hero's return to his lost Newark) and Herman Roth's death in *Patrimony*. Over all, *Sabbath's Theater* is no less a virtuoso performance than its predecessor, *Operation Shylock*, but it has a depth and resonance unattained there. In Roth's new theater it feels as if the lights were about to be extinguished for good, and that's unsettling.

The end of the novel—Sabbath's return to Madamaska Falls and what he discovers there—struck me as a shade arbitrary and contrived, after the absolute rightness of the New Jersey pages, although a flashback to Drenka's final hours in the hospital is as powerful as writing can be. As for the sexual affronts the book will cause some readers, it depends on where (or whether) you draw the line. (I had mixed feelings about an extended transcript of the phone-sex tape between Sabbath and the student, a tape that, Sabbath admits, was more than enough "to drive me out of every decent antiphallic educational institution in America.") But, as Yeats's Crazy Jane puts it, "Fair and foul are near of kin, / And fair needs foul." In Sabbath's formulation (and his creator surely agrees), "The unknown about any excess is how excessive it's been."

This novel is Roth's most ambitious effort at finding that out, and it is also one of the first such efforts to conduct itself, consciously, at the end of the century—"the century that had virtually reversed human destiny," Sabbath thinks. Matthew Arnold, who would have had his problems with *Sabbath's Theater*, knew, however, that a great work occurred only when the power of the man and the power of the moment came together, which is what happens in this novel. "Egypt and Greece goodbye, and goodbye, Rome!" Philip Roth seems to me to be saying something similarly terrifying and exhilarating about American life in 1995.

New York Times Book Review, September 10, 1995

CRITICS, BELLETRISTS

THE WRITERS surveyed here are, with the exception of Edward Gorey, who is a category all to himself, English: four of them novelists of reputation, all of them men of letters in various senses. Samuel Johnson, the prototype of such men, has been presented to us most vividly in Lawrence Lipking's literary biography, one of the best accounts we have of Johnson as a writer. John Churton Collins, by contrast, is probably the least-known and least-read of English critics who still—I argue in my essay—make a claim on our attention. My account of Aldous Huxley was prompted by reading the first two volumes of what will be his collected essays. Even though his standing as a novelist has slipped, Huxley still has interest for us as a vigorous writer and a learned man. "Impossible," the title of my review of Evelyn Waugh's letters, might with equal justice be applied to those of his fellow comic novelist and generally outrageous counterpart, Kingsley Amis. As for A. N. Wilson, perhaps the busiest of current English all-purpose writers, a survey of some of his best books in an already voluminous oeuvre makes the case for his appeal.

The short concluding piece on Edward Gorey is my tribute to an artist who has given me much pleasure.

Authorizing Samuel Johnson

"JOHNSON's reputation is of the most deadly kind," wrote Marvin Mudrick almost thirty years ago. Mudrick was reviewing the latest volume in the Yale edition of Samuel Johnson's works—in this case his periodical essays, diaries, and prayers—which Mudrick thought would do little to make his books more read. In his essay titled "The Ogre at the Feast of Life," Mudrick praised Boswell for having written, in his *Life of Samuel Johnson*, "a book immeasurably greater than the collected works of his subject." Such depreciation of Johnson's works by comparing them to Boswell's biography was long ago set in motion by Macaulay, in 1831, when he portrayed Johnson as a grotesque, freakish, Falstaffian character whose own works were fading away to obscurity. It is impossible, seventeen decades later, to inquire whether those works, in the eyes of the reading public, have faded any more than Pope's or Dryden's or Milton's or Ben Jonson's—who except academics and their dutiful students reads *any* older English writer? But most people interested in Johnson would agree that over the past fifty years he has received critical and biographical treatment that is distinguished and illuminating. Lawrence Lipking's fine new book is but the latest in a series that includes biographies by Joseph Wood Krutch, James Clifford, John Wain, Walter Jackson Bate, and Robert DeMaria Jr., along with critical studies by Bate, W. K. Wimsatt, Paul Fussell, and many others. Most recently, Bruce Redford has provided a handsomely edited five-volume collection of Johnson's correspondence. And there is even a book on the rhetoric of the *Rambler* essays, titled *Samuel Johnson after Deconstruction*, that brings to bear on Johnson, for better or worse, the work of our contemporary Great Chams, Jacques Derrida and Harold Bloom.

Samuel Johnson: The Life of an Author, by Lawrence Lipking. Cambridge: Harvard University Press, 1998. Before Lipking, the most useful introductory tours through Johnson's writing

Amidst all the specialist studies of Johnson in relation to this or that—to politics or religion or the arts or deconstruction—it is brave and admirable of Mr. Lipking to have written a "generalist" book about Johnson as author, addressed to the generalist reader. Lipking takes up, pretty much in chronological order, the main pieces of writing through which Johnson survives: the letter to Chesterfield, apropos of publication of Johnson's *Dictionary of The English Language;* the poem "London"; the "Life of Richard Savage"; "The Vanity of Human Wishes"; the *Dictionary;* the *Rambler* essays; *Rasselas;* the preface to the edition of Shakespeare; *A Journey to the Western Islands of Scotland;* and *The Lives of the English Poets.* The claim implicitly made in these choices is that Lipking has something forceful, even new, to tell us about items central to Johnson's achievement as a writer, an author; this claim is handsomely substantiated in the book he has written.

Lipking's credentials as an eighteenth-century scholar of impressive learning were established with his first book, *The Ordering of the Arts in Eighteenth-Century England.* Since then he has on numerous occasions written with an insider's authority about changing notions of the period over past decades, especially as critical focus has shifted from studying preeminent writers and their work—Dryden, Swift, Pope, Fielding, Richardson, Gray, Johnson—to social and political circumstances, to the contributions of women writers, to once marginal issues of labor, the poor, health, and other examples of what used to be called "background."[1] His assured purchase on what seems like virtually everything written on eighteenth-century writers is evident. With particular reference to Johnson, we see this in the scrupulous footnotes to chapters acknowledging someone's contribution that Lipking makes use of or at least informs us of. These acknowledgments are invariably generous, and he is generous as well to his predecessors who have written books about Johnson. Unlike some biographers and critics, he doesn't pretend that his point of view hasn't been touched, or enhanced, or altered, by some previous laborer in the vineyard. There is a confident sense of large-spiritedness about his whole critical enterprise.

---

may be found in Fussell's *Samuel Johnson and the Life of Writing* (W. W. Norton, 1971) and DeMaria's *The Life of Samuel Johnson* (Oxford: Blackwell, 1993). DeMaria has more recently published a fascinating account of Johnson's reading: *Samuel Johnson and the Life of Reading* (Baltimore: Johns Hopkins University Press, 1997).

1. See "Inventing the Eighteenth Centuries," in *The Profession of Eighteenth-Century Literature,* ed. Leo Damrosch (Madison: University of Wisconsin Press, 1992).

That enterprise is staked out in the introduction by Lipking's gloss on his subtitle, "The Life of an Author," as "not the life of a man but the life that he put in his work." The notion of authorship has become a contested one in recent decades, after the underminings practiced on it by Barthes ("The Death of the Author") and Foucault ("What Is an Author?"). But in fact there was an earlier detectable "slippage," as Lipking finds it, in the series of four definitions of "author" in Johnson's *Dictionary*; from "The first beginner or mover of any thing: he to whom any thing owes its original," down to the decidedly more modest "a writer in general." Lipking is concerned to show how Johnson made himself into an author; how, despite his doubts, self-lacerations and gloom about any human endeavor, he could eventually speak, in the preface to the *Dictionary,* in the first person and "for"—as its representative in this great work—the English nation. Indeed, in the preface to his edition of Shakespeare, Johnson speaks not for just a nation but the whole world:

> *Shakespeare* is above all writers, at least above all modern writers, the poet of nature; the poet that holds up to his readers a faithful mirror of manners and of life. . . . His persons act and speak by the influence of those general passions and principles by which all minds are agitated, and the whole system of life is continued in motion. In the writings of other poets a character is too often an individual; in those of *Shakespeare* it is commonly a species.

But it would be deeply mistaken to assume that this authority came easy to Johnson: from the beginning, Lipking shows, he maintained a doubleness of attitude toward authorship, of "enormous ambition combined with preemptive dejection." As a moralist his great, in some ways his only, theme was—as Bate described it decades ago and in Johnson's words—"the hunger of imagination which preys incessantly upon life," and which by its very nature, can never be satisfied. In Lipking's words, and with special reference to the case of his subject, "the dream itself precipitates its own disenchantment." Wordsworth gave that theme a slightly different spin at the famous moment in his poem "Resolution and Independence" when he declared, "As high as we have mounted in delight, / In our dejection do we sink as low." In terms of Johnson, the extent to which your imagination hungers will determine the power of the ensuing disenchantment, as in Wordsworth's "fears and fancies thick upon me came, / Dim sadness—and blind thoughts, I knew not, nor could name." Here, psychologically, Johnson and his Romantic successor were at one, though Johnson never managed to "solve" the problem as Wordsworth thought he did in his poem by producing, from nowhere, the Leech-gatherer.

Lipking's first chapter, "The Birth of the Author," is an especially strong one, containing as it does a brilliant close reading of the famous letter to Chesterfield, written after Chesterfield had anonymously recommended the forthcoming *Dictionary*. A few months afterward, Johnson wrote to him, reminding him of their past relation or lack of it ("Seven years, My lord have now past since I waited in your outward Rooms or was repulsed from your Door"), and delivered the goods to his putative—but only putative—patron:

> Is not a Patron, My Lord, one who looks with unconcern on a Man struggling for Life in the water and when he has reached ground encumbers him with help. The notice which you have been pleased to take of my Labours, had it been early, had been kind; but it has been delayed till I am indifferent and cannot enjoy it, till I am solitary and cannot impart it, till I am known and do not want it.

Lipking's commentary on this section may be quoted in full, as typical of his perspicuity. The climactic word of the letter is *known*—"till I am known and do not want it":

> The rule of emphasis that Johnson followed generally put most weight on the end of a period. Hence the third of three parallel clauses, completing a cadence, was meant to be very emphatic. Clearly, Johnson stresses how much he does not want Chesterfield's notice. "Want" means primarily "to be without something"; the would-be patron encumbers the writer with help he does not need. But "want" also stands for "desire," and the weight on the word conveys a great weariness, a desire to be free forever from that old yearning for favor. To be *known* is more solid than to be famous or praised; it implies an integrity that can stand out in public. Johnson no longer sues for favor or struggles for life. He is not the person whom Chesterfield thought he knew; his work will speak for itself.

It should be noted that such critical procedure on Lipking's part is as much a matter of registering something heard—the voice of the author—as something seen and understood.

His discussions of Johnson's major works are satisfyingly instructive for the way they combine old-fashioned virtues of setting the work historically and biographically, with internal commentary on its language. One example, a particularly enlightening one, is his handling of Johnson's great poem "The Vanity of Human Wishes." This reader at least has tended to engage with it as a timeless specimen of moral satire, the debt to Juvenal notwithstanding. Lipking reminds us that its date of appearance, 1749, was "postwar" (after the martial failures of "the bold Bavarian," Charles VII, and of Charles XII of Sweden), but also post-great-writers: Pope had died in 1744, Swift the next year, and (though not at all a "great writer") Johnson's friend Savage in 1743. As for the prevailing atmosphere in English verse, "Night thoughts and graveyards cast shadows on [it]," notes Lipking, noting as well that Johnson's wife was sick and approaching death. In opposition to forward-looking (or pre-Romantic) poets of his time, like Akenside or Gray or Collins, Johnson stayed loyal to the heroic couplet he inherited from his Augustan predecessors, but made of it something new, a resistant, massively individual idiom consisting of what Ezra Pound was later to call, with reference to "Vanity," a "triumph of the perfectly weighed and placed word." Such attention to words so placed would be natural, perhaps, to the operations of a lexicographer; but only Johnson could have turned his lexicographic virtues into the poem that resulted.

When Lipking descends to local demonstration of how perfectly weighted and placed are the poem's words, he quotes the concluding couplet in Johnson's portrait of the "sinking statesman" whose "burning to be great" has now suffered a serious dampening":

> For now no more we trace in ev'ry Line
> Heroic Worth, Benevolence Divine:
> The Form distorted justifies the Fall,
> And Detestation rids th' indignant Wall.

Lipking describes how we now see the picture "cut out of its frame in disgrace":

> Implicitly the couplets reproach the faithlessness of retinues and parasites, who justify themselves after the fall of their patron by looking askance at his portrait. "Line" packs in many meanings: not only features of the face, the painter's strokes, and a poet's flattering verses, but also genealogy. What viewers once recognized in the painted face was not mere family likeness but inherited virtues, Worth and Benevolence so unmistakable that they assumed a visible form, like members of the family.

But things have changed, England has changed, and the poet's feelings are "projected onto ideas and things":

> The personified Detestation and Wall collaborate on shedding the hated portrait, but they do not seem to like each other much. The Wall might be indignant not only about the face it has borne but also about being defaced (a touch of the Latin *indignitas,* indignity, may cling to it), and Detestation might be leaving an empty patch on the Wall as well as clearing it. At any rate, the amount of hatred seems excessive, directed at a mere form. Humanity is nowhere to be seen; and that is the point.

Lipking's contextual placing, followed by close engagement with couplets and lines of verse, makes the poem available to us as something more than a "timeless" anthology favorite. His close reading of selected passages shows us why, if we didn't know it already, Johnson's friend and onetime pupil, the actor David Garrick, said that "The Vanity of Human Wishes" was "as hard as Greek."

One finds similarly useful criticism in the pages devoted to *Rasselas* and to the Shakespeare preface. But Lipking's judgment—and any reader of Johnson will, I think, endorse it—is that *Lives of the Poets,* the last project in a life full of projects is Johnson's critical masterpiece, his most personal and also most "common" effort, inasmuch as he has become "surrogate for a literate nation." The famous sentences about Thomas Gray with which the volume originally closed (a life of the forgotten Lyttleton was later added) exploit the word "common": "In the character of his *Elegy* I rejoice to concur with the common reader; for by the common sense of readers uncorrupted with literary prejudices, after all the refinements of subtlety and the dogmatism of learning, must be finally decided all claim to poetical honours." Lipking describes this as a moment in which Johnson merges the public judgment with his own: "Johnson's whole career as an author has led to this moment." But we see everywhere in the *Lives* this deference to and concurrence with the common reader, a reader who no longer and perhaps never was on sea or land.

Still, Johnson invokes him, or wills him into being. My own favorite instance of this, one out of many, occurs in his commentary, from the life of Pope, on the *Essay on Man*—"certainly not the happiest of Pope's productions," says Johnson by way of beginning. In two longish paragraphs he teases Pope for his attempts at wisdom in the field of "metaphysical morality" and his provision, through four epistles, of "much that every man knows, and much that he does not know himself." Then, abruptly, the third paragraph changes perspectives and key, without even the ghost of a transition, into admiration of Pope's wizardry that Johnson assumes all readers must share:

> This essay affords an egregious instance of the predominance of genius, the dazzling splendor of imagery, and the seductive power of eloquence. Never was penury of knowledge and vulgarity of sentiment so happily disguised. The reader feels his mind full, though he learns nothing; and when he meets it in his new array, no longer knows the talk of his mother and his nurse.

The rightness of these declarations is inseparable from Johnson's own predominance of critical genius, his seductive powers of eloquence disarm us so that we scarcely think to question what this man so obviously knows to be the case.

Lipking says, interestingly, that in reviewing the poets from Cowley to Gray, in recording the great achievement of national genius to be observed in Milton, Dryden, Pope, Swift, and their minor brethren, Johnson was also reviewing his own career and looking once more into "the dream of authorship" he had so largely and continuously indulged. A few years before he wrote the *Lives*, and in a letter Lipking doesn't quote, Johnson wrote to Mrs. Thrale on the occasion of his just-passed sixty-fourth birthday:

> The return of my Birthday, if I remember it, fills me with thoughts which it seems to be the general care of humanity to escape. I can now look back upon threescore and four years, in which little has been done, and little has been enjoyed, a life diversified by misery, spent part in the sluggishness of penury, and part under the violence of pain, in gloomy discontent or importunate distress.

He says he will try to be "content," but then, as is his wont, adds a further grim reflection to the substantial one already expressed:

> In proportion as there is less pleasure in retrospective considerations the mind is more disposed to wander forward into futurity, but at Sixty four what promises, however liberal of imaginary good, can Futurity venture to make. Yet something will be always promised, and some promises will always be credited. I am hoping, and I am praying that I may live better in the time to come, whether long or short, than I have yet lived, and in the solace of that hope endeavour to repose.

However much "better" he lived in the eleven years that remained to him, however much he may have reposed in that hope, his active, combatively argumentative, and wholly personal performance in the *Lives* was something no previous English writer had come within miles of—and the intense pleasure that comes from reading this endlessly rereadable book has been amply testified to. But imagine, at age sixty-four, and after having authored the *Dictionary* and the edition of Shakespeare, *Rasselas,* the *Rambler,* and "The Vanity of Human Wishes," plus a raft of journalism, biography, poems, and translations—to say, and with full sincerity as it seems, that "little has been done"! Johnson could say it because he had, among others, Milton, Dryden, and Pope (not to say Shakespeare) to look back on and against whom to measure his achievement in letters. In writing these biographical and critical accounts he recalls, in Lipking's words, "his own journey through life."

In this connection it is a nice stroke of Lipking's to end his discussion of the *Lives* by considering Johnson's relation to Dryden, especially since Johnson himself suggested it in the tour de force that concludes the biographical section of the life of Pope. Through three paragraphs a comparison between Dryden and Pope is pursued with all the elegance and ingenuity of a writer at the top of his bent ("Dryden's page is a natural field, rising into inequalities, and diversified by the varied exuberance of abundant vegetation; Pope's is a velvet lawn, shaven by the scythe, and leveled by the roller"). Then, the parallel having been established at length, Johnson concludes: "And if the reader should suspect me, as I suspect myself, of some partial fondness for the memory of Dryden, let him not too hastily condemn me; for meditation and inquiry may, perhaps, show him the reasonableness of my determination." This moment is notable for its unique combination of the cautiously apologetic ("as I suspect myself") and its unambiguous conclusion—with all perhapses canceled out—in which "the reasonableness of my determination" is asserted.

Lipking has an ingenious, though not far-fetched explanation for Johnson's preferring Dryden, who, compared to Pope and Milton, was "all too human." Dryden is not, for Johnson, beyond the reach of lesser mortals; his foibles and faults—of negligence, hasty writing, the unevenness of many of his compositions—are part of a poetical character with which Johnson could identify. After all, his own work gave evidence of such imperfections. The roughness of temperament ("Dryden's was not one of the 'gentle bosoms,'" writes Johnson) is a further point of contact. Lipking reminds us of what I had forgotten or never knew—that in his earliest years Johnson had wanted to write Dryden's Life; now, nearing the end of his own literary career (Lipking's chapter on the *Lives* is titled "Touching the Shore"), his project of adding something to "English" has come to fulfillment. With a flourish, Lipking sums it up: "[Johnson's] life as an author has not, after all, been in vain; he has carried on Dryden's work."

As I read and assented to the lovely collocation between Johnson and his predecessor, I found myself thinking of a poem of Dryden's neither Johnson nor Lipking mentions. Written six years previous to Dryden's death, his verse epistle "To My Dear Friend Mr. Congreve" was prompted by the production of Congreve's second play, "The Double Dealer." In a way not unlike Johnson's own in the *Lives*, Dryden places the younger Congreve in relation to his contemporaries in the drama as well as to the ancestor of Congreve and the rest of us, in a triplet that ends with one of the best alexandrines ever written: "This is your Portion; this Your Native Store; / Heav'n that once was Prodigal before, / To *Shakespeare* gave as much; she cou'd not give him more." Dryden ends by presenting himself as "worn out with Cares and Age," as abandoning "th' Ungrateful Stage"; there follow the most moving ten lines he ever wrote, and ones that surely touched Johnson:

> Unprofitably kept at Heavn's expense,
> I live a Rent-charge on his Providence:
> But You, whom ev'ry Muse and Grace adorn,
> Whom I foresee to better Fortune born,
> Be kind to my Remains; and oh defend,
> Against Your Judgment, Your departed Friend!
> Let not the insulting Foe my Fame pursue;
> But shade those Lawrels which descend to You:
> And take for Tribute what these Lines express:
> You merit more; nor cou'd my Love do less.

Lawrence Lipking should be proud of his own tribute to Johnson, a work no less of learning than of love.

Hudson Review, Spring 1999

John Churton Collins:
Forgotten Man of Letters

WHEN was the following credo written and by whom?

> I believe, for the reasons already explained, that Belles Lettres are sinking
> deeper and deeper into degradation, that they are gradually passing out of
> the hands of their true representatives, and becoming almost the monop-
> oly of their false representatives, and that the consequences of this cannot
> but be most disastrous to us as a nation, to our reputation in the World of
> Letters, to taste, to tone, to morals. It is surely a shame and a crime in any
> one, and more especially in men occupying positions of influence and au-
> thority to assist in the work of corruption.

Jonathan Swift? William Wordsworth? John Ruskin? F. R. Leavis? The credo
contains sentiments that each of them on more than one occasion endorsed.
But in fact these words were set down a hundred years ago, by a man of letters whose name a century later is scarcely known, even to academics in English studies. For John Churton Collins is one of the great secrets of belles
lettres in English, a prophet without honor even in the writings of those—
such as Leavis—who might have recognized him as a forebear and fellow
spirit in the fight to make the criticism of literature a serious and valuable activity. The reasons for Collins being buried so deep in the ranks of those forgotten should be enquired into.

Insofar as he is remembered at all, it is as an irascible, if well-equipped,
attacker of his contemporary men of letters. Foremost of these attacks is the
one on Edmund Gosse, whose Cambridge Clark Lectures, published in book
form as *From Shakespeare to Pope* (1885), were taken to pieces by Collins as
a tissue of factual error and incompetent judgments. The review begins
famously:

That such a book as this should have been permitted to go forth to the world with the *imprimatur* of the University of Cambridge, affords matter for very grave reflection.

The forty pages to follow document the charge, citing chapter and verse. And Collins provided similar dismantlings of what he called dilettantism—loose, impressionistic commentary on literacy works—in books by John Addington Symonds, George Saintsbury, and other lesser-known belletrists. The attack on Gosse is understood to have provoked Gosse's friend Tennyson—about whom Collins had already written essays that displeased Tennyson—to call him, picturesquely, "a Louse on the locks of Literature." In fact as Christopher Ricks and, later, Gosse's biographer Ann Thwaite have pointed out, Tennyson employed the less picturesque "Jackass" by way of characterizing Collins.

Dilettantism was one-half of what Collins saw as the besetting sin of literary studies; the other half was philology, the discipline that controlled that study at both Oxford and Cambridge. His plea for the detaching of literature from philology as a legitimate subject of study was forcefully and scornfully made in the first part of a three-part essay titled "English Literature at the Universities" (*Ephemera Critica*). Collins describes philology's resistance to any attempt to widen and extend the audience for literature by making it a subject for "liberal" study. On the contrary, he says of philologists:

> In their eyes the Universities are simply nurseries for esoteric specialists, and to talk of bringing them into touch with national life is, in their estimation, mere cant. Their attitude toward Literature, generally, is precisely that of the classical party toward our own Literature: they regard it simply as the concern of men of letters, journalists, dilettantes, and Extension lecturers.

Collins goes on to admit that philology is a branch of learning "of immense importance," but also declares that as a science "it has no connection with Literature." He believed that the "instincts and faculties" of the study of philology, compared to the student of literature, were radically dissimilar, and that until the study of literature became separated from philological investigation, it would lack integrity.

Collins himself was an extension lecturer, perhaps the busiest and most devoted of them who ever lived. In the appendixes to the memoir *Life and Memoirs of John Churton Collins*, his son L. C. Collins tells us that his father began his career in the University Extension Society in 1880, continuing for twenty-seven years, by which time he had delivered over three thousand lectures. He possessed, we are told, a remarkable memory for prose as well as verse, and a flair for the dramatic, with the result that he was enormously popular and much in demand. L. C. Collins notes, "As his memory was so good, he was able to dispense for the most part with the use of his notebooks, and on this account the lecture was rendered more pleasing for its air of ease and spontaneity; he displayed, too, a genuine and never lacking enthusiasm in his subject and this usually became infectious." Yet for most of those twenty-seven years, despite repeated applications, Collins had no university post (he eventually received one at the University of Birmingham in 1905), which surely fueled his conviction that he was an outsider; while inside the universities lived philologists (and perhaps some dilettantes as well) resisting any attempt to open up the study of English to more systematically critical operations.

His hero was Matthew Arnold, whose great essay "The Study of Poetry" appeared the year Collins began work as an extension lecturer. But satiric urbanity of the sort Arnold deployed in that essay, when he treated Dryden and Pope as classics of prose, rather than of poetry, from our "excellent and indispensable eighteenth century," was not Collins's usual style. Arnold could deftly and smoothly expose the awkwardness of Francis Newman's translation of Homer, or the banalities of Mr. Roebuck and Sir Charles Adderley in the famous "Wragg is in custody" passage from "The Function of Criticism at the Present Time." By contrast Collins's attacks were the opposite of feline, and "urbane" would be scarcely the right adjective for their comportment. Consider sentences from his evisceration of Gosse in the *Quarterly Review*, 1886:

> There is not a chapter—nay, if we except the Appendices and index, it would be difficult to find five consecutive pages which do not swarm with errors and absurdities. And the peculiarity of Mr. Gosse's errors is, that they cannot be classed among those to which even well-informed men are liable. They are not mere slips of the pen, they are not clerical and superficial, nor such as, casually arising, may be easily excised, but they are, to borrow a metaphor from medicine, local manifestations of constitutional mischief. The ignorance which Mr. Gosse displays of the simplest facts of

Literature and History is sufficiently extraordinary, but the recklessness with which he exposes that ignorance transcends belief.

And he proceeds, damningly, to lay out the evidence.

This vigorous no-holds-barred relentlessness with which Collins prosecuted his victims has been unfortunate for his reputation, insofar as when critics recognize his work at all it is to focus on its demonstrable excesses. Rather than attention being paid to the truth or falsity of Collins's charges, it is directed at the psychology of the charger: thus Collins, rather than his victim, becomes the subject of analysis. For example, Phyllis Grosskurth, the biographer of John Addington Symonds, speaks of the "paranoiac envy and irascibility that characterized his [Collins's] work." Although she admits that Collins's rebuttal to Gosse's response to the attack on him was "far more specific about actual inaccuracies and incomparably better organized as a whole than Gosse's effort," we are left with the impression that Collins's effort proceeded from motives somewhat dishonorable, certainly less than the "disinterested" criticism Arnold had called for. Ann Thwaite, in her biography of Gosse, goes even further along this line, admitting that Collins was quite right in his pointing out Gosse's errors, but also calling Collins "a fanatic and a pedant," thereby undermining his worth.

In a similar vein, Grosskurth points to Collins's demonstration of how much Tennyson's poetry owed to his predecessors—how adept and inveterate a borrower was the poet—as a covert slur on Tennyson. She credits Collins's "fantastic memory, his ability to find allusions and parallels behind nearly every phrase of Tennyson's." But when she comes to Collins's declaration that his tracing of allusion was "offered as commentaries on works which will take their place beside the masterpieces of Greek and Roman genius," she finds that declaration to be "intoned sanctimoniously" and that what really happened was that "Collins had tasted blood." The significant fact that Collins's way of noting sources, allusions, and indebtednesses to his predecessors in Tennyson's poetry would be drawn upon and practiced in Christopher Ricks's great edition of his works seems to go for naught—at least when compared to the analyzing and demoting of the less than worthy motives out of which Collins's practice supposedly issued.

In *The Rise and Fall of the Man of Letters,* John Gross has some pages on Collins that give a more sympathetic picture of his contribution. But Gross too is bothered, at least slightly, by what he calls Collins's "licensed ferocity" as a critic. Gross admits that the errors Collins uncovered in other critics ought not to have been let pass, and that "other reviewers in the same situation might well have delivered equally unfavorable verdicts." But, Gross goes on to qualify, "he did bring to the task of demolition a peculiar intensity, which was over and above the call of scholarly duty, and which suggests the brooding assassin rather than the judge." This is fair enough, but leaves us to decide for ourselves just how attractive this peculiar intensity that goes beyond "the call of scholarly duty" remains for us today.

By drawing on his son's memoir we can suggest the nature of Collins's "intensity," then observe it in the literary work of a critic whose legacy is richer and more various than the demolition jobs on his contemporaries for which he is mainly remembered. Everyone was in awe of his wonderful memory—"the greatest since Macaulay," testified a Philadelphia host of Collins, who had been invited to lecture there in 1893 by the American Society for the Extension of University Teaching. He was not just good at quoting *poems* from memory, as his host, Mr. Miles, testified when Miles's son asked Collins where he could find a good description of a great battle. "In Napier's Peninsular War, Vittoria for instance," was the answer.

> "Of course, Mr. Collins," I said *in jest*, you can recite the whole of it?" Whereupon, he reeled off fifteen pages of Napier without a pause, or hesitation, to the great delight of the youthful Basil and all of us. He followed this, a little later, with the whole of Manzoni's hymn to Napoleon, *in Italian!*

Collins's familiarity with languages was also phenomenal: he could read Greek, Latin, French, Spanish, Italian, and, in his later years, German. He was especially devoted to Italian and issued a vigorous protest when the Civil Service abolished it from its examinations on the grounds that it was too easy to "get up." As for the classics, his campaign to bring English and Classical curricula into some kind of harmony went along with a number of practical suggestions in his *The Study of English Literature,* in his edition of Matthew Arnold's *Merope* along with Sophocles' *Electra,* and in his posthumously published series of lectures, *Greek Influence on English Poetry.*

The intensity of Collins's literary pursuits can be observed in the pattern of his daily activity. His son quotes from his father's notebook: "Have just completed, 3 a.m. a respectable feat. I have carefully annotated the whole of Pope's Essay on Criticism. I began it on Sunday midday, August 9th and have finished it at 3 a.m. on August 12th, 1896." The three a.m. end to the workday was not an isolated instance. At one point he speaks of "the most frightfully laborious six weeks I have ever known," in which he frequently worked sixteen or seventeen hours a day. In 1903, completing a month's visit to Oxford, where he had been working on a long article on nineteenth-century American poets, he says he has avoided "*deep* depression," though has had "a good deal of the milder kind." And he enumerates a typical day: "Always a plunge in the river at 8.30: then breakfast 9.15: work from 10.30 to 5 as a rule: then bicycle ride: then dinner 7.30: then rest: then work 9.30 to 3 a.m. nearly every day." Even for a nineteenth-century man of letters, this must be extreme. Saintsbury, after all, had his wine cellar for diversion; whether Collins felt anything about wine is unrecorded. L. C. Collins tells us that his father cared nothing for the theater or for picture galleries, and that he was especially bored "by music in any shape or form." He did take an active interest in criminology, and he loved cemeteries, which, his son tells us, were always the first places he visited in a new town.

Although prey to depression throughout his life, his physical constitution was strong and he scarcely missed a single one of the ten thousand or so lectures he was to deliver over his career. The depressions, which could last for months, were inexplicable, and they came and went. His marriage seems to have been a happy one, though it is hard to see what sort of time he could have spent with his wife and the seven children she bore him. His death, under mysterious circumstances—his body was found in a dike in the English countryside, a bottle of sedatives nearby—could have been intentional or accidental, or some blurry combination of these. Although it can't be proven by demonstration, he appears to have been an essentially solitary being in the midst of the domestic and educational society in which he was involved. An entry from his notebook suggests how he contrived to see himself in relation to other people, to society: he writes that our character seems to have been given us at birth ("*what* a man is *that* is he born")

> and that so far as the foundations of character are concerned, education has little or perhaps no weight. I cannot call to mind a single human being who has had *the slightest* influence on me. My *intense* love of literature was inspired by no one, encouraged by no one, influenced by *no one*. It awoke suddenly and spontaneously—my life, my deeper life, has been *essentially* and permanently *solitary*. At school, at College and since it has been quite apart from my surroundings.

This is really an extraordinary claim to make for oneself, with the italicized words pumping up the intensity, and it's no wonder that such a man should fail to be rewarded in his attempts at public, institutional success. At the beginning of the last century, he launched a campaign to found a scholarship at Oxford for the comparative study of classical and English literature. He found a philanthropist named John Passmore Edwards who expressed interest in the project; then Collins solicited many letters from leading intellectuals in the culture (Arnold, Jowett, Gladstone, John Morley). Eventually the project did succeed—the money came through and was accepted by Oxford. But at one point it looked as if the benefactor was pulling out, and Collins confided the following to his notebook; that it was "one more of the many illustrations of the ill-fortune which has pursued me through life":

> I have never succeeded in anything except as a lecturer, everything that I
> have essayed has broken down, even when there seemed every chance of
> my succeeding as here. Bitter indeed has been the disappointment. I had
> set my heart on this and it seemed so likely to succeed.

It almost must have been difficult for him, after things righted themselves in this instance, to grant an exception to the blanket wailing over himself as a perfect failure in everything.

Yet Collins succeeded in the most important way a literary man can be said to succeed: he produced a substantial number of commentaries on poets and critics that are permanently valuable examples of intelligent criticism. And he provided a passionate, still relevant example of a way of thinking about the study and teaching of literature. This is to make no claim for his endurance as someone whose writings will be consulted, looked up for critical insights: his books are out of print and will remain so. In a sense it could be argued that he didn't really write *books,* but essays rather, which he then cobbled together into his most important volumes of criticism, *Essays and Studies; Studies in Poetry and Criticism; Ephemera Critica.* His biographical works—studies of Bolingbroke and Swift, an account of Voltaire, Montesquieu, and Rousseau in England—are, though readable and clearheaded, perhaps the least original of his productions. But his work as an editor of texts, the plays of Cyril Tourneur (the introduction to which T. S. Eliot singled out for praise) and of Robert Greene (the editorial part of which was taken to task by a later scholar, W. W. Greg), were honorable projects that deserve at least mention. And his Clarendon Press editions, with introductions, of More's *Utopia* and Sidney's *Apologie for Poetry* are elegant little monuments to memorable texts.

But his most original work consisted in the critical commentaries on subjects he cared about with his peculiar intensity, and in his splendid polemic, *The Study of English Literature: A Plea for Its Recognition and Organization at the Universities.* To take up the latter first: Collins argues that when literature has been recognized at all as a subject for teaching in the universities, it has been done in a spirit similar to that in which classics has been taught:

> It has been regarded not as the expression of art and genius, but as mere material for the study of words, as mere pabulum for philology. All that constitutes its intrinsic value has been ignored. All that constitutes its value as a liberal study has been ignored. Its masterpieces have been resolved into exercises in grammar, syntax and etymology. Its history has been resolved into a barren catalogue of names, works, and dates. No faculty but the faculty of memory has been called into play in studying it. That it should therefore have failed as an instrument of education is no more than might have been expected.

This passionate declaration, issued we must remember from a man who had been lecturing for eleven years in the university extension program; who had been attempting to demonstrate to non-university audiences all over England the "intrinsic value" of literary masterpieces; and who believed—as Arnold believed—that poetry was a criticism of life and that the task of literary criticism was to elucidate (in Arnold's terms) how that poetry shows "a power of forming, sustaining, and delighting us as nothing else can." The study of literature in the universities was instead an exercise in how not to do things: "We have absolutely no provision for systematic critical training," declared Collins; the interpretation of literature, of "verbal analysis, analysis of form and style, analysis of sentiment, ethic, and thought," was not being performed. Instead, philological investigation took its place. Collins's strictures on philology, after he grants it a place in the academic groves, are pretty severely unqualified in their negative estimate:

> It must not be confounded with Literature. . . . Up to the present time, it has, in consequence of this confusion, been allowed to fill a place in education altogether disproportionate to its insignificance as an instrument of culture. As an instrument of culture it ranks—it surely ranks—very low indeed. It certainly contributes nothing to the cultivation of the taste. It as certainly contributes nothing to the education of the emotions. The mind it neither enlarges, stimulates, nor refines. On the contrary, it too

often induces or confirms that peculiar woodenness and opacity, that singular coarseness of feeling and purblindness of moral and intellectual vision, which has in all ages been characteristic of mere philologists.

He remembers suggesting to Mark Pattison, and receiving Pattison's approval, that Pope's lines from *Dunciad IV* should be inscribed over the doors of the Classical Schools:

> Since man from beasts by Words is known
> Words are man's province, Words we teach alone.
> When Reason doubtful, like the Samian letter,
> Points him two ways, the narrower is the better.
> Plac'd at the door of Learning, youth to guide,
> We never suffer it to stand too wide
>
> .   .   .   .
>
> Whate'er the talents, or howe'er designed,
> We hang one jingling padlock on the mind.

Collins's conviction that the philological study of literature frequently directs attention to "unprofitable topics" is substantiated by his quoting from a university "paper" on *Macbeth*, which consists of questions like the following (I am compressing them):

1. What reasons are there for believing that this play has been interpolated? Point out the parts probably interpolated.
2. What emendations have been proposed in the following passages? [There follow seven passages.]
5. Give the meanings and derivations of the following words. In what context do they appear?
7. Illustrate from the play important points of difference between Elizabethan and modern grammar.

Collins points out that the only mental faculty appealed to is that of memory, and that nothing in the questions "indicates the existence of what constitutes the life and power of the work." In like manner he adduces editions of Shakespeare and Milton from Oxford's Clarendon Press that, solid though their scholarly editing is, insist on regarding the work as a monument to language merely; on dwelling "with tedious and unnecessary minuteness" on that which is of interest only to philologists, and of confining themselves oppressively to these matters. As with the paper on *Macbeth*, Collins quotes from the editorial notes that accompany these editions.

Yet for all philology's anti-liberal pedantry, it is to Collins's mind a lesser evil than dilettantism. One of philology's arguments against "literary" rather than linguistic study of works was that it would too easily turn into vague, impressionistic remarks ("chatter about Shelley") testifying only to the professor's or student's pleasure or lack of it in a particular instance of art. How do you grade such "subjective" responses whose rightness or wrongness can't be measured the way interpolations to *Macbeth* can? Collins himself worries about the matter, especially when the subject is lyric poetry, and he admits that the "spectacle" of a lecturer with one of Tennyson's poems in hand ("Tears, Idle Tears," or "Mariana") attempting to show "what is graceful, what is fanciful, what is pathetic," would be "ludicrous and repulsive"; yet, he adds, anything can be ridiculed, and so long as the lecturer remembers that his task is "the interpretation of power and beauty as they reveal themselves in language"—so long as he remembers, with Arnold, that poetry is the criticism of life—he will be performing his proper function as a teacher, as a critic. (In an appendix to *The Study of English Literature* Collins provides, under various headings—historical, comparative, critical—sample questions that a serious, "liberal" study of literature might involve.)

Decades later, in the essays gathered together in *Education and the University* (especially "Literary Studies" and "A Sketch for an 'English School'"), F. R. Leavis would expand on some of the ways a literary-critical training might be conducted. "It is plain that in the work of a properly ordered English School . . . the training of reading capacity has first place. By training of reading capacity I mean the training of perception, judgment and analytic skill commonly referred to as 'practical criticism'—or, rather, the training that 'practical criticism' ought to be." By that time, with philology no longer so preeminent, Leavis took up arms against "literary history, as a matter of 'facts about' and accepted critical (or quasi-critical) description and commentary." Leavis called such history worthless unless the student could, as a critic, as "an intelligent and discerning reader," approach literature with a reading capacity trained in the practical criticism of language. Leavis was not given to generous recognition of his forebears in the fight to recognize "English" as a legitimate subject of study, but Collins deserves an important place among that number.

If Leavis should have given Collins a mention, so might have T. S. Eliot, who praised his introduction to the plays of Tourneur but appears not to have noticed how similar to Collins's are his, Eliot's, own strictures on impressionistic criticism. In the two essays that open *The Sacred Wood,* "The Perfect Critic," and "Imperfect Critics," Eliot was concerned to distinguish what he saw as appropriate "objective" criticism from the more subjective sort practiced by two of his predecessors, Swinburne and Arthur Symons. Eliot notes in Swinburne's critical essays important "faults of style," such as "the tumultuous outcry of adjectives, the headstrong rush of undisciplined sentences" that are "the index to the impatience and perhaps laziness of a disorderly mind." The resultant "blur" Eliot sees as continuous with Swinburne in his poetry. As for Symons, whose book on Symbolist poetry Eliot testified to having been influenced by, he is content to give us his sensations about *Antony and Cleopatra* ("the most wonderful, I think, of all Shakespeare's plays") without moving beyond those sensations to generalization, analysis, construction—"*ériger en lois ses impressions personnelles,*" as Eliot liked to quote from Remy de Gourmont.

Thirty-five years previously, in "The Predecessors of Shakespeare," Collins proceeded to give his own accounts of those playwrights, but first took to task John Addington Symonds—whose book on them occasioned the essay—and Swinburne, for the impressionistic excesses of their prose. Collins admits that Swinburne possessed a "powerful and accurate memory" but that this is his sole qualification as a critic (note the overlap with philology as also memory-oriented):

> His judgment is the sport sometimes of his emotions and sometimes of his imagination. A work of art has the same effect on Mr Swinburne as objects fraught with hateful or delightful associations have on persons with sensitive memories. The mind dwells not on the objects themselves, but on what is accidentally recalled or accidentally suggested by them. . . . Criticism is with him neither a process of analysis nor a process of interpretation, but a "lyrical cry." . . . What seem to be Mr. Swinburne's convictions are merely his temporary impressions.

Collins finds a continuation of Swinburne's hyperbole in J. A. Symonds's "wild and whirling verbiage, his plethora of extravagant and frequently nauseous metaphor," and he quotes a number of passages where Symonds has even outdone his master in such stylistic vices and deformations. Now of course—as with the evisceration of Edmund Gosse—it is possible to see these adverse reflections on Swinburne and Symonds solely as examples of Collins's destructive motives. (Especially with Swinburne, who had encouraged and supported Collins in his editing of Tourneur, we feel the feeding hand being bitten.) The alternative, one more appreciative of Collins, is to see these attacks, like those Eliot mounted decades later, as undertaken in order that stronger, more telling critical operations might proceed—operations that both Collins and Eliot practiced with impressive results.

As always seems to be the case with people who write about Collins's work, these pages have concentrated on his efforts as an adversarial critic of bêtes noires like philology and impressionistic criticism, and on some representative practitioners of them. What to my knowledge no one has remarked about his achievement overall, are the number of pages devoted to "positive," that is, encomiastic, criticism of writers: Shakespeare, Milton, Dryden, Chesterfield, Wordsworth, Crabbe, Byron, Arnold, and others, including (surprisingly) nineteenth-century American poets. The best of these show him operating in a manner his master Arnold (with Sainte-Beuve in mind) liked to call flexible and varied (*ondoyant et divers*), combining historical "placing" of the writer and his works with vigorous making of judgments on the relative virtues of those works and of the writer's rank compared to contemporaries and predecessors. In the range and openness of his taste, he compares favorably to Arnold who (as Eliot noted in *The Sacred Wood*) succumbed to the temptation "to put literature into the corner until he cleaned up the whole country first." Eliot wished Arnold had given us more judgments and analyses of particular writers; for all Collins's absorption in the "idea" of how literature should properly be taught, he seized plenty of occasions for exercising his more purely literary discriminations.

This is not to say that he doesn't present limitations that we are conscious of, from the standpoint of a century and more later. Two of these limitations are probably related. For all Collins's belief in the analysis and interpretation of a poet's words, he seldom if ever comes to particular grips with them the way his twentieth-century successors—I. A. Richards, Empson, Leavis, and the American New Critics—have shown us can be exciting. He doesn't attempt to enter into passages of poetry by describing (in words Arnold used in "The Study of Poetry") their rhythm and movement. (In fact Arnold didn't do much of such "entering" himself, preferring to stay back and remain external to the poetry, even as he pronounced it sound or unsound, great or not so great.) Related to this absence in Collins is his tendency to substitute for discussion of the poem's language, an insistence on its soundness, its goodness as a moral statement. This tendency is particularly marked in the volume of essays his son published after Collins's death—lectures, most of them, with plenty of passages quoted but too often simply affirmed as noble. The essay on Wordsworth, significantly titled "Wordsworth as a Teacher," is one of his weaker efforts, since it consists too frequently of such affirmations about various Wordsworthian passages of poetry. In these respects we can say, without complacency or finger-shaking, that Collins was of his age rather than ahead of it.

He never wrote better than in the four long essays published in the *Quarterly Review* between 1878 and 1892, which, along with a shorter one on Menander, were gathered to make up *Essays and Studies,* his best book. Along with the essay on Shakespeare's predecessors, with its attack on Symonds, are ones on Dryden, Lord Chesterfield, and Lewis Theobald— "The Porson of Shakspearian Criticism," as Collins calls him in the essay's title. In his book on Collins, Anthony Kearney speaks of his "tendentious" use of Dryden as a support for Collins's own fight against the excesses of late Victorian impressionism in criticism. Tendentious or not—and the word didn't occur to me as I read the essay—this ninety-page trip through Dryden's life and major works is a triumph of clear-eyed criticism, unafraid to make its preferences and judgments known. Its opening paragraph, running to nearly three pages, is a magisterial summary of Dryden's "services" to literature, sentence after sentence of which begins "He had rescued," "He had brought home to us," "He had given us," "He had shown us," as we are moved through Dryden's contributions in poetry and the criticism of poetry. Collins doesn't offer a new "take" on Dryden; his essay is continuous with Walter Scott's fine "Life" in his edition of Dryden, and with the accounts that were to follow by Saintsbury and Mark Van Doren (the latter precipitating Eliot's essay of 1920). But the distinguishing touch of his readerly sensibility is always evident.

A single example must suffice: late in the essay he comes to discuss Dryden's *Fables, Ancient and Modern,* and immediately tells us we must discriminate between the successes and failures of these translations. He finds Dryden to be essentially a "rhetorical" poet, and although Collins notes the lack of affinity between Dryden's temperament and Virgil's, he can with qualification praise Dryden's "re-writing" of the *Aeneid* as substituting a "masterpiece of rhetoric for a masterpiece of poetry." But such was not possible with Chaucer, where Dryden's failure is, to Collins, egregious:

All Chaucer's *naiveté*, simplicity, freshness, grace, pathos, humour, truth to nature and truth to life, all that attracts us in his temper, tone, and style, have not merely disappeared, but, what is much worse, have been represented by Drydenian equivalents. Where Chaucer is easy and natural with the easiness and naturalness of good breeding, Dryden is simply vulgar. It may be doubted whether there is a single touch of nature which Dryden has not missed or spoilt, or a single pathetic passage which he has not made ridiculous.

Illustrations follow, after which Collins names a number of "passages which admit of rhetorical treatment," in which, by contrast, Dryden is extremely successful. What is worth noting here and characteristic in general of Collins's criticism, is the willingness to speak harshly about parts of a poet's achievement that are unsatisfactory to the critic's eyes and ears. These adverse judgments make more convincing the praising of other work by Dryden, and make more telling the essay's concluding salute to "the manifold energy of that vigorous and plastic genius, which added to our literature so much which is excellent and so much which is admirable."

The distinction between the rhetorical and the truly "poetic" was an important one for Collins, and he uses it again in another of his best critical performances, "The Works of Lord Byron" (*Studies in Poetry and Criticism*). Singling out parts of the work where Byron's rhetorical or "falsetto" note is most heard (the dramas, the first two cantos of *Childe Harold*), he distinguishes them from the poems, or parts of poems, in which Byron is sincerely moved—in which he truly becomes Byron the poet:

> It is when we compare the dramas with *The Vision of Judgment* and *Don Juan,* that we measure the distance between Byron the rhetorician and Byron the poet, between degrees of talent and the pure accent of genius. A large proportion, perhaps two-thirds, of Byron's poetry resolves itself into the work of an extraordinarily gifted craftsman, with a rhetorical talent as brilliant and plastic as Dryden's, working on the material furnished by an unusually wide experience of life, by sleepless observation, and by a marvelously assimilative and retentive memory, incessantly if desultorily adding to its store.

But in *The Vision of Judgment* and in *Don Juan* we have something that goes beyond talent and reveals "the true, full man," reveals the "amazing versatility and dexterity of his genius for comedy and satire." Collins's account of

Byron's poetry, in its fullness and particular discriminations, supplies what Matthew Arnold, in his own essay on the poet, signally failed to give us, since Arnold was so busy comparing Byron to Wordsworth and Leopardi that he managed never once in the entire essay to mention either *Don Juan* or *The Vision of Judgment,* those poems Collins rightly saw as the peak of Byron's achievement.

In suggesting briefly the often invigorating character of Collins's criticism (as well as the sheer reading pleasure of the sentences as he lays them out), I should mention his eighty-page survey of American poetry, "Poets and Poetry of America" (*Studies in Poetry and Criticism*). He opens it by claiming that American poetry is underestimated in England, and his essay, published in 1905, is the first serious attempt of an English critic to recognize and come to critical grips with poets across the water. In his survey Collins does, among other things, the following: he singles out Philip Freneau as someone whose too voluminous work nevertheless presents "a few flowers"; he praises Bryant as America's first poet of distinction, mentioning "Thanatopsis" and "To a Waterfowl" especially; he calls Emerson one of the greatest American poets, but finds that claim best substantiated in Emerson's prose, since although the poetry is "absolutely original," it frequently shows Emerson's defective ear and unmusical blank verse. Collins anticipates Yvor Winters in having a good word to say for Jones Very, while he finds the more popular Whittier deficient in "high poetic quality." As for what are now called the Fireside Poets—Holmes, Longfellow, and Lowell—Collins calls them "genial, polished, and most accomplished men" but also judges that "from men so constituted and tempered great poetry we cannot hope to find." Poe, on the other hand, gives us a poetry that is both new and original, though his most famous poems are tours de force or "tuneful nonsense." Emily Dickinson is faulted for being "in her jerky transcendentalism and strained style, too faithful a disciple of Emerson," but Collins finds much real merit in her work. And Whitman, a figure of "monstrous and ludicrous egotism" (anticipating D. H. Lawrence's essay soon to come), is also in his art an "astute showman," able to "collect a crowd for a show which, in some respects, is well worth seeing."

Collins concludes his survey in a curious manner, pronouncing gloomily that the "future of American poetry is as dark as that of our own," and although in 1905 it would have been understandable to have such thoughts about the mainly genteel American products appearing, it is of a piece with Collins's inability to look at the future of literature with anything but low hopes. The few contemporary poets he wrote about—William Watson, Gerald Massey, Stephen Phillips—were hardly the bringers of a new style or point of view. Indeed it may be that as an omnivorous reader of everything—at least all the poetry and poetic drama—written prior to, say, 1885, Collins was a sufferer from the Burden of the Past. Knowing how much had been written and how much of it was good, he couldn't imagine there was anything notable to come. At any rate he was not the man to discover what Leavis was to call "new bearings" in English or American poetry.

These judgments, culled from his American poetry survey, are not produced to prove Collins's indisputable rightness as a critic of those poets, but to suggest that, as is always the case, his judgments—however summary and undemonstrated through particular analysis—are worth considering, qualifying, amending. In a word, Collins is an *interesting* voice to have in the conversation. And with respect to American poets, the conversation, at least in England, hadn't proceeded very far by the beginning of the last century.

It would be unprofitable, and perhaps unnecessary, to take up for discussion various of Collins's other essays: these pages have made, I hope, a case for his historical but also for his continuing value for us as a writer about literature. Instead I will close by quoting briefly, from two of his best essays, sentences that, ostensibly about the subject under examination, have also unmistakable application to the examiner. The first, longer, one is from his essay on Chesterfield, an impressive exercise in setting that writer in relation to Cicero, La Bruyère, La Rochefoucauld, and Voltaire and comparing him in intellectual honesty and moral candor to Montaigne and Swift. At a certain point in the essay, describing Chesterfield's importance, his particular message and value, Collins puts him in the class of the work "of men out of touch and out of sympathy with their surroundings, separated by differences of character, temper, intellect from their fellows, viewing things with other eyes, having other thoughts, other feelings—aliens without being strangers." He says that the judgments of these men provide the "tests of national life":

They put to the proof its intellectual and moral currency. They call to account its creeds, its opinions, its sentiments, its manners, its fashions. For conventional touchstones and standards of their own, derived, it may be ideally from speculation, or derived, as is much more commonly the case, from those of other nations . . . they are the upholders of the Ideal and of the Best.

If we substitute "national literature" for "national life," Collins would qualify as one of these men; at least, the peculiar intensity of his prose in this passage, in conjunction with his self-born, self-created myth quoted earlier ("My intense love of literature has been inspired by no one, encouraged by no one, influenced by *no one*"), encourages us to think of him as an "alien" like the Chesterfield he is writing about.

A similar affection for the outsider who has been reviled, at least his achievement underappreciated, shines through in the conclusion to "The Porson of Shakspearian Criticism," his convincing attempt to rehabilitate Lewis Theobald as a great textual critic of Shakespeare. Theobald, once of *The Dunciad* and a name thereafter dogged with the imputation of pedantry and obfuscation, is for Collins a hero, the first great editor of Shakespeare who provided a "settled text" that deserves the gratitude of mankind. Collins's words about Theobald—"He belonged to a class of men who are or ought to be the peculiar care of the friends of learning"—serve well as Collins's own epitaph.

A SELECT COLLINS BIBLIOGRAPHY

Illustrations of Tennyson (1891)
The Study of English Literature: A Plea for Its Recognition and Organization at the Universities (1891)
Essays and Studies (1895)
Ephemera Critica: or Plain Truths about Current Literature (1901)
Studies in Poetry and Criticism (1905)
L. C. Collins, *Life and Memoirs of John Churton Collins* (1912)
Anthony Kearney, *John Churton Collins: The Louse on the Locks of Literature* (1986)

Yale Review, October 2002

Cheers for Aldous Huxley

Here are the first two in a projected six volumes of Aldous Huxley's essays, ably edited by two academic Huxleyites. They appear at a time when, it's fair to claim, the writer's reputation has never been lower. This is not because Huxley over the past few decades has been the object of revisionary or adverse commentary, such as his contemporaries D. H. Lawrence and E. M. Forster provoked; since no one bothered to demote Huxley, no one needed to spring to his defense. Rather he has been left alone to molder—"stone dead," as Nabokov said of John Galsworthy. Huxley's reputation received little assistance from Sybille Bedford's biography (1973); the book was long on stories of travels and personal relationships but virtually devoid of critical sophistication brought to bear on Huxley's writings. And although the latest *Books in Print* lists a number of Huxley titles, the list is misleading: many editions of *Brave New World* (still a favorite, evidently, for assigning to high school students) and of the druggy *Doors of Perception,* his hymn to artificial paradises. But most of the other titles are from reprint houses, usually high-priced and suggesting—what is surely the case—that Huxley doesn't show up in the college and university courses where Lawrence, Virginia Woolf, Forster are standard fare.

It would be rash to expect that publishing the essays he wrote between 1920 and 1929—in two thick volumes coming to a thousand pages—will do much, if anything, for Huxley's stature; still it is good that a venturesome publishing house like Ivan Dee thought the project worth taking on and that the editors assiduously looked up Huxley's fugitive pieces and joined them with the books of essays he published in the 1920s: *On the Margin* (1923); *Along the Road* (1924); *Proper Studies* (1927); and *Do What You Will* (1929).

Complete Essays/Aldous Huxley, edited by Robert S. Baker and James Sexton. Vol. 1, *1920–1925;* vol. 2, *1926–1929.* Chicago: I. R. Dee, 2000.

Also included is *Jesting Pilate,* the around-the-world travel book he brought out in 1925. Huxley's heavy production in this period was stimulated by the contract he signed with Chatto & Windus, surely one of the most exacting of such agreements to be found. Early in 1923, after he had published his first two novels, *Crome Yellow* and *Antic Hay,* and some volumes of poems and short stories, Huxley agreed to supply Chatto with two new works of fiction a year (one of which was to be a full-length novel) for the next three years. For this, Chatto would pay him five hundred pounds a year, sufficient for him to devote himself to writing. Three years later the agreement was renewed. Huxley was a very fast worker: *Crome Yellow* was written in two months; *Antic Hay,* in four. Still, the pressure of deadlines was such as to make impossible any Flaubertlike search for the mot juste, or Joycean commitment to a massive fiction project.

Early in his career he had planned to write a book about Balzac, then abandoned the idea. But he may well at certain moments have seen his own enterprise as a writer in Balzacian terms, or so one might guess from one of his "Marginalia" columns of 1920, appearing in the *Athenaeum* under the pen name Autolycus. Huxley speculates: "Sooner or later there will arise a larger mind—tentacular as it were, with feelers spreading far and wide over the whole face of this epoch—and we shall get from it a new *Comédie Humaine.*" If we put the novels and stories from the 1920s together with the essays in these two volumes, something like a Balzacian "spread" can be observed. As for Huxley's own tentacular feelers, they extended to take in artists of the past and the present, not just in literature but in painting and architecture, in music, in drama. He also took on history, politics, religion, travel—you name it. "Encyclopedic" is an understatement for the range and grasp of Huxley's curiosity.

Volume 1 of the essays contains the pieces he wrote regularly for the *Athenaeum,* the weekly edited by John Middleton Murry and featuring contributions by T. S. Eliot, Pound, Forster, Bertrand Russell, Woolf, and a host of other now-notables. Huxley's "Marginalia" columns made up his first nonfiction prose collection (*On the Margin*), and the column format encouraged him at times to indulge the archly coy address of the all-too-personal essayists—as in a column about Francis Bacon where we get the likes of this: "Bacon's *De Sapientia Veterum* is a book to which I have always been particularly attached. I have a great weakness for wisdom. . . . From Solomon to Anatole France, all the sages are dear to me, and none dearer than Bacon . . ." Such cloying confidences occur less frequently as time goes on, and one learns to believe Huxley when he testifies to this or that personal attachment. He really *was*, I have no doubt, devoted to Bacon's book, unknown to some of us.

The editors chose a topical rather than chronological presentation, so the first volume is in four parts: "Architecture, Painting, Literature"; "Music"; "History, Politics, Social Criticism"; and "Travel." Let us take up the Literature rubric first. As a critic of contemporary poets and poetry, Huxley comes off poorly. In "The Subject-Matter of Poetry," he compares the present age unfavorably with that of the early seventeenth century in which a poet like Donne flourished—Donne whose "passionate apprehension of ideas" and "passionate curiosity about facts" "put the whole life and the whole mind of his age into poetry." Turning to the present, Huxley names Alfred Noyes (but why?) and Conrad Aiken as poets who try, though with no great success, to make "contemporary ideas" the subject of their verse. They and others unnamed are "minor" talents who fail to incorporate "the busy and incessant intellectual life" of the modern experience. Well, one thinks of some poems that appeared in the years 1919–1923, like Pound's *Hugh Selwyn Mauberley,* Eliot's "Gerontion" and *The Waste Land,* Yeats's "The Second Coming," and "Meditations in Time of Civil War." In his rather severe review of these collected essays, the always fair-minded P. N. Furbank noted that Huxley admitted to being and indeed was a "stick-in-the-mud" regarding the tradition of "the new." And not just in poetry: Huxley takes every opportunity in these essays to tell us how dull a book is Joyce's *Ulysses* ("one of the dullest books ever written") while Wyndham Lewis, Ford Madox Ford, and Woolf don't even come up for discussion. In fairness to him, he was able to salute two English writers as divergent as Edward Thomas and Lytton Strachey, and he was surely one of the first English critics to recognize and admire Proust (Proust gave him a mention in *À la recherche*). But it seems that Huxley's large pronouncements about the lack of a modern giant such as Donne (or Dante, or Lucretius) went along with an inability to extend himself very far in the direction of what actual poets and novelists were producing.

Still, it should not be forgotten that he called Lawrence, along with Proust, "another great renewer of love," and although in the 1922 essay where that phrase appears he demurred at the writer's too-great fondness for loins and solar plexuses, Huxley grew—especially after 1926, increasingly admir-

ing of Lawrence. His introduction, after the writer's death, to Lawrence's letters (published 1932) remains a key appreciation, and he is one of the few
people who moved closer to rather than away from Lawrence in the final
years of that writer's life. One thinks of Huxley, especially the early Huxley,
as the bright young man who had ideas about everything on earth and was
quite willing to advertise them. In fact, the essays show him becoming, as
the 1920s wore on, increasingly critical of rationalism in various forms; his
admiring (and excellent) essay on Pascal praises that writer for his critique
of rationalism; in other places he criticizes Enlightenment notions of reason
and equality. So Lawrence increasingly appealed, even as Huxley had the
temerity to portray him as Mark Rampion in *Point Counter Point* (Lawrence's response in a letter to Huxley: "your Rampion is the most boring
character in the book—a gas bag.")

As for the writings about art and architecture, they are stimulating on old
masters, less so on significant modern developments. There is an excellent
account of Breughel—"the first landscape painter of his century, the acutest
student of manners, and the wonderfully skillful pictorial expounder or sug-
gester of a view of life." There is a passionate tribute to Piero della Francesca,
whose *Resurrection* at Borgo San Sepulcro Huxley calls "the best picture in
the world." Piero's consummate artistry, to Huxley's mind, is brought out
by comparison with Botticelli and with Giotto, partly in terms of the hard
work of travel one had to do in 1925 to view Piero's art at Arezzo, San Sepulcro, and Urbino: to get to the last, notes Huxley, "you must travel by bus for
seven hours across the Apennines." (Although, remember that he had his
wife, Maria, to drive him about the hill towns in their excellent Citröen.) He
allows that he would be willing, if it were necessary, to sacrifice Botticelli's
works so that Piero's could be saved: "I should unhesitatingly commit the
Primavera and all the rest of them to the flames." (Up, Huxley!) And, again
with reference to the relative inaccessibility of Piero's works, he writes, "If
the Arena chapel were in the mountains of Calabria, instead of at Padua, we
should all have heard a good deal less of Giotto." This is salutary and probably true.

In the memorial volume that appeared soon after Huxley's death in 1963,
Kenneth Clark writes about his capacity for seeing, despite his impaired vision. (Huxley was actually blind for a year or more when, as a youth, he suffered from an inflammation of the cornea.) Clark calls him "one of the most
discerning lookers of our time" and cites his ability to enter into the life of a

picture and write it up with evocative skill. The description of Caravaggio's "Conversion of St. Paul" in *Crome Yellow* is Clark's example, but he also praises other descriptions of things seen—the interiors in *Antic Hay;* the Italian countryside in *Those Barren Leaves.* But few discerning lookers, among men of letters, are also discerning listeners to music, and on the basis of the hundred and some pages of review columns he wrote for the *Weekly Westminster Gazette* in 1922, along with some musical pieces that got into his fiction, Huxley qualifies.

In his writings about music he comes across as a gentler Bernard Shaw, although, curiously, he never mentions Shaw's music criticism as a distinguished predecessor (Shaw seems to have held no interest in any way for Huxley). There is an original piece on Brahms's Variations on a Theme by Haydn, a composition he says "that first made me realize, as a boy, the enormous richness and complexity, the endless intellectual potentialities of music." One essay compares Palestrina to Verdi, putting in a good word for Palestrina's polyphony; another singles out Delius as a composer who, in "On Hearing the First Cuckoo in the Spring," gets the "nature-emotion" into his work (Huxley compares him to Edward Thomas in his poetry). And there is occasionally a putdown, as when he wonders why on earth people go to hear Saint-Saëns's *Samson and Delilah.* Although he himself doesn't much like Wagner's operas, he can imagine why people go to see them: "But Saint-Saëns is very far indeed from being a Wagner. He is not exuberantly alive—he is hardly alive at all."

Like virtually every Englishman in the 1920s and 1930s, Huxley traveled and wrote about his travels. Here as elsewhere, the reader of eight decades later may be permitted to sample, and I found myself especially pleased with writing that focused on on-the-road discomforts, or that contemplated with a cold eye the efforts of other travelers to enjoy themselves. In "Why Not Stay at Home?," one of the essays that made up his attractive collection of travel pieces, *Along the Road,* he shakes his head over all the Anglo-Saxons trying to have a high old time in what they have been told is Gay Paree, where they will encounter something called Life: "Conscientiously, therefore, they strive when they come to Paris to be gay. Night after night the dance halls and the bordellos are thronged by serious young compatriots of Emerson and Matthew Arnold, earnestly engaged in trying to see life, neither very steadily nor whole, through the ever-thickening mists of Heidsieck and Roederer."

Or his heart goes out, sort of, to an American couple on an excursion to the island of Torcello, who have evidently had enough of churches and so resolutely remain in the boat while the others scramble ashore to look at Torcello's church. Huxley finds it a melancholy thing that they have paid all this money, come all this way, to end up sitting in a motor boat tied to a rotten wharf. And, remember, this is only Venice: "Their Italian ordeal had hardly begun. Padua, Ferrara, Ravenna, Bologna, Florence, Siena, Perugia, Assisi, and Rome, with all their innumerable churches and pictures, had still to be looked at, before—the blessed goal of Naples finally reached—they could be permitted to take the liner home again across the Atlantic." He concludes by deciding that travel is a vice, while knowing full well he will soon relapse "into [his] old bad ways" and head for the hills.

Occasionally he suffers his own travel ordeal, as, in "A Night at Pietramala," he is marooned in an Apennine village with a howling wind, an unheated room, and only the second volume of the *Encyclopedia Britannica* to console him (Huxley regularly brought along on his journeys one or another of the India paper volumes from what must have been the famous eleventh edition). He quotes from Browning's "De Gustibus" ("What I love best in the world / Is a castle, precipice-encurled, / In a gash of the wind-grieved Apennine" but declares that the Apennine wind for him "begets nothing but neuralgia and the profoundest depression. It is not 'Prospice' that I should write in the precipice-encurled castello; it is something in the style of the 'City of Dreadful Night.'" There are a number of other "positive" bits of appreciation, from the activity of reading old guidebooks, to the geometrical landscape of Holland, the latter evoked with great precision. There is even a fine diatribe at Tibet, where that country is invoked as a way to feel better about the fact of industrialized Europe: "The spectacle of an ancient and elaborate civilization of which almost no detail is not completely idiotic is in the highest degree comforting and refreshing." Cruel, yes, but tonic.

Volume two of the essays (1926–29) shows a distinct change of emphasis, as pieces on literature and the other arts markedly decrease. On the rise is attention to politics and society, science and religion, as represented by the essays originally published in *Proper Studies* and *Do What You Will.* I found my eyes frequently glazing over in front of many of these, especially the ones from *Proper Studies*—"The Idea of Equality," "Education," "The Political Democracy," "The Essence of Religion"—and decided that it is not so much their content that estranges (Huxley is eminently sensible about all these matters) but their style, or rather lack of style. For here we have the spectacle of the opinionated, mischievous voices of the novels, letters, and early prose pieces eschewed in favor of a relatively toneless, even solemn, laying out of ideas. For all their reasonableness they lack bite, lack the sense of fun of the earlier Huxley. In that way they are I'm afraid predictive of his career in its later stretches, his hungerings after mysticism, his piousness about the virtues of drugs. It's doubtful that anyone today, aside from the Huxley expert, will pick up his essays in order to canvass their ideas; his appeal lay rather in the original, personal style.

Huxley was evidently a kind man, very much without the sharp edges that made dealing with contemporaries like Lawrence and Wyndham Lewis—and later Evelyn Waugh—so fraught with peril. There is an occasion, even as he turns out yet another column, when he senses that his "strenuous journalistic career," as he calls it, may be just another instance of the vanity of human wishes. Writing for *Vanity Fair* in 1925 when the career had been cooking on all fronts, he shakes his head over how "boredom and the urgent need of distraction" must be filled with the curse of print: "Every day, every damned day, from forty thousand to a quarter of a million words have to be poured into the bottomless waste-paper baskets, the dustbins, the insatiable sewers of the world. And there is no respite; there can be no slackening off. However little there is to say, the pages must be filled."

Certainly there was no slackening off for him—it was just not in the cards. A modest epitaph for his own journalistic career would be that he filled the pages better than most.

Sewanee Review, Winter 2003

Impossible

WRITING recently about Edmund Wilson's journals, John Updike cheerfully remarked that there was something in them to offend everyone. But compared to these letters, by the writer Wilson once called "the only first-rate comic genius that has appeared in English since Bernard Shaw," they seem quietly inoffensive. Evelyn Waugh was truly what Wilson (with his curt "Edmund Wilson does not . . ." postcards of refusal) sometimes aspired to be: an impossible person. It was a role that came naturally to him, that he worked hard to perfect over the years, and that eventually didn't feel—and doesn't feel to us—like a role at all, just the truth. Waugh's diaries, published a few years back, are likely—in their eight hundred pages of sometimes monotonous recording and complaining—to defeat any but the most devoted fan. The letters, on the other hand, though not without their repetitions and an occasional patch or two of aridity, are eminently available, especially since they have been splendidly edited and selected by Mark Amory, a friend of the Waugh family who has spared himself no labor in doing a fully responsible job. (A trivial and amusing example of his assiduousness: in 1961, Waugh writes to Ann Fleming, describing a ball he's attended in Somerset at which the stables were floodlit and the horses consequently upset, "One bit an American pornographer who tried to give it vodka." The "pornographer" turned out to be Norman Mailer, who, when consulted by the scrupulous editor, admitted that the horse had bitten him, but that he was not feeding it vodka, just patting its nose.)

It is the exasperated Buck Mulligan who, in the first chapter of James Joyce's *Ulysses,* calls his friend Stephen Dedalus "an impossible person," this impossibleness lying in Stephen's ability to take everything said as personal to himself and thus as an occasion for offense. But Joyce was not "impossible" in his letters; among English contemporaries the best challenger to Waugh in this regard is most certainly Wyndham Lewis, whose own letters (finely edited by W. K. Rose) are relatively unknown. (As far as I can tell, Waugh and Lewis were unaware of each other's existence; at least neither ever referred to the other.) The liberal consensus has it, I should guess, that D. H. Lawrence and Virginia Woolf are the major modern letter writers among English novelists of this century, and Lawrence was, to boot, as impossible a person as one could hope for. But their reputations may suffer from a glut on the market: six large volumes of Woolfian epistles and the prospect of eight Lawrentian tomes. Waugh and Lewis make their concentrated impact on us through a single fat volume of letters each. And both Waugh and Lewis were blessed, or cursed, by a wildness of humor neither Lawrence nor Virginia Woolf possessed.

It is this curse of humor (the phrase is from Lewis's *Tarr*) that turns the impossible person into not just a possible but a desired presence in Waugh's letters. Tired of hearing Berenson's *I Tatti* mentioned in hushed tones by someone who stopped there for a visit? Here is Waugh's *I Tatti:* "We went to see B. Berenson, like Trotsky, in a house which after Harold's [Acton] is a miserable hole." Tired of trying to convince yourself how, really, you love all your children equally, but in different ways? Here is Waugh: "My unhealthy affection for my second daughter has waned. I now dislike them all equally." Tired of expressing your complex ambivalence toward Dickens as a novelist? "I have just read *Dombey and Son*. The worst book in the world." (Nabokov, by comparison to this, is a moderate, judicious critic.) Admittedly, one-liners like the above, impossible to answer in any reasonable way, speak to our secret wishes that things could be simpler and more final than they usually seem. But at moments, Waugh's "simplicity," his stubborn refusal to accede to the social and psychological imperatives by which the liberal conscience directs its life, result in strikingly new and valuable perspectives. A prime example of this comes when, after his first wife (Evelyn Gardner, "she-Evelyn") has run away with John Heygate, throwing Waugh into humiliation and bewilderment, he tells Harold Acton that he is going to divorce her because "I cannot live with anyone who is avowedly in love with someone else. Everyone is talking so much nonsense on all sides of me about my affairs that my wits reel. Evelyn's family & mine join in asking me to 'forgive' her whatever that may mean." Coming up against that "forgive," in the chilly contempt provided by quotation marks, one suddenly entertains a new way of thinking about things. Is it only the impossible person who doesn't know what "forgive" means? Are the rest of us sanely clear about it?

Of course it is easy enough to be impossible about non-Englishmen (with Dickens's Mr. Podsnap as a role model), especially when they are of other races and creeds. But it is not so easy to put them into creative fantasies whose comic energy outshines any moral depravity. So in 1933, upon returning to British Guiana from a trip up the Amazon ("The streets are entirely paved with gold which gives a very pretty effect especially towards sunset. But otherwise it is rather dull"), he writes to his correspondent that "the delight of these simple people at my return is very touching. A public holiday has been declared and all the men & women prostrate themselves in the dust and bring me their children to bless . . . several elderly niggers have already died of excitement." Writing from Jerusalem a couple of years later, he notes that "they have a wall here where the Jews blub, V. sensible idea," an observation made especially memorable by the verb choice and by its "sensible" English approval of the odd custom. Or consider the aggrieved self-righteousness of the following confession, written from California, about how Randolph Churchill has behaved abominably, has been "brutishly" drunk, and has "mocked the Jews." We are invited to consider, by comparison, the innocent Evelyn: "I was not in the least anti-Semitic before I came here. I am now. It is intolerable to see them enjoying themselves." What could the poor fellow have done in the face of such frolicking Californian Jews but embrace anti-Semitism? (He later admitted to Nancy Mitford that he possessed a bit of "anti-Jew feeling" but "not anti-Semite. I rather like Arabs.")

Or there is the impossible anecdote, often involving an animal that has somehow wandered into and disrupted Waugh's civilized routine. Here is the young student at Oxford enjoying a delightful adventure: "I went out for a long and solitary walk, as is my custom, accompanied only with my big stick. In an obscure village miles away I met a white dog and—as is also my custom—addressed it with courtesy." But the promising relationship is shattered when the white dog sees the stick, sets up a howl, causing a "virago of a woman" to appear and accuse Waugh of beating the dog. Crestfallen, he departs. As a journalist in Ethiopia in 1935, enduring much boredom so that a "funny novel" can come out of it, Waugh reveals to his wife Laura the failure of his efforts with a different sort of animal: "I had a baboon but he seemed incapable of affection and he kept me awake in the afternoons so I threw him away." Quite right too; there is only one thing to do with a baboon who has no decent human feelings and is also noisy in the afternoon— throw him away, however one does that. Or there is the witty bawdry and wonderfully bad jokes like this public school one about what wines Princess Mary and her new husband will drink on their wedding night: "She will open her 24 year old port and he will indulge in cider (inside her)." As for proper behavior in the London Library (Lady Mary Lygon has just been elected to membership): "Always go to the closet appointed for the purpose if you wish to make water. Far too many female members have lately taken to squatting behind the Genealogy section. Never write 'balls' with an indelible pencil on the margins of the books provided. Do not solicit the female librarians to acts of unnatural vices." After all, standards must be kept up.

The single most extraordinary letter in the whole collection is one written in 1936 to Laura Herbert, who was to become Waugh's second wife and the mother of his children. A months before, he had revealed to his confidante Mary Lygon that he felt he was cutting a less than glorious figure with Laura, who "came to London with me yesterday but it was not a success for I had a hangover & could only eat 3 oysters and some soda water and I was sick a good deal on the table so perhaps that romance is shattered." Evidently not, but in his letter to Laura asking her to marry him, he takes pains to lay out the assets and liabilities of his character, without aid of romance:

> I can't advise you in my favour because I think it would be beastly for you, but think how nice it would be for me. I am restless & moody & misanthropic & lazy & have no money except what I earn and if I got ill you would starve. In fact its a lousy proposition.

On the other hand,

> you wouldn't find yourself confined to any particular place or group. Also I have practically no living relatives except one brother whom I scarcely know. You would not find yourself involved in a large family & all their rows & you would not be patronized & interfered with by odious sisters in law & aunts as it often happens.

Still, it should be remembered,

> all these are very small advantages compared with the awfulness of my character. I have always tried to be nice to you and you may have got it into your head that I am nice really, but that is all rot.

Who could resist such impossible sincerity? Not Laura Herbert, who married him, bore him one child after another, and stayed home during World

War II while Waugh engaged in various odd military enterprises, occasionally taking time out to keep his wife up to the epistolary mark: "I know you lead a dull life now. . . . But that is no reason to make your letters as dull as your life. I simply am not interested in Bridget's children. Do grasp that. A letter should be a form of conversation; write as though you were talking to me." Nor was it simply "Bridget's children" he didn't want to hear about: "No particular interest in your doings [he wrote to Laura from White's, his London club]: to hear that Teresa has sneezed or Bron fallen down does not excite me." He had previously begun a letter to her, also written from White's, with the news that "I have regretfully come to the conclusion that the boy Auberon is not yet a suitable companion for me"—this after a day spent together in London.

It was incredibly lucky for Waugh that he married a woman who was, truly, the Angel in the House. The other stroke of luck was his Catholicism, of which there is of course much in the letters and in respect to which he is at his most serious, most fierce. (There is a particularly striking trio of letters to John Betjeman, trying to argue or bully Betjeman out of his halfway Anglicanism.) Unfortunately, at least for this reviewer (a lapsed Protestant and, worse yet, an American), much of the in-chat among those of the true church is less than gripping, probably because by the standards set in other letters it's not impossible enough. So in 1955, when Edith Sitwell converts, and Alec Guinness has converted, Waugh writes to the former about how "one great sadness in Catholic life is year by year to count the apostasies—seldom from reason, almost always through marrying outside the Church. . . . Then one hears of the Grace of God steadily reinforcing the ranks. It is a great consolation." Left outside this charmed circle, I'm eager to hustle on to the next letter, when suddenly the convert sounds like something more: "I heard a rousing sermon on Sunday against the dangers of immodest bathing-dresses and thought that you and I were innocent of that offence at least." Saved by the comic bell.

Finally, though Waugh will not be remembered for his magnanimity toward other novelists, it's interesting that he treats his equals without condescension, often with affection and admiration. These qualities are to be found in the letters to Henry Yorke (Henry Green) and particularly in the ones to George Orwell, about *Animal Farm* and *1984*, and to Anthony Powell. "I don't quite know how I would define my admiration," he wrote to Powell on the appearance of volume three of *A Dance to the Music of Time*,

"I feel each volume of this series is like a great sustaining slice of Melton Pie. [Editor Amory precisely glosses it as 'Elaborate cold meat pie, specialty of Melton Mowbray, Leicestershire.'] I can go on eating it with the recurring seasons until I drop." Alas, he dropped, while the Music of Time played on. The letters from his last years are few and short. "Since we last met," he writes his old pal Nancy Mitford, "I have become an old man, not diseased but enfeebled [he was then in his sixty-first year]." Other letters speak about bereavements, "No work, Feeble health." Still, at moments, something caught his fancy, tickled it into the old style of creating, as in this to Ann Fleming:

> When I saw the doctor he asked about my habits. I said, "I have practically given up drinking—only about 7 bottles of wine & 3 of spirits a week." "A week? Surely you mean a month?" "No, and I smoke 30 cigars a week & take 40 grains of sodium amytal." He looked graver & graver. "Oh, yes, a bottle of paraldehyde a week." He brightened greatly & said: "Now that is an excellent thing. Far too few people use it."

Not even the grave physician could resist, or so it seems, this particularly impossible patient. The reader may be similarly disarmed.

American Scholar, Summer 1981

Talking Piss: Kingsley Amis in His Letters

THIS book is a handsome physical object, with many appealing illustrations, a chronology of Amis's life, and notes on the major recipients of his letters, followed in some cases by bracketed notations of how the recipient is referred to—thus "Anthony Powell [Tony, A.P., Horse Faced Dwarf, HFD]." There are appendices containing a number of poems, many of them parodies of other poets, sent by Amis to Philip Larkin. There is Amis's short and telling speech at Larkin's funeral. There are three "Alibi Notes" he wrote to Robert Conquest, cover-ups for extramarital adventures, and three "Bunny" household notes to his second wife, Elizabeth Jane Howard ("Piney"), with a signature rabbity signoff drawing. All this material, edited within an inch of its life, we owe to the incredibly industrious and imaginatively resourceful Zachary Leader. The old devil himself, if he could read this volume, would, I am convinced, be pleased.

When Larkin's letters were published in 1992, they elicited surprised responses from readers who had admired the poems but were appalled or disgusted by moments of racism and sexism in the correspondence. My guess is there won't be a similar problem with Amis's, since no one familiar with his novels will pick up the letters expecting sweetness and light. Indeed some readers of this volume already suspect that the man who speaks therein may be the great comic writer in English of our just-concluded century. Amis's comedy, increasingly in the later novels but there from the beginning, is instinct with animus, indeed animosity, often more than tinged with a bit of cruelty. Especially notable in this respect is his *Memoirs,* which contains sometimes unsettling remarks about his enemies and friends (including Larkin), nastily if humorously directed.

The Letters of Kingsley Amis, edited by Zachary Leader. London: HarperCollins, 2000.

The letters are full of such high-spirited animosity, and I quote one of the best of them in order to establish the usual pitch of things. In one of his last letters to Larkin a couple of months before the latter died, Amis reports on a luncheon at Iris Murdoch's:

> Went to lunch at ole I Murdoch's flat today. A Polish Jew held the floor, not up to much but at least pro-Franco, which "shocked" the others. All loved culture and thought everything was marvellous. Isn't Yeats marvellous? Isn't TSE marvellous? Isn't Magritte marv[el]lous? Isn't Flaubert marvellous? One of them "couldn't wait" for some exhibish to open. Another was "very excited" that some mouldering pile had been "saved." And what did I think of Terry K[ilmartin]'s Proust compared with that other fellow's? Ruh-beeble de bobbledy beezle. It is against *that* that we are fighting. And all's to do again. Francophile, a word they used several times unsarcastically, they pronounced Fronko-feel. Starsky and Hutch at 7.40. Oh come on Kingers this plain-man stuff doesn't get yoooghgh

He knows that Larkin is ill and hopes to cheer him up the only way Amis knows how and the way he has been practicing (with Larkin especially) for over four decades: by bringing out the worst in any person or event that falls his way. Larkin's "Vers de Société" opens with the Larkin-figure pondering a social invitation—"My wife and I have asked a crowd of craps / To come and waste their time and ours / Perhaps you'd like to join us?"—to which his first answer is, of course, "in a pig's arse, friend." Amis, having accepted the invite to lunch with a crowd of craps at "Ole Iris M's" couldn't wait to get home so he could write it up, make it live for Philip. "Shocked" by the Polish Jew's defense of Franco, "excited" by an art show about to open or a cultural monument saved, full of enthusiasm for "marvellous" modernist writers and painters, enunciating French matters in an unnatural (that is, un-English) accent rendered perfectly as "Fronko-feel," they are forces against which Amis—like Wordsworth in *The Prelude* but with something other than Wordsworthian fervor—and Larkin have been fighting. What this leaves out however is the TV cop show that "Kingers" looks forward to but allusion to which is also mocked for its plain man, too-easy righteousness. It also leaves out the best moment in the sequence, coming from nowhere: "Ruh-beeble de bobbledy beezle." Is that what the "craps" in their excited chattering sound like? What the silent, registering Amis thinks about their talk? What, in a memorable formulation, "social life" amounts to? Take your pick, but the words were at least as fortifying to me as Amis hoped they would be for Larkin.

I remember some relative or teacher informing me when I was growing up that if you couldn't say something nice about a person you had better not say anything at all. This principle, absolutely inverted, is the driving force of Amis's epistolary performance. For example, talking bad about one's in-laws is undeniably a common way to behave, but nothing quite matches in my experience the creative abuse Amis lavishes on his father-in-law, Leonard Bardwell. As early as 1949, he writes Larkin that "I don't see how I can avoid doing him in fiction if I am to refrain from stabbing him under the fifth rib in fact." Accordingly, "Daddy B." became the inspiration for Professor Welch, who would appear five years later in *Lucky Jim*. Like the professor, Leonard Bardwell was a devotee of folk music—"And the father does folk dancing (polk dancing? pock dancing? fock dancing?)"—so it was to Amis's delight that his father-in-law injured himself while engaging in "some lunatic folk fandango" involving staves. Bardwell reminds Amis of some "imbecile brother of Yeats," who, when asked how he was, "launched into an incoherent account of his recent ailments and protractions." In retaliation, writes Amis, "I now find his sense of smell is defective, so make a point of farting silently in his presence." (He has conveyed this same information to Larkin a few letters previously.)

Meeting him at the train station in Swansea at the beginning of a visit, Amis sings the rondo theme from Beethoven's first concerto (the "Welch theme" in *Lucky Jim*—"You ignorant clod, you stupid old sod") until spotting "his resentful ape's face peering about all round me without seeing me." One of Daddy B's activities while visiting Kingsley and Hilly is recounted thus:

> He's gone out today to see how much he remembers of the geography of Swansea; those are the *ipsissima verba*. Now why, I wonder, does he want to do that? What will he do if he finds he remembers a lot of it? And what will he do if he finds he doesn't remember a lot of it? He goes round in a blue shirt, with his braces in full view, trying to disgrace me.

As the letter to Larkin draws to a close, with a flurry of the signoff word ("bum") he and Larkin use ("Billy go and talk to Daddy; he's in there all on his bum, *bum,* bum bum, bum, *bum*"), it becomes necessary for Amis to contrive a postscript:

> You won't believe me, but while I was doing the above, he came and twisted the handle of the study door, behind which I am. He said, Are you in there, Kingsley? Yes, I said, in a cordial, eager tone. All right, he said. What the hell did he want? Did he confuse this room with the shithouse next door? Is it any longer just to speak of him confusing anything with anything? OOoogh, the old . . . the old

The consensus seems to be that Leonard Bardwell was a harmless enough fellow, but in Amis's practice if you can't turn the fellow into something really dreadful and funny you had better not bother at all. Eliot observed that Ben Jonson's satire was great "not by hitting off the object, but by creating it; the satire is merely the means which leads to the aesthetic result, the impulse which projects a new world into a new orbit." Something like this happens when Amis goes to work on Daddy Bardwell.

The letters to Larkin, who is by far the largest recipient, especially in earlier days of Amis's correspondence, bring out the worst—that is, the best—in him. By trying to amuse his friend, by showing off, by being funnier than (even) Larkin, he adopts a no-holds-barred mode of disparagement fiercer and wilder than either Amis the man or the more reasonable Amis we often see when he's writing to others. (Conquest is second only to Larkin in eliciting "bad" epistolary behavior.) Especially appealing are the letters to Larkin written in the 1940s when Amis is reading for his Oxford degrees, the second of which (B. Litt) he never received, since his thesis was rejected thanks to Lord David Cecil. One knew from previous remarks how contemptuous he was of Old and Middle English poems, especially long ones, so when he has to write "a bleeding essay all about the sodding old bore Langlad gland I mean," you know *Piers Plowman* may be in for less than full appreciation. Even more hateful, because more studied and revered, was "Bare-wolf," that "anonymous, crass, purblind, infantile, *featureless* HEAP OF GANGRENED ELEPHANT'S SPUTUM." Nor is there a letup when Chaucer appears, on whom he is writing an essay referred to as the "levels of C's art as shown in the Cuntherbelly Tails." What he thought of those levels, scatalogically described to Larkin, was suppressed in the essay he handed in to his tutor, J. B. Leishmann, who "has pronounced himself 'very pleased' with my essay on the levels of Cah warrggh Chaucer's fart. He kept on talking about Chaucer's humour and I could hardly keep myself from *breaking wind in his face.*"

But Langland, *Beowulf,* Chaucer, all take a back seat when the writer to be essayed is Dryden:

> I have stopped reading Dryden. He is very like Chaucer, isn't he? I mean, however hard you try, you cannot see *what people mean* who admired them. Now I can see what people *mean* (though I don't *agree* with them) who like DONNE or POPE or WORDSWORTH, or KEATS, or even MILTON, but I cannot with Dryden. A second-rate fucking journalist ("OH?"). A SECOND-RATE FUCKING JOURNALIST. ("Oh.").

An irresponsible judgment, but good knockabout fun, of the sort a very clever, very literary young man "getting up" Eng lit, might indulge in. I did something similar with a friend, trading praise and abuse of writers as we studied for our Ph.D. orals. But not to the creative/destructive level Amis takes things, perhaps an expression of his own developing passion to be a great writer—at least better than the likes of Dryden and Chaucer.

Other patches of saying the worst about a writer may speak to the secret hearts of readers who would never themselves admit to harboring such thoughts. About Hopkins, for example (and once again to Larkin):

> I find him a bad poet—all this how to keép is there ány any stuff strikes me as a bit unnecessary—and so his defence of his work to Bridges, in spite of Bridges being a bumblock of the first order, seems arrogant to me: You must be wrong when you don't like my stuff, d'you see, because *I know* my stuff's good, d'you see? And his silly private language annoys me—"what I am in the habit of calling *inscape*" well *getoutofthehabitthen.* I had another go at his poetry the other day, and confirmed my previous impressions of it as *going after the wrong thing,* trying to treat words as if they were music. They aren't, are they? If his verse can't be read properly without key-signatures and sharps and flats, *so much the worse for it.* And as for this bitch batch bum come cock cork fork fuck stuff, *what is the point of it?* Eh?

He adds, assuagingly, that he can see why Hopkins appeals—"a sensible man, outside religion and poetry." This paragraph of promising literary criticism gains some of its charm by being sandwiched between thanking Larkin for the "dirty magazine" he sent him and a little slavering over the Italian film star Silvana Mangano ("I bought the Tit bits with Mangano in it and am prepared to believe all you say"). So if readers of these letters aren't prepared to condemn Amis for insensitivity to Hopkins's genius, they can deplore his unblushing, adolescent leer at pornography. In other words, there is something for everyone in this correspondence.

It has been noted how often the scales fall from Amis's eyes; for example, he had thought Keats was merely a bad poet ("I stood tip-toe upon a little hill so I could fart better" was his creative extension of a Keats opening line) but that, as universal opinion had it, a wiser, nicer, much more percipient man was to be found in his letters. Not a bit of it:

> I know now that Keats was a boring, conceited, self-pitying, self-indul-
> gent, silly little fool (My dear Girl bum) as well as an incompetent, un-
> interesting, affected, non-visualising, Royal-Academy-picture, salacious,
> mouthing poet. He's still better than Shelley though.

We are to thank him for the measured putting of his abuse of Keats into perspective by reminding us of Shelley. Sometimes a single sentence is enough to snare and smear one English don (David Cecil) and two English poets (Crabbe and Cowper), as in "that POSTURING QUACK Cess-hole thinks Crab's good, doesn't he along with that lunatic stricken-deer bastard who couldn't spell his own name properly." (Yet in *Memoirs,* some years later, Amis would admit that awful as Lord David was, his book on Cowper "really has something to say about Cowper.") On another occasion he does a pretend version of scales-falling-from-eyes, in writing to Larkin about Sylvia Plath (Larkin had treated Plath's work with some sympathy), "You did know she didn't mean to kill herself"? On another occasion, while compiling the *New Oxford Book of Light Verse,* he suggests it would be "fun to include in the anth a poem by Sylvia Plath, one of the really balls-aching ones, and refer in the Intro to her sadly undervalued comic manner."

Some of the best moments occur when Amis engages in teasing Larkin by being impious about Larkin's favorite, Thomas Hardy ("ole Hardy"), whose poems are filled with "all those rotten old words nobody uses and those horrible double-barrelled ones he made up out of his own head, like all-uncared and eve-damps and self-wrapt and fore-folk. . . . Still you use words like that yourself don't you so Iyyyeeeeeghghgh . . ." On the eve of one of Larkin's visits to London, Amis contrives the following hellish entertainment:

> We thought we'd lay on a bit of a show for you since you don't come to
> London all that often. A cocktail party about 5.30 with some of your ad-

mirers—George Steiner, Ian Hamilton, Arnold Wesker; Alvarez of course, and I hope A. L. Rowse, though I haven't heard from him yet. Then I've booked seats at *Equus,* which is really the most *exciting* thing to hit the stage for years, and after that a place I know with a marvellous group of young West Indiaaaaeeeeoooghghgh

Or, in response to Larkin's opening an exhibition on D. H. Lawrence at Nottingham in 1980, the following [Amis always refers to Lawrence as DEL] :

> You really are potty about old DEL. How the fuck do you GET THRU him? CAN'T YOU SEE he's just like Wagner and Pound, a self-solving mystery? Fellows say, "Here's a GRINDING SHIT who never did *Anything* nice to or for *anybody,* and yet he's written all this stuff which is supposed to be frightfully good Funny. But then some of them look closely at the stuff and find that, instead of being frightfully good, it is in fact INSULTINGLY BAD IN EXACTLY THE KIND OF WAY YOU'D EXPECT FROM THE WAY HE BEHAVED. All of a piece. End of problem. Oh well. We all have our little foibles. Wouldn't do if we all thought the same OH YES IT FUCKING WELL WOU

The remarks about contemporaries and recent predecessors in the literary line would make a splendid anthology of what Amis called "horsepissing." Here, without comment, are a few of them: "I don't like Henry Green much, by the way: it takes me too long to understand what he means by the things he says." "The extracts from Mrs. Woolf she gives [Q. D. Leavis in *Fiction and the Reading Public*] show me why I hate her so much. She is guilty *most of the time* of a forcing of sensibility . . . what we get is a kind of intellectual melodrama, the exacerbation of *totally fictitious* states of feeling into a sentimental pipe dream untouched by discipline. . . ." "Reading some of Rilke's letters (You are mad, you know?). He seems on first acquaintance to be one of those Henry James men who are too busy wondering what a writer is to be one." "Ruskin is a clown but quite a funny one." "I have just come back from my weekly lecture on modern literature, in which I dealt with Ezra Pained and old man T.S.E's *Waste country.* Honestly, can you see anything in EP? Buggered if I can." "I've read *The days of the locust* by Nathanael West . . . I feel when reading him as I do with Virginia Wolf: I want to keep saying, 'No, he didn't,' 'No, it didn't happen as you describe it,' 'No, that isn't what he thought,' 'No, that's just what she didn't say.'" "With Prof. Kermode's implied assessment of Robert Lowell as fit to stand alongside Pound I for one have no quarrel." "What do I find in the Observer but a great puff for that John Ashbery whom I excoriated in my last. Greatest living poet in English, the reviewer thought, or possibly so, and 'exciting,' that horrible word—an exciting new film isn't one with lots of car-chases and gun-battles, but a piece of trendy, pretentious stodge."

In concentrating on and quoting extensively from Amis's recurring extravagances in saying and imagining the worst—his refusal or inability to take a moderate, "balanced" view of anything—I risk convincing no one not already convinced of the great exhilarations these letters produce. An alternative way to "review" them would be to understand or explain them by invoking Amis's psychological limitations, his phobias and fears (of flying, car-driving, being alone), his self-destructive drinking, his sometime cruelty to others. The most egregious example of that latter quality may be found in a chilling letter he wrote his American biographer, Dale Salwak, whom for a number of years Amis had cooperated with, if not encouraged, in various labors. When Salwak sent him the first three chapters of the finished manuscript for comment, Amis replied by saying he considered them "altogether unsatisfactory," that Salwak's "level of performance was so low as not to rate publication." As if that weren't sufficient, there is a capping paragraph:

> Please realise that no imaginable rewriting would rectify the situation. The fact that I have left many passages and pages of your typescript unmarked testifies to my weariness and boredom with them, not to their correctness or adequacy.

Imagine receiving that in the mail, of a morning. I experienced a very minor version of what Salwak must have felt, when in 1980 I published a review, in this journal, of Amis's Collected Poems. In a letter to Larkin, he mentions the piece ("my first highbrow crit"), then mocks it a bit, then writes in another letter to Larkin a month later, "Yes (re Pritchard) it's a bugger, the people who think you're (one is) good while getting you wrong." I don't know how I got him wrong but, after wincing a bit, decided that trying to "explain" it was not the way to behave—better to relax and enjoy. Wyndham Lewis once said about Joyce's Ulysses that no one who ever looked at it would ever want to look behind it. What there is to look at in these twelve hundred pages of letters is something like God's plenty, as Amis's hated Dryden remarked about Amis's hated Chaucer. Or is it the Devil's plenty? At any rate there seems to be nothing that remotely approaches it in modern English letters, and for that we're in Amis's—and Zachary Leader's—debt.

Essays in Criticism, October 2001

A. N. Wilson's Literary Life

THE recent publication of *God's Funeral*, by my count his thirtieth book, is occasion for singling out A. N. (Andrew Norman) Wilson as, if not England's foremost man of letters, surely its most prolific and entertaining one. Not yet fifty—he will become so this year—he has produced a varied and appealing series of books, beginning in 1977 with *The Sweets of Pimlico*, a novel. There have followed novels, biographies, works of religious speculation and scholarship on Jesus and Paul, a group of nineteenth-century portraits (*Eminent Victorians*), and a highly seasoned look at the royal family (*The Rise and Fall of the House of Windsor*). He has edited *The Faber Book of London* and *The Faber Book of Church and Clergy*, as well as Scott's *Ivanhoe* with a revealing introduction and good notes. As with his precursor, Anthony Burgess, whom he resembles in comic wit, theological obsessions, and immense productivity (even in name—Burgess's given one was John Anthony Burgess Wilson), A. N. Wilson's reputation is lessened in the eyes of some by such striking productivity. (Burgess's response in the early 1960s to the charge of overproduction was to publish two novels under the pen name of Joseph Kell.) No one can be that good who writes that much, runs the logic, and ambivalence about Wilson is heightened by his willingness to say on one occasion or another all sorts of outrageous things, while moving about from Catholicism to atheism in ways that confuse a reader trying to keep track.

God's Funeral is an immensely readable excursion through a large number of literary and philosophical figures, mainly from England in the nineteenth century, who occupied themselves with what he calls in his preface "the God-question." It is a question, Wilson believes, that does not go away, as it has not gone away for him. Although he admits to not being a theolo-

---

God's Funeral, by A. N. Wilson. New York: W. W. Norton, 1999.

gian, a philosopher, or a scientist, as a man of letters he has no hesitations
about taking them on—from Hume and Kant to Darwin and Baron von
Hügel.[1] Wilson's method of presentation is old-fashioned: a portrait of the
man (or woman); liberal use of memorable anecdotes about him; extracts
from his writings of attitudes about God, religion, the church, science etc.;
then a personal un-dispassionate judgment, on the critic's part of the man's
contribution and importance. He has his heroes, an eclectic collection including Newman, Swinburne, Ruskin, William James, even "funny old Herbert Spencer," who wrote "millions of words which no one now reads." For
good measure there are also a couple of villains, or at least pretenders—like
Matthew Arnold and G. B. Shaw. In his chapter on William James, Wilson
describes the philosopher's famous style—so irritating to James's contemporary, Charles Sanders Peirce—as "an intelligible, even a chatty style, laced
with amusing asides and jokes." There is no better description of Wilson's
own style, not just in the new book but throughout his work.

A few facts about Wilson's life may be of interest.[2] Born in Staffordshire in
1950, he was the youngest of three children whose father was a designer of
pottery, also managing director of Wedgwood. At age seven he was sent to
boarding school in Wales, which he has lovingly characterized as "a crummy
hateful little place," but which he has made good use of as a source for comic
fiction. At thirteen he entered Rugby, then New College, Oxford, where at
the end of his second year he married his tutor, Katherine Duncan-Jones, a
prominent Shakespearean scholar. By that time he had already embraced
and renounced more than one "faith"; in his book of religious speculation,
How Can We Know?, he described his youthful self: "At the time, I was very
young for my fifteen or sixteen years, very impressionable and very enthusiastic. I had already been by turns, a convert to a simple sort of evangelical
Christianity; an atheist; a Marxist with particular devotion to the teachings
of Chairman Mao."

He also fell into the grip of Tolstoy for two years, tried to practice vege-
tarianism, joined the Peace Pledge Union, and read the sage with devotion
until he found his mind "in a new place," this one under the auspices of

1. Compare Wyndham Lewis in *Time and Western Man:* "I do not feel impelled to explain
myself when I am examining a mere philosopher: he speaks my language, usually with less
skill, but otherwise much the same as I do."

2. My source here is "The Busy, *Busy* Wasp," by James Atlas (*New York Times Magazine,*
October 18, 1992).

Cardinal Newman. After taking a "bad" degree at Oxford (a second) he spent a year at a nearby theological seminary, St. Stephen's. This he accords about as much respect as he gave his Welsh boarding school, calling the seminary "a madhouse . . . a homosexual world of a particularly high-camp kind—a girls' names and feather dusters sort of world. . . . It was beyond belief." Something like that school would receive memorable presentation in his second novel, *Unguarded Hours*. Wilson and Duncan-Jones had two children; he returned to the Church of England when his wife balked at raising them as Catholics. He taught a year at a public school, then lectured at New College, Oxford, a lectureship eventually not renewed. At age twenty-eight he published *The Sweets of Pimlico*, a delightful and also vaguely disturbing novel that won the John Llewelyn Rhys Memorial Prize. He became literary editor of *The Spectator*, thus launching his journalistic career; was dismissed two years later when he altered without permission some sentences by one of his reviewers; later wrote a weekly column for the *Evening Standard* and generally turned out much literary commentary. His first marriage ended in 1989; he then married Ruth Goulding, an art historian, and moved to London.

Before remarking briefly on his latest book, I want to survey Wilson's achievement as novelist, biographer, and all-purpose reviewer. We may begin by noting that he has declared George and Weedon Grossmith's *Diary of a Nobody* the best comic novel in English. This is enough perhaps to locate Wilson's essential bourgeois pleasure in the absurdities of Mr. Pooter and his family. When you think about it (and if you have read the wonderful *Diary of a Nobody*), how many novels are in serious competition for the accolade? *Decline and Fall, From a View to a Death,* and *Lucky Jim* come to mind—and not surprisingly, since Wilson is a comic writer of the post-Waugh-Powell-Amis axis. His books, especially his earlier novels, don't presume to take their characters seriously, deeply, sympathetically; rather, like the Dickens who revels in "superficial" creation of character, Wilson's theatrical comedy displays the antic absurdities of types chosen for their outrageousness—like the seminarians in *Unguarded Hours*. Here is a typical exchange among some of these students at St. Cuthbert's, a theological college where the hapless and wholly engaging protagonist of the novel, Norman Shotover, has landed in his bid to be ordained. Father Arnold Fogg is vice-principal of the college and is referred to in the exchange that follows about "cottas," waist-length surplices:

"I knew Felicity Fogg would get her knickers in a twist over those cottas."

"Sometimes I think she's a bloody Protestant."

"Mind you, Father, I can see some of the embroidery was, shall we say, extreme?"

"What's extreme about a few emblems of the Immaculate Heart of Mary?"

"Temper, temper! What do you think, Sheila dear?"

"I thought the cottas were quite pretty," said Norman. "A bit gaudy, perhaps, but quite pretty."

The next paragraph informs us that Norman has adapted fairly happily to life at St. Cuthbert's, though he admits that the students "had an odd way of speaking." This impression dated perhaps from his first day there when a fellow student says to him admiringly, "You really are a saucy little beast!" The running gag is uncomplicated but nonetheless amusing.

Unguarded Hours and its successor of a year later, *Kindly Light*, both featuring Norman as protagonist whirled from this escapade to that, are Wilson at his breeziest, most unguardedly inventive. *Kindly Light*, for example, begins with a mass performed by Father Sporran and his dancing nuns (the nuns are clad in "black fish-net stockings and the briefest of gym-tunics"). who sing the Beatles' "All You Need Is Love" while Father Sporran serves up communion with slices of Hovis (English all-purpose bread) and Sainsbury's Beaujolais. There are various other "modern" improvements on the Eucharist; Wilson is especially keen on travestying post–Vatican II goings-on in the Roman Catholic Church, and "satire" is hardly the word to fit the extravagance with which various awful "advances" are treated. (Wilson might say no extravagance was needed, since in themselves they constituted a travesty.) But he is equally at home in the schoolroom where Norman teaches after he flees the church and where he attempts to have his students read aloud from *Macbeth*. One of the Hassif twins, whose English is weak but whose father, a Middle East oil magnate, has promised to finance a new language laboratory named The Hassif Block, is being encouraged to read aloud some lines, over the protests of an obstreperous boy named Macracken:

"Come on Hassif—Thou hast it now: King, Cawdor, Glamis, all. As the weird women promised . . ."

"Ooh! Weird!"

"Macracken! That is your last chance. The next time it will be three hundred lines."

"*Zoo harst eet naking. Cow-door Glamees . . .*"

"Sir, he's lousy, he can't read; let me read, sir. Please, sir. I promise, I'll do it properly, sir. Honestly, sir."

And so on. Paul Pennyfeather's teaching debacle with the boys at Llanabba Castle in *Decline and Fall* is of course behind this, but Wilson provides many commendably original touches of his own.

In contrast to this "superficial" treatment of character, there are interesting moments in Wilson's early novels when he manages to take us convincingly into the mind of a protagonist who, on occasion, has or has developed over the novel an inner life. In Wilson's (for a first novel) extremely assured *The Streets of Pimlico*, Evelyn Tradescant's love for the strange old man Theodore Gormann flowers when Theo dies at a seaside resort where Evelyn has taken him to recuperate after he falls victim to a bombing in the National Gallery: "Her inability to believe that Mr. Gormann any longer existed produced a nervous blankness which stemmed even the desire to weep." Even more convincingly, at the end of *Wise Virgin*, the blind medieval scholar Giles Fox, his affections three parts iced over, finally proposes to Louise Agar, his far-from-stunning research assistant whose devotion has proved itself on his pulses. These novels, along with *Who Was Oswald Fish?*, *Scandal*, and *Love Unknown*, remind us in places of Iris Murdoch, to whom, along with John Bayley, *The Sweets of Pimlico* was dedicated. (Wilson began work on but never wrote a biography of Murdoch.) Wilson's novels, however, are a lot less murky and not as long as Murdoch's, also better written page by page, even while—to some readers' disappointment—less philosophically dense.

His novels usually tend toward excess in their later stages, with farce and madcap behavior taking over from more subtle comedy and the sort of precise observation that is given to, say, academic Oxford social life and why one academic left it behind:

> Three years was enough of it. Dinner parties at which gross quantities of ill-chosen wine washed down food that would have been regarded as penitential in a boarding-school; repeated talk of college appointments and disappointments; fog in the winter; torrid humidity in summer; water so hard that one could barely wash one's hands; constant catarrh and quarrels with the neighbors.

These sentiments from *Unguarded Hours* were ones Wilson gave the character of Gussy Mason at about the time he himself was no longer a lecturer at Oxford. But there is much similarly and strongly directed observation in *Wise Virgin* and in more recent fiction like *The Vicar of Sorrows* and *Dream*

Children (his best novels). Wilson's most ambitious, certainly most extended, piece of observed manners is to be found in the five novels that make up *The Lampitt Chronicles,* a wide-ranging portrait of English middle-class and "bohemian" life in the second half of this century. Here the precursor is Anthony Powell's *A Dance to the Music of Time,* and my feeling is that Wilson's chronicle, lacking the highly wrought, wholly deliberative style that Powell perfected in those books, produces something much less memorable. Compared to Powell's hero, Nicholas Jenkins, Julian Ramsay (protagonist of *The Lampitt Chronicles*) is granted no such distinctive style, so that while the Lampitt books are filled with lively, humorous bits of mordant life, they don't stay in the mind forcefully; one doesn't think to reread them, as one does with other Wilson novels.

Astonishingly, in addition to this impressive output of fiction, he produced in the 1980s five substantial biographies, beginning with Sir Walter Scott and proceeding through Milton, Hilaire Belloc, Tolstoy, and C. S. Lewis. Each of them (except the Belloc, which I haven't been able to get through) is never less than thoroughly agreeable and informative about both its subject's life and work. In particular, the one on Scott (*The Laird of Abbotsford*) offers many fresh readings and judgments of the novels; while the exemplary one on Lewis reveals a sympathetic insight into the man, his writings, and Oxbridge life in decades past. The life-and-works approach, so central to Wilson's procedure as a biographer, is also evident in the six essays that make up *Eminent Victorians,* a handsomely illustrated presentation of Prince Albert, Charlotte Brontë, Gladstone, Newman, Josephine Butler, and Julia Margaret Cameron. Justifying his appropriation of Lytton Strachey's title, Wilson quotes Strachey's claim in the latter's *Eminent Victorians:* "*Je n'impose rien; Je ne propose rien; j'expose*"—suggesting that in saying this, Strachey had his tongue so firmly in his cheek he could barely get the words out. Wilson allows that his predecessor's book "will still be read when mine is forgotten," but he adds, rightly, that "when both Strachey and I are forgotten, they will still be reading *Jane Eyre* and Newman's *Apologia.*" Let's hope so; at any rate, Wilson writes about his eminences with an engagement both shrewd and sympathetic, avoiding—as Strachey did not—making himself out to be much more knowing and clever than his subjects. He likes, and with some justice, to think of his own motive as that of befriending rather than patronizing the dead, and practices what he preaches in his book on the Victorians and in much of *God's Funeral.*

Wilson's single collection of essays and reviews is titled *Penfriends from Porlock,* and its best parts are portraits of figures, many of whom are forgotten. There is a lovely one, for example, of William Ralph Inge, a.k.a. "The Gloomy Dean"; also of Montague Summers, "Peter Simple," and the not-forgotten G. K. Chesterton. There are as well two nasty carvings-up, of Lyndon Johnson and of Sir Charles Snow. The essay on Dean Inge is an example of Wilson's "befriending" the dead: "I like his family life, the devotion to Kitty [Inge's wife] and the children, his desolation when two of his children and finally his wife die." But when he decides to be less friendly, the results are devastating. Discussing English journalism, he once spoke of its "tradition of organized rudeness," and latterly a review by him of Paul Theroux's book on Sir Vidia Naipaul concludes with the following salute to the American writer: "Of all the lice on the locks of literature at present crawling, he is one of the lustiest. The rudeness is usually witty: reviewing a dull biography of an interesting man, John Sparrow, the Warden of All Souls, Wilson produces a priceless exchange between Sparrow and the historian A. L. Rowse, who used to complain that Sparrow hadn't read his (many) books. "Do you know my *Tudor Cornwall,* John?" "No," replied Sparrow and gestured to the figure on his right: "Do you know Stuart Hampshire?" Sparrow's biographer thinks such a riposte was quick-witted, but Wilson suggests that Sparrow must have taken Hampshire into dinner at All Souls many times before he could trap Rowse into saying the line about *Tudor Cornwall.*

Such English common-room aggression might have merely turned into the sort of spiteful entertainment produced by an Auberon Waugh (who once, reviewing something I'd published, called it "this idiotic little book"). But Auberon could not have written *God's Funeral,* the essential richness of which lies not in any speculative insights it gives us about what happened to God over the past two hundred years, but in the individual "penfriends" brought to life in its pages. In the essay on Dean Inge, an address given to something Catholic-sounding called The Ambrose Society in 1985, Wilson speaks as a Christian; and his *How Can We Know?* of the same year has a preface declaring that his writing of the book made him discover "that in spite of everything, I did believe the Christian religion to be inescapably and irresistibly true." In the final paragraph of *How Can We Know?,* however, the word "but" appears four times. Six years later he contributed an essay to a pamphlet series, "Against Religions," in which he declared organized religion to be "a form of moral blackmail." And in *The Faber Book of Church and*

Clergy, which he selected and edited in 1992, he declared "I stand outside the church these days." It's not easy, perhaps not possible, to decide on the evidence of *God's Funeral* where Wilson "really stands" now with regard to Christianity, but he writes a concluding paragraph that asserts, contra Death-of-God talk—"One of the most extraordinary things about the twentieth century has been the palpable and visible strength of the Christian thing, the Christian idea." Certainly he sounds exhilarated rather than dismayed by that fact. But unceasingly, "the Christian thing" has provided the energy fueling Wilson's writing, fictional and otherwise.

I see no overall "argument" to *God's Funeral;* its life instead is in its parts, its portraits that add up to what Wilson calls "a story of bereavement as much as of adventure." This story is borne out from the opening poem by Thomas Hardy ("God's Funeral") to concluding accounts of some embattled, "modernist" religious thinkers. Many of the judgments are expressed in the language of high admiration, guaranteed to give us pause. Is Swinburne "an unjustly neglected great poet"? (Perhaps so, but who can actually read the poems line by line?); Is Rossetti's painting *Beata Beatrix* "perhaps the greatest work of art of the 19th century?" (Well . . .) Can you guess what book Wilson would keep if all the others written in the reign of Victoria—like *David Copperfield, In Memoriam, The Origin of Species*—were destroyed? (Ruskin's *Fors Clavigera:* "Impossible to summarize either what the letters are like or what they are about." So there.) Sometimes the epithets make one just a shade nervous: Kant is "the dwarfish genius of Königsberg"; Benjamin Jowett is "the endearing if slightly absurd master of Balliol"; Mark Pattison is "the crabby old Rector of Lincoln." The ghost of Strachey lurks. And when Wilson takes arms against figures he dislikes (and whom I admire) like Arnold and Shaw, I bristle a bit. Shaw's crank beliefs, as in the virtues of the all-wool Jaeger suit, are held up for ridicule, but there's no indication that Wilson is at all moved, or even entertained, by the plays. Perhaps he isn't, and he certainly is in no way responsive, except with contempt, to Arnold, "lofty Matt," who got all soft about "those delicate, beautiful Greeks." Arnold's poetry, or rather "Dover Beach," is dismissed by claiming that its sea of faith metaphor is confused. But Wilson is himself confused— to the extent that he misrepresents *Culture and Anarchy*—in identifying Arnold's Philistines as "the governing aristocratic class." Arnold called that class the Barbarians, a name Wilson gives instead to the rising middle-class Philistines. In telling us that Swinburne found Arnold's lectures on poetry "boring," Wilson adds, parenthetically, "which they are," as if we needed to be assured they really were. As for the "Wragg is in custody" passage in "The Function of Criticism," Wilson reduces it to effete snobbery. And although he admires George Eliot much more than he does Arnold, his comment on F. W .H. Myers's famous description of walking with her in the Fellows' Garden at Trinity College, Cambridge, is surely odd. Eliot told Myers on that occasion that of the three great words—God, Immortality, and Duty—the first and second were, respectively, inconceivable and unbelievable. But the third was peremptory and absolute. Myers writes, "I listened, and night fell; her grave, majestic countenance turned toward me like a sibyl's in the gloom; it was as though she withdrew from my grasp, one by one, the two scrolls of promise, and left me the third scroll only, awful with inevitable fates." Wilson quotes this as an example of how some of Eliot's contemporaries found her position on unbelief "somewhat arid." I should have called Myers's response anything but that.

But this is to niggle about a book full of fine things (like urging us to *read* Kant rather than swallow a summary of his "thought") and always instinct with Wilson's highly original, cultivatedly aggressive mind and style. Who else could write, by way of characterizing one's impatience with certain kinds of religious fundamentalists, "You just want to shout 'yah boo sucks.'" (This must be good English schoolboy lingo.) Like Ruskin, about whom he has some vivid pages, Wilson's "intemperate judgments," expressed in a twenty-three-year career's worth of books, "contribute to his charm." Surely he would not mind his assertion about Ruskin being applied to himself: "You never quite know which way he will jump."

An A. N. Wilson Bibliography

The Sweets of Pimlico (1977)
Unguarded Hours (1978)
Kindly Light (1979)
The Healing Art (1980)
The Laird of Abbotsford (1980, biography)
Who Was Oswald Fish? (1981)
Wise Virgin (1982)
A Life of John Milton (1983, biography)
Hilaire Belloc (1984, biography)

Scandal (1984)
Gentlemen in England (1985)
How Can We Know? (1985, religious inquiry)
Love Unknown (1986)
Stray (1987, children's)
Tolstoy (1988, biography)
Penfriends from Porlock (1988, essays)
Tabitha (1989, children's)
Eminent Victorians (1989, biographical essays)
C. S. Lewis: A Biography (1990)
The Lampitt Chronicles
   Incline Our Hearts (1989)
   A Bottle in the Smoke (1990)
   Daughters of Albion (1992)
   Hearing Voices (1995)
   A Watch in the Night (1996)
Jesus (1992)
(ed.) *The Faber Book of Church and Clergy* (1992)
(ed.) *The Faber Book of London* (1993)
The Vicar of Sorrows (1993)
The Rise and Fall of the House of Windsor (1993)
Paul: The Mind of the Apostle (1997)
Dream Children (1998)
God's Funeral (1999, intellectual history)

Hudson Review, Winter 2000

At the Goreyworks

I was introduced to the work of Edward Gorey in the fall of 1954 when a Cambridge friend of mine who knew Gorey, already a legend in Boston literary circles (he had by then moved to New York City), urged me to pick up copies of his first two books. Accordingly I purchased *The Unstrung Harp* (1953) and *The Listing Attic* (1954) at a bookstore in Harvard Square, each of the volumes priced at two dollars and providing me with delighted entry into the world of a unique talent. *The Unstrung Harp*, subtitled "Mr. Earbrass Writes a Novel," had a jacket design featuring a figure in evening dress, overpowered so it seemed by a very large harp visibly without strings. He is doubtless the protagonist of Mr. Earbrass's novel, indeed he looks very much like Mr. Earbrass—as do all the other figures in Gorey's book. That is, he wears, always, an expressionless expression; he is bald, with a mustache, a lidless eye, and a nose that is more or less parallel to his chin. We always see this figure in profile.

The Unstrung Harp consists of thirty panels with a hefty bit of text for each, more words than Gorey would ever again provide for his illustrations. In the first one, the well-known novelist, author of the Hipdeep Trilogy, is seen on the croquet lawn of his home, Hobbies Old, situated near Collapsed Pudding in Mortshire: "He is studying a game left unfinished at the end of summer," the remains of which consist of two lonely wickets and a ball more or less encased in snow. In the distance are some statuary and a bit of unadorned, bleak nature. Mr. Earbrass is clad in one of his fur coats; his extremely elongated feet and footwear (spats?) look ineffective against the snow. A croquet mallet droops from his left hand as he stares off into some unpictured distance.

The World of Edward Gorey, by Clifford Ross and Karen Wilkin. New York: Harry N. Abrams, 1996.

In her fine account of Gorey, the centerpiece of this handsome book about the artist, Karen Wilkin speaks of the "charm" of his writing. *The Unstrung Harp* gave me plenty of that charm, as Mr. Earbrass's "verbs seem to have withered away and his adjectives to be proliferating beyond control." In the penultimate panel we see him, his novel finally published and reviewed, standing on his terrace at twilight: "It is bleak; it is cold; and the virtue has gone out of everything." Various words drift through his mind, a few of which are as follows: "ANGUISH TURNIPS CONJUNCTIONS ILLNESS DEFEAT STRING PARTIES NO PARTIES URNS DESUETUDE DISAFFECTION." The juxtaposing of ANGUISH with TURNIPS; the sudden appearance of the unmemorable STRING in the midst of ILLNESS DEFEAT PARTIES and NO PARTIES; the lovely DESUETUDE, not even in my vocabulary at that point—all this was extremely appealing and quite unlike anything taking place in graduate classrooms at Harvard.

Anyway I didn't have to write a paper on Gorey and could content myself rather with memorizing some of the amazing limericks from *The Listing Attic*:

> To his clubfooted child said Lord Stipple,
> As he poured his post-prandial tipple,
>   "Your mother's behavior
>   Gave pain to Our Saviour,
> And that's why he made you a cripple."

In the accompanying drawing a merciless adult, in the act of filling his glass from a large decanter, peers down at a bandy-legged little fellow in shorts and tie, a crutch supporting his right arm. *The Listing Attic* was filled with that sort of unhealthy humor: a curate beating a small child to death with his cane; a woman whose stammer "was atrocious and so was her grammar; / But they were not improved / When her husband was moved / To knock out her teeth with a hammer." There was also the gentleman who detested leeks so much he clouted the maid who offered him one; or there was the about-to-be-immolated victim of "Some Harvard men, stalwart and hairy," who, in their drunken masculinity, cavorted about Harvard Yard at 3:00 A.M. shrieking, "Come on out, we are burning a fairy." All this, though of dubious moral value, felt inspiriting as one looked at the miniature design and perfect five lines below. Compared to Gorey, Edward Lear, inventor of the limerick (whom Karen Wilkin names as an obvious "influence" on the artist) seemed of another age and rather too tame.

With reference to *The Unstrung Harp,* Wilkin identifies the main constituents of Gorey's art:

> Painstaking drawings with an eloquent orchestration of hatchings and tickings, marvelous period details of costume and setting, a narrative that leapfrogs from the precise to the unexplained, a tone of vague melancholy, and an author who manifestly delights in both visual and linguistic oddities.

I'm sure the vague melancholy had much to do with what appealed to me, and still does, in these productions. In *The Willowdale Handcar* (1962), for example, the feckless tourists visit "the ruins of the Crampton vinegar works, which had been destroyed by a mysterious explosion the preceding fall." *Où sont les neiges d'antan?* It isn't clear just what the visitors take away from their visit to the ruins—it's not even clear from the drawing that they're looking at them—but there's something vulnerable and affecting about the whole enterprise.

Gorey's melancholy is there in his books all right, but for me was most strikingly expressed in the sixty or so covers he did for Anchor paperbacks during his term at Doubleday. *The World of Edward Gorey* contains two of these: one for Gogol's tales, consisting of furred Russians up to no good; one for Gide's *Lafcadio's Adventures.* But the covers I love most are five in number: there is Melville's *Redburn,* in which the red-shirted muscular hero, with strongly emphasized crotch, looks over his shoulder at three sailors eyeing him; there is James's *What Maisie Knew,* in which the little girl (who would reappear as Charlotte Sophia in Gorey's *The Hapless Child,* 1961) is observing a very tall, black-suited male (probably Beale Farrange) importuning or threatening a female (Mrs. Beale?) against a background of grey wallpaper and gold drapery. There is Conrad's *The Secret Agent,* in which a Verlocian figure with a briefcase contemplates, all by himself, Greenwich observatory; or Kafka's *Amerika,* in which two passengers aboard a ship approaching New York stare at the towers of lower Manhattan. The sky is streaked with flashes of sunset-red fire; one of the watchers looks through binoculars, the other— probably our hero, Karl Rossmann—has one hand on the rail, another holding a folded-up umbrella. A black suitcase stands some feet away from him

on the strongly hatched grey deck. Perhaps best of all is Gorey's cover for Ler-
montov's *A Hero of Our Time,* a Caucasian mountain wildness humanized
scarcely at all by two tiny figures, one on horseback, the other standing at
the edge of a precipice and (perhaps) declaiming Pushkin or Byron to the
depths. All these designs have amazing force and appeal, hardly suggested by
my crude descriptions. Of course they have also the flavor of a distant time,
four decades ago, when "quality" books, handsomely designed, were first
made available in paperback for the price of seventy-five or ninety-five cents.
But they represent some of Gorey's most intense, secretive, and disturbing
portraiture, especially appropriate for books, like *What Maisie Knew, The Secret Agent,* and *Amerika,* that display ambiguous events and furtive characters. Gorey would not be the right illustrator for Jane Austen; he could have
done Emily Dickinson up proper.

Gorey left New York in 1986, his regular attendance at Balanchine's New
York City Ballet now at an end.[1] In an interview conducted by Clifford Ross
at Gorey's house on Cape Cod, the artist is at his most insouciant, reminding me at times of Auden's rebuke to a Philip Larkin comment—"Naughty,
naughty." We are told that Manet "ruined" painting and that Picasso is detestable. On the other hand, Gorey loves surrealism, collects postcards of
dead babies and "ravishingly beautiful crime scenes." His house is filled with
little animals, finials, "an occasional driftwood," and "lots of iron utensils."
He adores Flaubert, reads him "over and over again, albeit with a good deal
of boredom." His relation to fiction is strictly an occasional one: "I haven't
read a novel for a long time. Actually I did read one. I didn't like it." He
swoons over the painter Francis Bacon but notes that "no matter how horri-
fying anything is, or how interesting, sooner or later it's just so much wallpaper on the wall." He should know: we are reminded of all that splendid
wallpaper in his own drawings of interiors. At the end of the interview he
speaks up for the kind of art that "is just sort of lukewarm." "Blessed are the
nonchalant," he declares, then adds, "Well, the kinds of things I'm attracted
to are nonchalant."

All very much the pronouncements of a coterie artist, not about to lay his
head on the line or his heart on his sleeve. I imagine him as the sort of per-

---

1. Wilkin suggests there may be a connection between Gorey's art and Balanchine's ballets,
of which Gorey saw so many so often. The "taut economies of Gorey's compositions, the expressive gestures of his figures, and his way of arranging them within the confines of the
definite rectangles of his drawings" have their analogue in Balanchine's art.

son you couldn't talk to without saying something gauche or self-betraying, and I don't plan to have a conversation with him. Karen Wilkin is astute in naming some of his ancestors: Lear and Lewis Carroll, of course, along with Beardsley, Max Ernst, and Paul Klee. But also Buster Keaton, the "Lucia" books of E. F. Benson, and—in an excellent thought on Wilkin's part—the novels of Ivy Compton-Burnett, coterie writer par excellence. I am grateful for Wilkin's directing my attention to many Gorey products I didn't know about, especially his sets and costume designs for a performance of Gilbert and Sullivan's *Mikado*. She describes the designs (three of them reproduced here) astutely:

> His vision of the town and population of Titipu is a delicately balanced gallimaufry of, among other things, traditional Japanese prints, turn-of-the-century postcards of English "watering places," the posters of Henri de Toulouse-Lautrec and a famous photograph of Lautrec himself in Japanese costume.

"An amalgam of British good taste and Kurasawa," she calls Gorey's costumes for the work, and she concludes her essay with a sympathetic and definitive summary of the virtues of this extraordinary artist by noting, with regard to Mr. Earbrass the novelist, "There is no equivalent Gorey-artist figure." Nevertheless, for this "connoisseur of the arcane and the obsolete":

> Pictures are probably more crucial than words to our sense of what Gorey is about. Important as his love of language, his carefully shaped sentences, and his tight rhymes may be to the character of his entrancing books, it is Gorey's imagery that etches itself in the memory, like an album of fading photographs from a vanished era, a series of isolated moments from a world at once unsettling, even baffling, but at the same time immensely appealing and wholly convincing.

Hudson Review, Spring 1997

Music, Teaching, and Teachers

THE autobiographical inclination can usually be detected, for better or worse, in anything I write. But it stands front and center in the writings that make up this final section, each piece an instance of what, in an earlier essay, I called Ear Training. Although I've spent most of my life playing the piano, singing, and listening to music—classical, jazz, popular—I seem to have been chary of writing about it. As often, the arrival of someone else's big book (James Parakilas's on the piano, Richard Sudhalter's on American jazz) provided the focus for reflection. The very short tribute to some favorite hymns is wholly inadequate to the experience of playing and singing them.

Teaching, on the other hand, I've done a lot of and written a lot about, especially in my memoir, *English Papers*. "The Classroom in Literature" is a short tour of what some good writers had to say about someone up there behind the desk going on about something. "Teaching Shakespeare" is a look at my own classroom performance on the podium. The book concludes, in "Amherst English," with two portraits of teachers whose examples meant everything to me.

Keyboard Reflections

THE surprise delight of last spring for me was the appearance of a 461-page treasure book containing all I ever didn't know about the piano. I began piano lessons just before turning age five, continuing up through high school, and during those years became a performer and accompanist in countless guises. But I was never interested in the physical instrument itself, never worried like a fiddle player about strings breaking, or an oboist whose double reed has suddenly gone bad; nor did I think at all about the piano as a cultural and historical phenomenon. I was busy getting the job done, as it were, and while a good sight reader of piano music, I never learned to "read" the piano. So this book has prompted some autobiographical reflections.

Although Arthur Loesser's classic of the 1950s, *Men, Women and Pianos,* is a sizeable compendium of information, mainly historical and cultural, *Piano Roles* is richly illustrated as well, with sixty-five color and one hundred forty-two black-and-white examples, cleverly chosen. And although Loesser's one-man survey provides agreeable continuity of viewpoint, this James Parakilas-cum-associates volume makes use of various scholarly and technical expertise in the writings of historians, musicologists, and musical curators, united by their interest in the instrument whose three hundredth anniversary is being celebrated. You can read about the piano's invention; its design and marketing; the difference it made to the great musical period of 1770–1820; the fierce exertions of its performers—especially Czerny and Liszt; and its more recent use in Hollywood and in jazz. There are shorter takes and sidebars on matters such as the piano tuner; silent movies with piano accompaniment; its significance as a cultural monitor in Jane Austen's novels; and, apropos of the metronome and piano stool, as occasion for

Piano Roles: Three Hundred Years of Life with the Piano, by James Parakilas and others. New Haven: Yale University Press, 1999.

"creative" (certainly breathless) excursions by the Russian writer Marina Tsvetaeva.

The guiding spirit behind the whole enterprise is Mr. Parakilas, a professor of music at Bates College, himself an accomplished pianist as well as a music man with a keen literary sense. (It is he who writes the pages on Jane Austen.) Parakilas is most generous in his acknowledgments of the "group" nature of "Piano 300," the project from which this book resulted. He gives thanks to his fourteen co-contributors and also acknowledges institutions including the Smithsonian, Bates College, and Yale University Press, which have cooperated in making this beautiful and surprisingly affordable volume. Parakilas, however, is the major writer, and he names in his introduction the motive behind *Piano Roles:*

> The theme of this cultural history of the piano is that the piano has always exhibited a unique power to act as a cultural go-between, as a medium through which social spheres that stood in opposition to each other could nonetheless nourish each other.

The piano's "voice," he explains, has a "gift for impersonating other musical natures":

> Although its sound comes from the decaying notes of hammered strings, it impersonates the sustained singing of the human voice. With a single set of strings, it evokes the harmony of a choir, the textural richness of an orchestra, and the rhythmic impetus of a dance band, . . . Played by itself, it puts whole worlds of musical sound at the fingertips of one player. Joining other instruments and voices, it supplies whatever they need to make their illusion complete.

One sees, then, why this introduction begins with reference to a 1915 Irving Berlin musical that featured the song "I Love a Piano" ("I love to stop right / beside an Upright, / Or a high toned Baby Grand"), in which the singer and attendant chorus girls were accompanied by six pianists on six pianos and a giant keyboard that reached across the stage. The show was before my time, nor have I seen the movie *King of Jazz*, in which the Paul Whiteman Orchestra is stationed atop a giant piano, at the massive keyboard of which sit five musicians, in tails, doing whatever they're pretending to do. (A marvelous full-page photograph of this event provides the lead-in to *Piano Roles*.) It's a long way back to Bartolomeo Cristofori, who built the first instrument at the turn of the eighteenth century.

The piano's expressive powers compared to the harpsichord's were greater in that—according to an article of 1711 on the Cristofori piano by its publicist, Scipione Maffei—it could imitate such effects as the orchestra or singers in a chorus while transporting (in Parakilas's words) "the rhetoric and drama of music making in the opera house or church into the private chamber." Such power was what Maffei claimed for the piano, and the harpsichord accordingly lost ground over the century, although it hung on to its position in the orchestra (Haydn switched from harpsichord to piano in 1792). The major press-man and establisher of a piano-centered musical culture was Muzio Clementi, who moved in 1766, at age fourteen, from Rome to England, and was taken up by a rich Englishman, Peter Beckford, at whose Dorset estate Clementi practiced eight hours a day and turned himself into a virtuoso. He went on to perform in European capitals, wrote many sonatas for piano students, and invested in piano manufacturing and music publishing firms. He could play passages—in thirds, sixths, and octaves—at a speed available to no one else, earning the opprobrium of Mozart, who said that Clementi "doesn't have a Kreutzer's worth of feeling or taste—in other words a mere machine." But Clementi's *Introduction to the Art of Playing on the Piano Forte* (1801) was extremely influential and contained original and transcribed music from composers including Bach, Corelli, and Haydn. Music journals sprang up concurrently, and by 1820 there were three of them in England, devoted especially to publicizing Clementi company publications. At age seventy-eight he brought out the first of a series of "keepsake" albums with facsimiles of musical handwriting from the likes of Haydn, Mozart, Beethoven, Weber, and Clementi himself, thus contributing to the "composer worship" that would only increase in intensity over the century.

My impression is that, as with English studies, academic musicologists have become increasingly concerned—as this book's emphasis suggests—with "cultural" matters: such as where the piano was played and by whom (man or woman) and for what sort of audience; or what the particular historical factors were that conspired to produce or further a certain kind of musical style. A recent conference of Haydn scholars, held at my college, gave on the whole much more attention to circumstances of performance than to the aesthetic qualities of the works performed. (Similarly, if you write about Pope's poetry these days you're probably not likely to be analyzing or judging rhetorical effects from one couplet to the next, but talking rather about Pope's relation to The Body or to Gender.) So I was particularly interested in and gratified by what seemed to me the best piece of musical criticism in the book, Gretchen A. Wheelock's (herself a Haydn scholar) "The Classical Repertory Revisited: Instruments, Players and Style." In this essay, while keeping an always sharp eye on the gradual supplanting of harpsichord by piano (coming into its full glory with Beethoven), Wheelock surveys keyboard piano writing by Haydn, Mozart, and Beethoven. An example of her way of combining critical description of the individual piece with situating it in the culture, comes as she discusses Haydn's "big" E-flat Major Sonata, Hob. xvi: 52, which she distinguishes from his earlier sonatas—though she notes an earlier "departure" from harpsichord writing in the 1771 C Minor Sonata with its "Sturm und Drang" qualities:

> The markedly different profile [of the E-flat Sonata] is obvious from the grand French-overture-style chords of the opening to the rousing dash of the Presto's final close. This is a fully theatrical work, public in style if not in performance venue, and its fistfuls of notes don't bring delicate hands to mind.

Or she distinguishes among some of Mozart's finest piano concerti:

> Ranging from such works as the C Major Concerto, K. 467, which echoes the pacing and diction of buffo intrigues in *Le Nozze di Figaro,* to the ominous world of *Don Giovanni,* previewed in the opening movement of the D Minor Concerto K. 466, Mozart's handling of both theatrical and intimate gestures is wondrously matched to the versatile persona of the piano and its relation to the varying textures and timbres of orchestral voices. Whereas the opening movement of the A Major Concerto, K. 488, highlights the suave vocal capacity of the piano, that of the C Major Concerto, K. 503, displays the instrument at its most majestic in the confident march of fully "orchestrated" chords and dazzling passagework.

She points out, later on, the difference between Beethoven's use of the damper pedal in middle period works like the "Moonlight" and "Waldstein" sonatas, and its presence in the opening bars (illustrated with a full page) of the adagio section to the A-flat Sonata, op. 110. This is criticism that helps us hear more of what we have already sensed in the music.

At the other end of the book (and skipping over completely its nineteenth-century sections on piano virtuosity, especially Liszt's), we have fascinating excursions on the piano in Hollywood film, on different ways of aggressively, even violently making it new (Jerry Lee Lewis grinding it out while standing atop the upright), and on modernist examples of avant-garde exploitations of the instrument in Henry Cowell, Charles Ives, John Cage, George Crumb. Of special interest to me was a deft, brief survey of the piano in jazz conducted by Mark Tucker, a Duke Ellington scholar and himself a fine jazz pianist. With the aid of excellent pictorial shots, Tucker gives us a look at keyboard greats from Jelly Roll Morton to Cecil Taylor, by way of suggesting how pianists in jazz are "middle" men who "can step forward into the spotlight to shine as soloists or stay in the background to join bass and drums in rhythm section chores." He imagines a distinct personality for jazz pianists, "authority figures, sages, intellectuals, teachers, control freaks," sometimes with a "formal, bookish air" and often called "professor," as they assume professor-like roles (Lennie Tristano, Billy Taylor). Tucker even provides a list of "great bespectacled pianists" whose willingness to look vulnerable suggests "an arduous process of acquiring knowledge, of paying dues, but also a certain vulnerability." This is musical portraiture of a high order.

> Softly, in the dusk, a woman is singing to me;
> Taking me back down the vista of years, till I see
> A child, sitting, under the piano, in the boom of the tingling strings
> And pressing the small, poised feet of a mother who smiles as she sings.

I was glad to see that Parakilas honors D. H. Lawrence's poem as giving beautiful voice to, among other things, "the glamour of childish days" for Lawrence and others, stirred up by hearing the instrument so central to the lives of those who studied or listened to it. *Piano Roles* is appropriately and charmingly dedicated jointly, by sixteen of its contributors and associates, to the sixteen piano teachers "who gave us our first piano lessons." Except for one "Mr. Meyers," they appear to be women, and for most of us I suspect it was our mothers who got us started. My own took me to a Mr. Donald Grey, one of the few male teachers in our area, and he sat me down in September of 1937 in a basement studio room in Binghamton's Arlington Hotel and talked to me about what study of the piano with him would involve. He provided a book, the introductory one in the Mason-Hammond series for piano beginners, then helped me get comfortable around middle C, from which the first easy and soon more difficult pieces to come would receive their bearings. This book's opening challenge, a little excursion featuring middle C and its ascending neighbors D and E, came equipped with unforgettable lyrics: "Loudly brays the donkey / As he goes to hay; / Singing on the wrong key, / In his favorite way." From there it was on to the next, a similarly focused piece about falling leaves: "Red, gold, brown [E, D, C], Flutt'ring down / Leaves are dropping, never stopping, Down, down, down" [E, D, C].

All I remember saying that afternoon was something to the effect of wondering how I would ever be able to play this instrument, which, though only an upright, seemed blackly huge to a four-year-old. At home there was an even larger object, a Steinway studio grand my mother had purchased with $1,500 of her young woman's savings. A capable pianist herself (she supervised music in the public schools of Johnson City, New York), she was much in demand to accompany singing at various events or conduct bits of musical entertainment. She was clear that it would not do for her to become my official teacher, but from the outset she acted as goad to and sustainer of my keyboard efforts, indeed my best critic as—on a daily basis—she would call in from the kitchen, "Play that section again, HANDS ALONE" This is really all the advice any young student needs, and I flourished under it with weekly lessons throughout the year (a couple of vacation weeks off in summer) and progressed from "Loudly Brays the Donkey" to playable bits from Mozart and Haydn.

Don Grey worked on my technique, taught me how to play three notes against two (a valuable skill), and avoided all "cute" pieces that other teachers assigned to lure reluctant or flagging pupils. He stuck to the classical canon and it wasn't too long before I was navigating Chopin's "Raindrop" prelude, refingered for my inadequate reach. Soon I was presumably delighting all sorts of local gatherings from Hadassah to University Women's Club to the Johnson City chapter of Kiwanis, along with seizing the innumerable opportunities for display afforded by school and church. In yearly contests (tournaments, we called them) one presented a program of memorized selections to be judged by some outside authority. There were festivals and recitals and endless ways in which a competent pianist could help out the community, such as, in my case, accompanying the Czech Sokolovna drill team, or doing an intermission number at YM or YWCA dances, the latter an especially dreary chore, even as it held out the remote possibility of meeting there a Young Christian Woman.[1]

---

1. Sure-fire applause-getters on these occasions were Debussy's "Claire de Lune" and de Falla's "Ritual Fire Dance." I suppose you could do worse, and it has since been done, surely.

World War II summoned my teacher to its service, and I was unmoored until a friend of the family's took me, aged eleven, to play for Ethel Newcomb. Miss Newcomb had been a student of Theodor Leschetizky's, among whose many pupils were numbered, most famously, Artur Schnabel. (Parakilas has a couple of good pages on Leschetizky as master teacher.) Newcomb agreed to take me on for a biweekly or monthly lesson at ten dollars per, an immense sum, so it seemed. These were vivid experiences, consisting mainly of anecdotal reflection by Miss Newcomb (along with servings of shortbread), a forbidding figure who lived in an old farmhouse in Whitney Point, New York. Sessions would last two hours or more (once stretching to six), and in her piano room with its two enormous Steinways I was introduced to the piano concerto, first Mozart's D Minor K. 466, then Beethoven's Third in C Minor. Miss Newcomb played the orchestral part on the other grand and insisted that I respect the score and its markings: "For ten cents you've got it all down there," she would insist. And she provided stories of the greats—Schnabel, Ossip Gabrilowitch, Vladimir de Pachman—that suggested there was something exciting, even romantic, about a musical career.

But such a professional career was not to be mine. I never practiced with the required intensity or for the length of time she recommended (never exceeded two hours a day, and seldom made that). My parents wanted me to be well rounded, and so did I, this condition more likely to be achieved in a liberal arts college than a conservatory. Perhaps the apex of my piano career came in six weeks spent at a rather broken-down music camp in the Catskills, where I discovered, as if by chance, the wonder of classical orchestral music. It was the overture to *Meistersinger* that did it, along with bits from Tchaikovsky's fourth and fifth symphonies. At one of the regular Sunday afternoon concerts I had the dubious honor of playing Henry Cowell's "Aeolian Harp" (it is touched on in *Piano Roles* as an example of 1923's avantgarde), in which one stood to pluck the piano strings while making awkward use of the damper pedal. A freak piece but doubtless amusing to see the young boy straining to reach the strings while standing on tiptoe in front of the keyboard.

The Parakilas book pays some attention to the piano as site of seduction, and in high school and college I put in a lot of service in dance bands under the illusion that there was something irresistible to the opposite sex in my thoughtful expertise. Nothing turned out to be further from the truth, and although I eventually met my life partner while accompanying Gilbert and

Sullivan's *Mikado* (she had the lead role), it was probably my high moral character to which she responded. As for any aspirations to be a performing soloist, I turned into a creditable amateur pianist, devoting myself in graduate school and beyond to learning as much of the repertory—especially the nineteenth-century composers—as I could take in. Here the giving of a recital every few years, attended mainly by loyal and discreet friends, acted as the essential spur. There were enough good moments in these, so I fancy, to justify the time spent practicing and the sickening nervousness that overtook me when the hour approached and it was time to walk out on the stage. Anyone who finds speaking in public an usettling challenge should hire a hall and give a concert, so as to experience something really unnerving, in a different league.

Is there anything to be gleaned from these reflections, stimulated by Parakilas's enlivening book? One of the characters in John Updike's first novel, *The Poorhouse Fair,* has lived into his nineties and is at times convinced he will persist on the earth forever if he carefully treats "each day of life as the day impossible to die on." I like to think that, occupied at the piano bench, I have felt something like such an intimation of immortality, since like nothing else I have known or am likely to know about, the piano represents—presents—the promise of happiness. Parakilas quotes from an inspiring article that appeared in 1910 in *Musical America,* a magazine my mother subscribed to: "One's piano is a kind of magic mirror which is capable of reflecting to one the whole musical world from classic times to the present, and throughout all lands. It requires only that one put the music on his piano-rack and play it, or, at least play at it." *Only* do that, and things will come out right, even help one resist the temptation to dwell too much on what has been. Perhaps if D. H. Lawrence had been fortunate enough to have learned to *play* the piano, not just listen to his mother singing and playing it, he would have avoided the piercing sensations in the final stanza of his poem:

> So now it is vain for the singer to burst into clamour
> With the great black piano appassionato. The glamour
> Of childish days is upon me, my manhood is cast
> Down in the flood of remembrance, I weep like a child for the past.

Hymns in Another Man's Life

THERE is a fine moment in John Irving's novel *A Prayer for Owen Meany* when the funeral service for the narrator's mother concludes with what is called "a real organ-breaker:"

> Crown him with man-y crowns,
> The Lamb up-on the throne;
> Hark! how the heaven-ly anthem drowns
> All mu-sic but its own:
> A-wake, my soul, and sing
> Of him who died for thee,
> And hail him as thy match-less king
> Through all e-ter-nity.

I know it well, number 352 in the *Hymnal of the Protestant Episcopal Church in the United States of America* (1940). I sang it innumerable times in Sunday school and church; indeed, I played it on the organ (innumerable times), accompanying junior or senior choirs at rehearsals where I squirmed with boredom and distaste and wished I were playing basketball or asleep or somewhere out of churchly oppressiveness. Now, forty years and more later, reading the Irving novel, I felt moved and exhilarated by the sudden mention of that old "organ-breaker." For there is truth in what Irving goes on to say: that the nature of hymns is such as to "make us want to repeat them, and repeat them; they are a part of any service, and often the only part of a funeral service that makes us feel everything is acceptable."

I haven't attended church in many years and don't plan on changing my habits, but the 1940 Episcopal hymnal sits right next to our piano, and more than once of an evening—often after eating and drinking with friends—it gets taken down and run through for an hour or so in which we belt out stalwarts such as "The Son of God Goes Forth to War," "Ten Thousand Times

Ten Thousand," "Hail to the Lord's Anointed," "For All the Saints Who from Their Labors Rest," "Ancient of Days, Who Sittest Throned in Glory," and—most all-purpose of them all—"Holy, Holy, Holy! Lord God Almighty." By my count there are fifty or sixty additional hymns in this book that are matchless, sometimes both musically and verbally.

In his short reminiscence, "Hymns in a Man's Life," D. H. Lawrence recalls a "rather banal Nonconformist hymn" of his childhood that contained the lines "O Galilee, sweet Galilee, / Where Jesus loved so much to be," and he noted that "To me the word Galilee has a wonderful sound. The Lake of Galilee! I don't want to know where it is. I never want to go to Palestine. Galilee is one of those lovely, glamorous worlds not places, that exist in the golden haze of a child's half-formed imagination." And, Lawrence insists, "in my man's imagination it is just the same." I would make the same claim, even down to that same word, since one of the lovely, glamorous worlds I still carry about with me is evoked in the hymn that begins "Jesus calls us; o'er the tumult," and the second verse says about the calling, "As of old, St. Andrew heard. it / By the Gal-i-le-an lake." The Galilean lake was an exciting place to hear about, just as was, more alliteratively and ominously, the "Cross-crowned Calvary" of the hymn that begins "In the hour of trial, Jesus plead for me."

I don't know the hymns Lawrence quotes from his Congregational upbringing, and I can't believe they're as good as my favorite Episcopalian ones, almost all of which were composed by Englishmen in the mid and latter parts of the nineteenth century. The foremost musical contributor (for me the music is a shade more important than the words in generating the hymn's power) is John B. Dykes, who is responsible not only for "Holy, Holy, Holy!" but "Eternal Father, Strong to Save" (the "sailor's hymn"), "The King of Love My Shepherd Is," and numerous other beauties. Then there is Sir Arthur Seymour Sullivan, partner of Gilbert, who provided the music to such Easter hymns as "Come, Ye Faithful, Raise the Strain," "Alleluia, Alleluia, Hearts and Voices Heav'nward Raise," and "'Welcome Happy Morning!' Age to Age Shall Say." Sullivan also wrote the music to "Golden Harps Are Sounding," an extravagant hymn that, perhaps because of its overripe language and harmonies, hardly ever got sung in our church. One the other hand "Onward Christian Soldiers" (again, music by Sullivan) was heard all too frequently, especially in Sunday school. And I remember disliking most of the hymns from the "missions" section of the book which admonished us to "Remember all the people who live in far-off lands." Evidently I didn't want to do that ("Some work in sultry forests / Where apes swing to and fro" just reminded me of Tarzan), preferring to concentrate on more passionately worded supplications such as "O Lamb of God, still keep me near to the wounded side."

Philip Larkin's poem "Church Going" ends by saying that churches will never be obsolete (never "go") because they speak to "a hunger in ourselves to be more serious." Perhaps that's what hymns do, by saying what we like now to think we once were or could have been, had we been more . . . serious. What to do with words and music woven into the fiber of one's being?

> Be-neath the cross of Je-sus I fain would take my stand,
> The sha-dow of a migh-ty rock With-in a wea-ry land
> A home with-in the wil-der-ness, A rest up-on the way,
> From the burn-ing of the noon-tide heat, And the burden of the day.

The only thing to do is sing it, all verses, then repeat it, for life will never be more acceptable than in such a shape.

All That Jazz

As THE millennium nears, writers about American jazz have been especially busy surveying the terrain of eight decades and more, describing and
evaluating yet again the major achievements as well as unearthing the minor,
agreeable talents that have slipped into obscurity. Two years ago Ted Gioia,
in *The History of Jazz*, gave us a compact, well-written, and well-selected account—in four hundred pages—of jazz from New Orleans to the present.
Now the able Gary Giddins, music critic for many years on the *Village Voice*,
and Richard Sudhalter, coauthor of a biography of Bix Beiderbecke, have
produced hefty tomes combining the fruits of far-ranging intelligent listening with social and historical acuity. Mr. Sudhalter's book has as well the
virtue of frequent musical illustrations that put in front of our eyes and ears
a particular instrumental solo or comparison of solos. This, of course, has
the good effect of sending one to the turntable and disc player by way of con-
firmation. So my only regret was at the size of my record collection, a good
one, but hardly equipped to produce everything alluded to here. Accepting
that limitation along with the fact that there is far too much in Giddins and
Sudhalter to take adequate account of, I fell back on Wordsworth's lines from
"Tintern Abbey" and read the books "not only with the sense / Of present
pleasure, but with pleasing thoughts / That in this moment there is life and
food / For future years."

The two jazz critics from this century's latter half with whom Giddins and
Sudhalter may be compared are Whitney Balliett and Gunther Schuller. Or
at least they figure as indispensable analysts of hot music who have been of

Visions of Jazz: The First Century, by Gary Giddins. New York: Oxford University Press,
1998. *Lost Chords: White Musicians and Their Contributions to Jazz, 1915–1945*, by Richard Sudhalter. New York: Oxford University Press, 1999. Much credit is due Sheldon Meyer of Oxford
for his making the press a pioneer in the field of writing on jazz. (Oxford has published, in addition to Giddins and Sudhalter, Ted Gioia, Gunther Schuller, and James Lincoln Collier.)

much listening use to me and, I presume, to other literary types who listen to jazz. Balliett's slew of books, appearing over the past forty years, most of them made up of his pieces in *The New Yorker,* contain countless artful descriptions of (as one of his titles has it) "The Sound of Surprise"—of the soloists and solos jazz has produced. If you want the verbal equivalent of a Sid Catlett drum break, or a cornet solo by Beiderbecke or Buck Clayton, Balliett is your man. (Interestingly, he is not once alluded to by Giddins, who as a journalist himself may feel slightly competitive.) Gunther Schuller's two books, *Early Jazz* (1968) and *The Swing Era* (1989) are, especially the latter, encyclopedic in the musicians, groups, and compositions treated; also systematic in their musical and musicological "readings" of particular pieces and sequences. Both Giddins and Sudhalter—especially the latter—frequently refer to Schuller's work, Sudhalter often by way of intelligent disagreement. But their approaches to jazz share one central agreement: that of putting the emphasis on listening, in the faith that language about what is heard, if strenuously and delicately used, can tell us much about the musical performance.

Gary Giddins is a jaunty writer, not averse to humor by way of putting irony in his style. "As jazz saunters past its one hundredth anniversary," he says in the introduction to *Visions of Jazz,* the music has a favorable press and is good at attracting Big Money to subsidize festivals, partly by way of a reaction to the more dangerous rock. At the same time it isn't producing many household names. Giddins quotes himself in an earlier book from 1985: "Few educated Americans can name even five jazz musicians under the age of forty." (He suggests that the average listener will blank out after mentioning Wynton Marsalis and perhaps a couple of others.) Whereas in 1960, Giddins notes "the roll of active musicians under the age of forty" included Miles Davis, Sonny Rollins, John Coltrane, Stan Getz, Charles Mingus, Sarah Vaughan, and about twenty-five other well-known names. And indeed the latter stretches of Giddins's book, containing many names from the last couple of decades, marked unknown territory for this listener, an out-of-date moldy fig/swing era/early bop amalgam whose tastes formed themselves in the late 1940s.

Giddins's taste is admirably catholic, and he delights in making the best case for his individual subjects, admiring strengths rather than deploring weaknesses. Although in his introduction he disclaims pretensions to writing a history of jazz, and mentions all the significant figures he hasn't discussed (his book is in fact a compendium of articles and reviews, arranged roughly chronologically), the individual sections on Jelly Roll Morton, Armstrong, Ellington (in three parts), Coleman Hawkins, Pee Wee Russell, Chick Webb, Dizzy Gillespie, Charlie Parker, and many others, are substantial enough exercises in life-and-works appreciation to count as a serious introduction to the music. And when he addresses himself to an extended piece of analysis, the results are impressive, perhaps the showcase here being a transcription and description of Parker's amazing solo on "Koko" (1945). That solo takes a little over four pages to transcribe, a much more leisurely effect than is made by the music itself, about which Giddins says:

> The tempo is brutally fast ($\downarrow$ = 300–310), but despite the speed and the general impression of volatility, Parker colors his solo with ingenious conceits, such as the clanging riff in measures five to eight; the dramatic, arpeggiated figure in bars thirty-three to thirty-four; the casual reference to the piccolo obbligato from "High Society" and its development at the outset of the second chorus (bars sixty-five to seventy) . . .

And on in this manner, while the reader tries to keep track, breathlessly following along. Then the summation:

> Note, too, the extended rests, the unexpected places where phrases begin and end, and the range of the solo, which climbs to high G . . . down to an E-flat below middle C. . . . Parker's sound is fat and sensuous yet jagged and hard, utterly unlike the cultivated approach of his great predecessors on alto, Johnny Hodges and Benny Carter.

Bernard Shaw once mocked the pedantry of music critics who "parsed" their subject as comparable literary pedant might have parsed Shakespeare's "To Be or Not to Be." But in fact Giddins's directings and pointings, if we take the time to follow them as we listen to the solo, get at what's indeed there in the music. And compared to the musicological and diagrammatical complexities of many of Gunther Schuller's illustrations, this one on "Koko" is a piece of cake.

In addition, Giddins has chapters on figures who don't spring to mind in our visions of jazz. There is a fine appreciation of Irving Berlin, including admiring paragraphs on *Annie Get Your Gun*, Berlin at his very best in "purebred ballads" like "They Say It's Wonderful" and "I Got Lost in His Arms" (the latter an especially beautiful and underrated number), or "remarkable sunny soliloquies" like "You Can't Get a Man with a Gun" and "I Got the Sun in the Morning." I was pleased also to be reintroduced to someone I haven't listened to since, delightedly, I did so in high school days: Spike Jones and his City Slickers, who gave us such immortal tracks as "Hawaiian War Chant" and "The Glow Worm," in which "a battery of percussive proxies and vocal sounds" managed to portray "the entire panoply of bodily functions." As Giddins truly puts it: "Like no other musician before or since, Spike had the upper and lower digestive tracts covered." Almost invariably in this book, when I had in my ears the musical number to which Giddins is referring, I found my own sense confirmed, a major exception occurring when he speaks about what seems to me Fletcher Henderson's greatest singlerecording, "The Stampede" (1926), and calls it—in some inexplicable failure of hearing—"starchy and unswinging."

Richard Sudhalter's book, the product of exhaustive, prolonged research and listening (the richly informed footnotes themselves occupy nearly one hundred pages), has a thesis, or at least an overriding motive driving it; namely, that in recognizing the central contribution made by black American musicians to the history of jazz—especially when the recognizing is done under a multicultural aegis—the contributions of white American musicians have been slighted. In his introduction he describes the distortion thus:

> Applied to jazz history, such thinking has spawned a view of early white efforts as musically insignificant and—particularly in the 1920s and '30s—vastly overpublicized. Jazz, says the now accepted canon, is black; there have been no white innovators, few white soloists of real distinction; the best white musicians (with an exception or two) were only dilute copies of black originals, and in any case exerted lasting influence only on other white musicians.

Sudhalter's efforts are made in the conviction that jazz music "may not be so much a black American experience as an *American* experience, with various racial and ethnic groups playing indispensable and interlocking roles." So that it was natural, rather than surprising, for Louis Armstrong to love Bunny Berigan's trumpet or Bobby Hackett's cornet playing, or the sound of Jack Teagarden's trombone; it was unsurprising that Coleman Hawkins's favorite band was Glen Gray's Casa Loma Orchestra, unsurprising that white musicians like Beiderbecke, Adrian Rollini, Miff Mole, Frank Trumbauer, Dave Tough, Bud Freeman, Pee Wee Russell, and many others were held in more than respect by black jazz musicians. The tale Sudhalter sets out to tell—and tell it he does, brilliantly—is of jazz as "a picaresque tale of cooperation, mutual admiration, cross-fertilization; comings-together and driftings-apart, all *despite,* rather than because of, the segregation of the larger society."

Over the long stretch of pages, Sudhalter artfully combines biography and historical-social commentary with enthusiastic, informed treatments of the different musicians, small combos, and larger New Orleans and swing bands, from early groups like the Original Dixieland Jazz Band (ODJB) and the New Orleans Rhythm Kings (NORK), up to the various notable bands of Artie Shaw in the late 1930s and beyond. (Sudhalter has promised a further volume dealing with forties and post-forties jazz.) His eclecticism shows itself in the conviction that in the "short rapid evolution of jazz, new styles and approaches seem to supplement, rather than supplant their predecessors." I found this particularly enlightening, since it got me listening to sides I'd forgotten I owned, to the "New York"-based style of the late 1920s and beyond, first as led by the entrepreneurial trumpet player Red Nichols, and his frequent sidekick Miff Mole—before the arrival of Teagarden, the hottest of white trombonists. Red Nichols and his Five Pennies, Miff Mole and his Little Molers (splendid name for a band!), and The Charleston Chasers, were recording groups on which can be heard musicians who haven't had their due—pianists such as Arthur Schutt and Lennie Hayton; the tenor sax man and arranger Fud Livingston; the guitar virtuoso Dick McDonough; Jimmy Dorsey, a capable alto sax "hot" man before he became a bandleader; Russell on clarinet; the drummer Vic Berton; Eddie Lang and Joe Venuti on guitar and violin respectively. One of the greatest delights of these records is the performance of Adrian Rollini on bass sax, first in the California Ramblers band of the middle 1920s, then with Mole and Nichols, and on many sides with Beiderbecke's small groups. Adrian Rollini managed, in his firm, swinging fullness, to make the unwieldy bass sax sound quite different from the "dyspeptic bullfrog" noises that lesser players produced. Rollini also experimented with the Couesnophone, a Paris product that was "a kind of harmonica in the shape of a toy saxophone." Rollini played solos on this instrument, dubbed the "goofus," in various Ramblers performances. Part of what makes Sudhalter fun to read is his willingness to describe the virtues and limitations of instruments we don't think too much about—like the bass and C-melody saxophone (the latter as played by Trumbauer), or the xylophone-marimba and the vibraphone, as played by Red Norvo. There is a chapter devoted to guitars and guitarists. Throughout the book Sudhalter keeps us in touch with the physical realities of instrumental performance and does so with relish.

Although it's a simplification, New York white jazz, in the persons of Nichols, Mole, Rollini, and their cohorts, had a somewhat angular quality, featuring solos that were tightly organized and punched out in staccato lines. Something analogous can be heard in the Bob Crosby band of the 1930s, which Sudhalter makes a strong case for as producing an ensemble "most certainly contrapuntal, wholly linear, its texture dependent on the melodic parity of its components." There is a different, cooler sound to such music than the "hot" brilliance of Armstrong, Hawkins, and other great black soloists. But as Sudhalter reminds us, no "period" style was there for long—new approaches supplemented, but didn't supplant, older ones. In his recording dates Nichols made excellent use of new musicians, especially ones arriving from Chicago—Goodman, Bud Freeman, Gene Krupa, the Teagardens, Glenn Miller, and others—who turn up on these dates and make for original sounds, shifting styles. The point may be, as in the words of one musician quoted here, to keep out of one another's way while occasionally straying into that way.

Sudhalter's assiduity in making comparative distinctions among solos and soloists is exemplary, as when he provides three different choruses by the tenor sax man Bud Freeman of "China Boy" (1928, 1939, 1957), in order to show the "refinement process" they demonstrate. His remarks about the process are detailed and doubtless accurate; I say "doubtless" because I own none of these recordings of "China Boy," and to follow the illustrated solo by hearing it in one's head or playing it on the piano is difficult if not impossible to do. (I did much better with an illustrated comparison of Trumbauer's and Beiderbecke's solos on the 1929 Whiteman recording of the tune, familiar to me.) This is just to say that all you need to use Sudhalter's material to the full is more time and more records: his is a book at the furthest extreme from something to be read and digested "all at once." Sometimes I can't share his high enthusiasm for an artist: he especially loves Bud Freeman's playing (the chapter on Freeman ends with Sudhalter paying him a visit when he was near death), calling his "one of the three significant tenor styles of the 1930s" (along with Hawkins's and Lester Young's). I've listened to enough Freeman (and heard him in person) to be bothered by what sounds to these ears like frequently out-of-tune playing; but Sudhalter admits that opinion about Freeman tends to be polarized.

The heart of the book for me is the chapter titled "Bix Beiderbecke and His Friends," in which the great man's career is reviewed, with abundant musical examples, by way of bringing out what Sudhalter calls the "inner voice" so strongly and unmistakably heard in the cornetist's recordings with the Jean Goldkette Orchestra, with Trumbauer and other pickup groups, with the Whiteman band. A number of critics, including Sudhalter himself, have written well about Beiderbecke[1] and have, at one point or another, realized that they must move into some sort of verbal poetry to convey the sense of his playing. Here is Otis Ferguson in 1940, addressing himself to this matter of Beiderbecke's "voice":

> Perhaps you will have to hear him a lot, perhaps you won't have any ear for the jazz music that grew up around you and in your time, and so will never hear the voice, almost as if speaking: but there is something in these records that goes beyond a mere instrument or the improviser on it, some unconquerable bright spirit that leaves no slops even in confusion and defeat and darkness gathering; some gallant human thing which is as near to us as it is completely marvelous . . . something, grown in this country out of the Iowa dirt, that didn't die and could not be buried so long as there should be a record left in the world and a turntable to spin it on.

Compelling, sentimental, or both? But Sudhalter, along with quoting these words, goes beyond the "completely marvelous," "unconquerable bright spirit" direction. He is bold enough, for example, to compare Beiderbecke with Armstrong, even the most magnificent of whose solos, he argues, "are emotional monoliths; they make their statements plainly, unequivocally, unalloyed by contrasting or contradictory impulses." Except for perhaps not noting enough how Armstrong's great solos (as in "Struttin' with Some Barbeque") *build* in intensity as one brilliant musical idea and technique leads to another, this statement seems fair and interesting. Beiderbecke's best solos do give us that sense of "contrasting or contradictory impulses" being explored, as a way of "looking *within* every piece of material, regardless of

---

1. Including William H. Youngren, whose excellent "Bix," in part a review of Sudhalter's biography, appeared in *Hudson Review* (Spring 1975), 87–96.

tempo or surface character." Sudhalter extends the comparison, not just to Armstrong but to other great black soloists, by considering Beiderbecke's great solo on "Singin' the Blues" (1927) as touchstone for his peculiar "inner voice":

> The tone is that of a brass-band cornetist—clean, ringing, silvery, every note struck head-on. Colorational devices . . . growls, buzzes, smears, half-valve effects—occur seldom; even vibrato, where present at all, is feather-light, dramatic contrast to its expressive prominence in the work of Armstrong, Bechet, Johnny Dodds and others.

And he proceeds to illustrate and describe the texture and logic of the solo. That Sudhalter is an excellent trumpet player may help make his appreciation of Beiderbecke especially telling, except that he writes with equal ease about sax, trombone, and percussion.

There are a number of informative and fully-packed chapters after the Beiderbecke one, including ones on Bunny Berigan, on Red Norvo and Mildred Bailey, on Bobby Hackett, and a concluding chapter on Jack Teagarden and Pee Wee Russell, two musical geniuses Sudhalter seems to have special affection for, and why not? Since he has deferred 1940s big band music until the subsequent volume, his treatment of later 1930s big bands is confined to Goodman and Artie Shaw. And since the Goodman consists only of an earlier published interview with the King, it's the Shaw chapter that's of particular interest. Sudhalter plays him off against Goodman, comparing their respective solos on "It Had to Be You" but also bringing out their differences as clarinetists and as bandleaders. Shaw's playing, as it developed in the late 1930s, exemplifies what Sudhalter calls "Apollonian ideals"—"logic, structural integrity, melodic balance, harmonic subtlety, introspection, emotional restraint, and great tonal beauty"—and Sudhalter places him in the line of Bix and Trumbauer. He quotes a revealing comment of Shaw's on the difference in attitude toward music between him and Goodman: "To me [said Shaw] listening to Benny talk about the clarinet was like listening to a surgeon getting hung up on a scalpel. He was totally tied up in it, to the exclusion of all else. He'd point at the horn and say, 'This thing will never let you down.'" Shaw found that strange, since for him mastery of the clarinet was "a way to get to something, to realize a greater goal." There is further lively speculation on the difference between the two as leaders: Goodman's band a collection of vivid individuals producing an overall chemistry that was exciting; Shaw's, by contrast, molded by the person of the leader into a unit, with arrangements that emphasized "balance, placement of solos, matters of key, texture, and ensemble density"—ways of voicing each section.

Like the other treatments in this book, the chapter on Artie Shaw sends you back to the recordings with new anticipation and curiosity. It is this activity that is the main fruit of what, in a short epilogue, Sudhalter calls "the vast and sprawling chronicle" he has written. Almost without thinking about it, we assent to his concluding assertions that jazz is "profoundly pluralistic" and that the "blacks invented, whites appropriated" way of thinking is based on "ignorance or willful misreading." In fact, perhaps the best praise of this book is that, in the countless, sometimes bewildering examples of musical performance it considers, we pretty much forget—in our lively engagement with those examples and what Sudhalter does with them—about the overall thesis impelling the project. Instead we have been, without knowing it, under the directive of Armstrong's much-quoted if apocryphal remark to Teagarden, which Sudhalter quotes once more in his introduction: "You an Ofay, I'm a Spade—let's blow."

Hudson Review, Summer 1999

The Classroom in Literature

As a professor of English, I've always been attentive to fictional portraits of life as it goes on in a classroom, elementary or "advanced." The once much talked-of (now no longer) "academic novel" typically confined its treatment to matters of university or departmental skullduggery and sex, figuring that readers would respond to these more than to teachers actually teaching students. On the whole, professors in books seem scarcely more real than they were in campus musicals from the 1930s, in which Dr. Fuddy Duddy is eventually inveigled into the Campus Sweet Shop by Betty Co-ed and her friends, whereupon music is put on the jukebox and Prof. Duddy proceeds to cut a mean rug with a cute chick in saddle shoes and white sox. We never find out whether the experience markedly improves his skills as a teacher. A variant on this sort of self-discovery occurs in more than one short story where the teacher, droning on about Eliot's "The Love Song of J. Alfred Prufrock" to the young ones, suddenly realizes that his own life is passionless, that indeed he *is* Prufrock. Anything can happen after that.

Since, as Tolstoy wrote, happy families resemble one another but each unhappy family is unhappy in its own way, happy schoolrooms have had little interest for novelists. We remember the chapter in Dickens's *Hard Times* that begins with the Schoolmaster, Thomas Gradgrind, berating Sissy Jupe for her inability to define a horse. The classmate who is able to do so ("Quadruped, Graminivorous, Forty teeth, namely twenty-four grinders, four eye-teeth, and twelve incisors") is named Bitzer, a boy with "cold eyes and a skin that looked as though, if he were cut, he would bleed white." Nothing double-minded in Dickens's attitude toward the classroom, one presided over by adults named Gradgrind, M'Choakumchild, supported by the "Bully of humility," Mr. Bounderby, all of them dedicated to maiming and distorting the "robber Fancy" that lurks within poor children. Dickens's caricature is brilliant and memorable (even if "unfair"), not the least for its satiric thrust.

Without satire, the picture of oppressed children dully assembled for instruction becomes merely depressing, as it does for D. H. Lawrence's heroine in *The Rainbow*, Ursula Brangwen, when she tries her hand at teaching a class of fifty-five boys and girls: "There were so many, that they were not children. They were a squadron . . . a collective inhuman thing," and she finds that words like "prison" and "brutal" are the right ones for her classroom. So, desperately caning one recalcitrant boy, she becomes "hard and impersonal, almost avengeful on herself as on them." The only positive breath of life in Lawrence's portrayal of education occurs when Ursula lets the pupils get their sums wrong, tells them stories instead of making them learn history and dates, neglects grammar, and gives them lines from a Wordsworth "Lucy" poem ("She shall be sportive as a fawn / That wild with glee across the lawn, / Or up the mountain springs"). Not "school" but "playing at school," with flowers and birds and all that lovely nature outside the classroom. Ursula knows she will never be a success as an elementary school teacher.

Nor will Joyce's Stephen Dedalus in *Ulysses*, who has even less luck with his dispirited attempt to teach history to the boys at Dalkey, mainly because his own head is full of self- recrimination and apocalyptic excess ("I hear the ruin of all space, shattered glass and toppling masonry"). He is moved to pity for and identification with an unhappy lad named Cyril Sargent, who brings him a book of "Sums" that Stephen's superior, Mr. Deasy, has made the boy copy out. Sargent is "ugly and futile: lean neck and tangled hair," yet "some one had loved him, borne him in her arms and in her heart." As Sargent works out one of the sums, Stephen looks on with something like sympathy while rising to a lyrically alliterative silent pronouncement: "Secrets, silent, stony sit in the dark palaces of both our hearts: secrets weary of their tyranny; tyrants willing to be dethroned." So the classroom becomes just one more place for Stephen to compose a romantic poem about the depth and mystery of the human soul. Like Ursula Brangwen, he's not destined for long to be employed by any school system.

It fell to Evelyn Waugh to give the pathetic/lyrical sadness of Lawrence's and Joyce's classrooms a much needed kick from behind. In *Decline and Fall*, a hapless young man named (haplessly) Paul Pennyfeather, expelled from Oxford, takes a job as master in a wholly improbable public school in Wales called Llanabba Castle. Panic-stricken his first day on duty, Paul asks another master, "But what am I to do with them" and receives the sensible answer, "Oh, I wouldn't try to *teach* them anything; not just yet, anyway. Just keep them quiet." "Dumb with terror," Paul enters the room where ten boys sit, hands folded. Each of them in response to Paul's "Good morning" answers "Good morning, sir," until Paul tells one of them to shut up. The silenced boy begins to cry (he's of Welsh blood, the other boys explain), and eventually Paul turns to inquiring their names, to which the first asked replies "Tangent, sir," the second "Tangent, sir," and likewise about the room. After Paul protests that they can't all be Tangent, one boy replies "No sir, *I'm* Tangent. He's just trying to be funny." In desperation Paul asks, "Well, is there any one who isn't Tangent?" to which four or five voices reply "I'm not, sir; I'm not Tangent. I wouldn't be called Tangent, not on the end of a barge pole." The narrator explains, helpfully, "In a few seconds the room had become divided into two parties: those who were Tangent and those who were not." Paul seizes things into his hands by threatening them with death ("I shall very near kill you with this stick") and assigning each to write an essay on "Self-Indulgence," to which will be awarded "a prize of half a crown for the longest . . . irrespective of any possible merit."

Fiction from more recent years that takes the school or college as its scene, mainly stands clear of what happens in those rooms where education does or doesn't occur. Mary McCarthy's *The Groves of Academe*, Randall Jarrell's *Pictures from an Institution*, Kingsley Amis's *Lucky Jim*, have their eyes focused on other institutional and personal matters. John Knowles's popular novel about a New England private school, *A Separate Peace*, was similarly unengaged by teacher-student interaction over the desk. The movie *Dead Poets Society*, a vehicle for Robin Williams's enthusiastic "human" teaching of poetry, came across as sentimental travesty, and not just because the mythical textbook on poetry, which Williams directs his students to rip to pieces, was composed by a mythical Professor Pritchard.

Two exceptions to this general avoidance of the pedagogical scene come to mind: James Guetti's little-known novel *Action* (1972) and Lionel Trilling's often-anthologized short story from the 1940s, "Of This Time, Of That Place." Guetti's novel is about a professor named Hatcher, addicted to various forms of gambling. In one chapter he is preoccupied with placing bets on the horses running at Aqueduct, but first must get through an introductory English class on Keats's "Chapman's Homer" sonnet, "a poem that once, hundreds of classes before, he had liked. Now he did not even admire his own tricky remarks about it." Class begins, Hatcher hands back the bad papers they wrote on the poem, pushes the class around a bit, then takes them through the sonnet with provocative questions just ahead of their conventional answers. Some students do become interested, as does the teacher, surprising himself. When class ends, Hatcher enters the corridor thinking "It might have been a good class. A few years ago he would have been sure of it." This wistful and self-critical ambivalence makes Guetti's take on the classroom distinctive. (It was the note Hollywood left out when they made a movie titled *The Gambler,* in which James Caan, the professor, talked grandly and inspiringly about—not a Keats sonnet, but Dostoevsky.)

Trilling's "Of This Time, Of That Place" is similarly true to the teaching life in imagining ambivalence and complication as marks of an interesting classroom. His story is about teacher Joseph Howe's discovery that one of his students may well be mad: the student, Frederick Tertan, has concluded his strange opening-day composition by writing, "Tertan I am, but what is Tertan? Of this time, of that place, of some parentage, what does it matter?" Stunned by the "splendid confusion of the boy's mind," Howe picks up another student's paper that identifies himself as "Arthur J. Casebeer," provides his parents' names ("My mother is Nina Wimble Casebeer"), and discloses that he was born in St. Louis eighteen years ago and lives there still. To which Howe's response is, "Arthur J. Casebeer, who knew who he was, was less interesting than Tertan but more coherent." The moment when Howe decides that Tertan truly is mad occurs during a finely rendered classroom argument about Ibsen's *Ghosts,* in which different participants state their claims and in which, after Tertan gives a long, confusing disquisition ("Speaking from one sense there is no blame ascribable"), a disgusted football player at the back of the room sinks out of sight in exasperation. As the story develops, questions of sanity and madness, of who the professor thinks he is in relation to this disturbing young man (there is a tradition that claims the Tertan character was based on Allen Ginsberg), as well as larger questions about education and society, are explored within compelling turns of event.

Both James Guetti's classroom scene in *Action* and the one in Lionel Trilling's story are exceptional in conveying some of the surprise, the uncertainty, the mixed feelings about what one has done, which characterize those occasions when the teacher and perhaps some of the students can say "That was a good class" and not be talking cant. But since, as Spinoza put it, all things excellent are as difficult as they are rare, such excellent things are rarely found in fiction.

Boston Sunday Globe, November 14, 1999

Teaching Shakespeare

Last January a *Washington Post* opinion piece by Jonathan Yardley lamented university and college English departments' lack of requirements, noting that at many prestigious institutions today (he named Amherst College as one) students can graduate without having read a single play of Shakespeare's. The column and a subsequent news story in the *New York Times* produced a number of letters from concerned alumni (say it isn't so, please) and a call to me from the chairman of Amherst's board of trustees requesting information on the subject. I told him that yes, it's possible though highly unlikely for an English major at Amherst to graduate without having read a single play of Shakespeare's—that indeed there had been no required course in Shakespeare, even for majors, for thirty years. I refrained from asking if he thought many alumni spent their evenings perusing *Twelfth Night* or *Troilus and Cressida* or *The Winter's Tale*—even good old reliable *Hamlet* or *Macbeth*. But I did say that, for the first time, I was about to give a lecture course on Shakespeare to fifty or so students and that I would apprise him of the results.

In the catalogue, I had rather tersely described the course by saying that we would read selected plays with attention to their "power and beauty as poetic dramas." A colleague in another department jokingly said that the description sounded like me, by which he meant it was provocative to claim that in studying a great writer we should have in view such old-fashioned, not to mention indefinable, qualities as power and beauty. Of course I had meant to be provocative, at least to remind myself—with a lift from Wordsworth—that poetry was an homage "to the grand elementary principle of pleasure" by which, Wordsworth claimed, we lived and moved—perhaps even when we were reading poetic drama for course credit.

In the opening class I told them it was a dangerous venture we were embarking on, since a recent headline in the *Times* announced "At Colleges, Sun Is Setting on Shakespeare." I quoted the president of Dartmouth College warning that "We mustn't deify Shakespeare," and I asked Why mustn't we do that?, since it had been done by larger spirits than ourselves (Samuel Johnson, Charlotte Brontë, Thomas Carlyle, to name three). More recently T. S. Eliot has adduced Shakespeare as a writer with "the most prodigious memory for words" that ever existed. In this course we would read nine plays, from *Midsummer Night's Dream* and *Romeo*, to *Coriolanus* and *The Winter's Tale*—the central sequence consisting of *Othello, Lear,* and *Antony and Cleopatra*. I told them the kind of course it wasn't going to be, the sorts of things I wouldn't be inviting them to do with Shakespeare. For example, they would not be invited to provide large-scale "readings" or interpretations of the plays, nor would they be asked to explain or account for the motives of this or that character. "Plot" was a word they would not hear from my lips. The Elizabethan audience and what it would or wouldn't have responded to; matters of stagecraft and dramaturgy in the playhouses of the times; editorial questions of text and emendation—these and other important matters they could read about in our Riverside edition of Shakespeare, but would come up only incidentally in class. Nor was I a proponent of one or another recent "approaches" to Shakespeare, whether new historicist, psychoanalytical, materialist, feminist, or deconstructive: these they could also read about in the Riverside.

By now we were deep in one of those respectful-if-wary silences I unfailingly produce on opening day. Changing pace, I suggested we consider a particular moment in a play they might not yet have read, *Othello*, where near the close of act 3 the Moor has been persuaded by Iago of Desdemona's guilt. He vows revenge, calls for blood, and in response to Iago's pretense of caution—"Patience, I say, Your mind perhaps may change"—bursts forth with

> Never, Iago. Like to the Pontic sea
> Whose icy current and compulsive course
> Ne'er feels retiring ebb, but keeps due on
> To the Propontic and the Hellespont;
> Even so my bloody thoughts, with violent pace,
> Shall ne'er look back, ne'er ebb to humble love,
> Till that a capable and wide revenge
> Swallow them up.

What were we interested in here? Othello's resolved mind, his fixity of purpose? ventured a student. I didn't say anything, and another student, probably trying to figure out where I was headed, said that it was Othello's language we respond to. But was it Othello's language? Did it believably emanate from his character? Or was it somehow "out of character"? (Alexander Pope, for one, said that the lines should be omitted as an "unnatural excursion.") Yet out of character or not, I said, these lines are thrilling; while not calling out for complex interpretation, they give us the thrill of intense pleasure, even as Othello is signing on for tragic destruction. How does this happen? The answer, we agreed (did "we"? were we a "we"?) was somehow "Shakespeare," and that was our subject this term. In our classes and in the papers they would write, the focus would be unfailingly on what I called the "expressive value" of lines in sequence, how we heard and registered them in our thoughts and feelings.

To talk about expressive value in a passage turned out, not surprisingly, to be a very difficult thing for the majority of the class to do. Largely a group of second-term freshmen and sophomores, their study of literature in secondary school had obviously been conducted in quite different terms. They had been taught, especially with regard to poetry, that the object was to tease out meanings, deep ones if possible, rather than describe how the verse sounded, what it was like to read it. Many of them had been warned against using first person singular, as if that were an inappropriately subjective way to proceed. Now I was asking them to talk in the first person, about what they saw and heard in a sequence of lines. Especially heard: in the early stages of the course I referred more than once to Bernard Shaw's phrase "word music" by way of pointing to Shakespeare's greatness; or to Virginia Woolf declaring, "From the echo of one word is born another word, for which reason, perhaps, the play seems as we read it to tremble perpetually on the brink of music"; or to Robert Frost's insisting that the "ear does it; the ear is the only true writer and the only true reader." But as any teacher knows, it doesn't help much to tell students what you want them to do; only after their not doing it can education perhaps begin.

An example of what I didn't want from them came when a student tried in the first paper to write about expressive value in *Henry IV*, part 1. In that play's opening scene, the king compares Hotspur ("the very spur of honor's tongue") to the wayward Prince Hal, whose brow is stained "with riot and dishonour." The student wrote:

> Every character in the play has a great deal of respect for Hotspur. . . . Even
> his greatest foe and the source of his deep-rooted anger respects his
> courage. This respect is in direct contrast to how the king feels about his
> son. . . . He wishes that Hal had Hotspur's natural noble temperament be-
> cause they are admirable and necessary qualities for a prince.

True, and so forth, but not nearly true enough insofar as it gives no sense of
Shakespeare as a writer, a maker of arresting sentence sounds. For that, the
student would need to "sound" Henry's rueful shame, and the place to begin was with something heard, with tones of voice—a way of addressing
something or someone. Why not point, I suggested, at the poignant exclamation in which the king allows himself to wish that Hotspur, rather than
Harry, were his son:

> O that it could be proved
> That some night-tripping fairy had exchanged
> In cradle clothes our children where they lay,
> And called mine Percy, his Plantagenet!

What are the feelings expressed in such a momentarily indulged wish? Why
is this rueful exclamation both shocking and satisfying, inadmissible yet
beautiful? Since "character" was an inference from such matters, rather than
a given, why not address themselves to Shakespeare's language—to the play
of the play—rather than to Hotspur or Hal or Bolingbroke?

After class a student who had had trouble with the paper came to my
office to discuss how she might rewrite it and, in trying to ascertain "what I
was after," said what I would hear more than once over the term—that she
hadn't been asked to do this before: "You mean you want us to write about
the writing"? Well, I replied, everyone says Shakespeare is such a great writer;
yes, maybe we should face up to the writing. Easier said than done, of course,
and her rewritten paper, in its attempt to pay attention to how the writing
sounds, moved from loose paraphrase to the other extreme, concentrating
instead on consonant and vowel repetition—as if that were what "sound"
essentially consisted of. "I can hear it in class when you read it aloud," said
another student, the mysterious "it" being (perhaps) the pace, the swing, the
tonal and human feel of a passage. Of course it is difficult in the extreme to
write well about such matters. I had been trained to practice, nay revere,
"close reading," but any professional, interpretive approach to Shakespeare
would claim itself as a close reading of the text. My own teaching seemed to

be, in its preoccupation with the sound of sense, a different sort of approach, and the student's remark about reading aloud reminded me of how absolutely central that activity was to my classroom procedure. No wonder students who didn't have the ear for it remained, by necessity, mainly eye-readers. A few were dissatisfied, and one young woman, when I asked them on the final exam to write a little about their experience during the term, found that we had insufficiently attended to characters, plots, motifs, "ideas." Indeed we had, but in the interests of what I believed to be even more important than such emphases—the life of the poetry.

Perhaps the most interesting remark on that exam came from a student who had performed at an average level and who now spoke about the nature of what I'd asked them to do. Many teachers at the college, he wrote, "focus on appropriate readings for the purpose of analyzing them in the context of a social movement," the focus being on "an agenda rather than on the works themselves." This course in Shakespeare was something new to him, and, in a formulation that gave me pleasure, he wondered whether he should consider it "a throwback to an older style of teaching, or innovative, since it is now so rare." Thinking of myself as an innovative throwback helped check the impulse toward self-congratulation, but also reinforced me in believing that the only way to keep the sun from setting on Shakespeare is for innovative throwbacks in English classrooms to focus on what really and finally matters: the power of words to raise the spirit and touch the heart.

Newsletter (Association of Literary Scholars and Teachers),
Autumn 1997

Amherst English: Theodore Baird

As someone interviewed in these pages more than once as both student and teacher in the composition course described, I am a less than disinterested commentator on Robin Varnum's account of writing instruction at Amherst College. That won't, however, deter me from singling out the book as a piece of documentation whose appeal should extend beyond local curiosity, even beyond the audience of English professors especially concerned with the teaching of composition. "The Era of Theodore Baird," pompously self-important as it sounds, is not an extravagant rubric to name decades in which flourished a bold and inventive approach to the teaching of writing, probably *the* most inventive one ever tried at an American college or university. Over the years, myths of all sorts have proliferated about what was a required course for Amherst freshmen, English 1-2: Composition. *Fencing with Words* provides a reliable and mainly sympathetic history of what went on in this course; it also raises critical questions about what it means to look back on the past, on one's predecessors, on a past "era" in education, without claiming too glibly to "understand" it.

First some facts, as gathered together by the scrupulous researcher. From beginning to end, the heart, soul, and wit of the Amherst composition course was Theodore Baird, who came to teach at the college in 1927. As a graduate student at Harvard he had studied with Irving Babbitt, but Baird was no humanist, nor did he speak from any announced platform of beliefs—religious, social, or moral-ethical. As a young teacher he discovered *The Education of Henry Adams* and at Amherst did the surprising thing of making it the sole text for a semester of freshman composition. This was

Fencing with Words: A History of Writing Instruction at Amherst College during the Era of Theodore Baird, 1938–1966, by Robin Varnum. Urbana, Illinois: National Council of Teachers of English, 1996.

quite extraordinary, since Adams's book offered a formidable challenge not only to young readers, but to the teacher concerned to "do" something with it in an English class. In fact, and as he admits, the *Education* was one of the books that changed Baird's mind. Varnum quotes a famous passage from its first chapter that Baird would more than once have recourse to: "From cradle to grave this problem of running order through chaos, direction through space, discipline through freedom, unity through multiplicity, has always been, and must always be, the task of education." Varnum misreads Adams's singular "order" as plural "orders," but she is right to say that Baird found the notion appealing ("one man's order is another man's chaos," he liked to say) since the human orders we make are diverse and conflicting. It was a principle that consistently informed the writing assignments he would construct for Amherst undergraduates.

Adams exerted a more covert and profound force upon Baird, insofar as a recurrent pattern in Adams's narrative shows him learning the limitations of his own language—the "ignorance" he confronts after he has failed to dispel it by employing one or another "order." Perhaps the most powerful chapter in the *Education* is titled "Chaos," in which, after a slow and painful illness, Adams's sister dies and his "first serious consciousness of Nature's gesture" takes the form of "a phantasm, a nightmare, an insanity of force." The following chapter, "Failure," describes on a more relaxed, comic note his attempt at instructing undergraduates at Harvard College. One of Baird's homely revisions of this failure-note was to say that "Education doesn't work," a slogan not popular on college campuses, especially when fund-raising is in the air. Indeed Baird seemed to take a wicked delight in the fact that our attempts to order chaos in one or another way are prone to failure, though usually in less than tragic ways, and that the experience of failure may lead to a sharpened, even exhilarated, notion of what it might be like to succeed. ("Success is counted sweetest / By those who ne'er succeed," wrote the Belle of Amherst.)

Soon after he arrived at Amherst, Baird put together an anthology of autobiographical selections titled *The First Years*, "an attempt to provide materials for a course in the writing of English by directing the student's attention to his own resources of experience." He knew, he wrote, that in a general way this was a long-established approach to the teaching of writing; his own idea was to help the individual student attend to his experience by giving him means of comparing "what he has written with the autobiographical memories of skilled writers." There follows a key assumption: "When the student attacks the problem of writing with subject matter rather than form as the end in view, his interest will be aroused and matters of form will be subordinated to their proper place. . . . The student cannot, except by admitting his own deficiencies as a human being, ascribe his lack of interest in his subjects to his opinion that they are dull and uninspiring."

Although the course Baird would eventually invent and direct, English 1-2, made no use of this textbook or indeed of any texts other than what students wrote, its principle was one Baird never retreated from: that you could make students care about their writing not by teaching them "good English"—the elements of grammar and punctuation—but by asking them to write about their own lives, a subject that presumably only a very few would claim to be devoid of interest.

The First Years (1931, revised 1935) contained selections from Adams, from Edmund Gosse's *Father and Son* and Howells's *A Boy's Town,* and other autobiographical works. But the writer given the most pages, and with whom the anthology concludes, is Marcel Proust, the last volume of whose great work had appeared in English the year Baird came to Amherst. In passages he chose for the anthology, like those having to do with the madeleine, the steeple of St. Hilaire in Combray, or the excitements and disappointments of going to see Berma perform, Baird found what he called in the introduction "the perfection of a kind of writing, occasionally hinted at, occasionally well done, in autobiography, but never before sustained for so long a time nor with such brilliant success." To speak of Proust as an "influence" on the course Baird was inventing would doubtless be crude; yet it is fair to say that *Á la recherche* was a supreme effort at running various orders through the chaos of thoughts and feeling of a single mind. On a suitably smaller scale, the effort might be something the Amherst freshman could be invited to try his hand at.

I'm suggesting that the energies Baird would direct into his composition course were continuous with literary experiences he was having of modern masterworks by writers who hadn't yet become objects of academic literary study. The third modern writer whose example—right down to the most intimate matters of tone and temperament—made all the difference to Baird, was Robert Frost. As with Adams and Proust, it seems ridiculous to talk about Frost's influence on a composition course that—as Varnum points out, quoting an essay on Baird by Walker Gibson—Frost liked to dismiss as "kid stuff." But pretty much any kind of academic course was kid stuff to Frost, who had spent his time at Amherst and other institutions playing against the system. When Varnum asked Baird if his course owed a debt to Frost in its emphasis on what Frost called "sentence sounds," Baird said he had no interest in talking about any such debt. This seems fair enough, yet when Frost published his first books of poems and filled letters home from England with his notions of the speaking voice, sentence sounds, "the sound of sense" and its importance for poetry, he also insisted on its importance for education. Just before sailing home, he wrote a letter to his fellow teacher at Dartmouth, Sidney Cox, about the difference between what Frost called "the grammatical sentence" and "the vital sentence," the latter being what he was after and what any teaching of writing should also be after. In a sentence that has never been commented on, as far as I know, Frost told Cox, "We will shake the old unity-emphasis-and-coherence Rhetoric to its foundations." In this gesture of solidarity, which he was not to act on in any systematic-academic way (such as founding a new kind of English course), there can nevertheless be heard an animus against conventional instruction in Good English, at the "correct" grammatical sentence as what could be taught, in grammar school, high school, and, if need be, once again at college. Baird shared this animus.

"Perhaps you think I am joking. I am never so serious as when I am," Frost also wrote to Cox, and the interpenetration of seriousness and joking he shared with Baird, who developed his version independently of Frost. Both men delighted in playfulness of utterance and were similarly hard to pin down when an interlocutor ventured the equivalent of "But seriously . . ." Both liked to shock, to discomfit, to put their listeners momentarily at a loss. Varnum quotes an apt sentence from the introduction to *The First Years,* in which Baird's acerbic yet playful manner may be glimpsed: he has been attacking rhetoric books that, aiming to teach students about various kinds of exposition, teach them instead how to write the deadly dull five-paragraph Perfect Theme (as Baird termed it). He assumes it is better for students to discover for themselves some of the difficulties in writing about their own thoughts and emotions; but he also supposes a certain level of attained literacy:

> I also assume, without undue belief in the natural goodness of the human heart, that if at college age a student has not learned how to spell *re-*

> *ceive,* how to punctuate, how to write sentences of greater complexity than those of Arthur Brisbane, he has so successfully resisted the pressure of former teachers that he ought to be considered immune and be allowed the precious privilege of discovering these intricacies for himself.

In the second edition these sentences (and the now forgotten Arthur Brisbane, a journalist) were cut. Baird, however, remained true to their sentiment throughout his teaching career: the composition classroom was a place where you could talk about ideas, consider interesting questions, look at human experience in various ways. In order to do this, the mechanics of composition were assumed, in a way that they scarcely could be now even at the most "elite" institution of higher learning.

Adams; Proust; Frost: are these the true progenitors of a course in freshman composition that was, so the word went round, really derived from William James's *Pragmatism,* Wittgenstein, Count Alfred Korzybski, or S. S. Hayakawa? In the course's heyday in the 1940s and 1950s, students—I was one of them—tried to look for a magic name at whose door might be laid responsibility for the puzzling assignments set by the English 1 staff. Baird denied that there was any such primal figure behind the inventive questions he made into semester-long sequences of writing exercises. (Varnum, in an appendix, gives the entire thirty-one short papers, final paper, and final exam that constituted the course in the Fall of 1946.) Before assuming that his denial was merely obfuscatory or coy, one might remember that Wittgenstein's *Philosophic Investigations* was not published until 1953 (Baird has said he didn't read Wittgenstein before or afterward); that Korzybski's *General Semantics* was promulgated in a messianic from-on-high manner quite alien to Baird's playfulness; and that James's massively influential *Pragmatism,* which surely Baird *had* read, cannot, except at a level of abstraction so high as to be meaningless, account for the imaginative pedagogy that informed English 1. He did acknowledge the importance of the Harvard physicist Percy Bridgman, whose work on "operational definition" contributed to the insistence that Amherst students define their terms and describe the order of actions they had engaged in. But the books Baird cared most about in his sustained and massive amount of reading were mainly not works of philosophical analysis. Literature, history, biography, travel narrative, scientific accounts (at the nonspecialist level) were his main passions; Shakespeare, Clarendon, Samuel Johnson, Gibbon, Jane Austen, Emerson, Thoreau, Darwin—along with Adams, Proust, and Frost—were the writers he returned to again and again and who informed his sensibility. There was a particular turn to that sensibility, and it provided an essential quality of the composition course. But before addressing this matter, a few remarks about the logistics of English 1-2, drawing upon the facts Varnum has assembled. "The Era of Theodore Baird" takes in years occupied largely by World War II and the postwar Amherst "New Curriculum" that institutionalized, for what turned out to be two decades, a year-long required course in Freshman Composition. During the war years, various Army and Air Force contingents succeeded one another at the college in rapid succession. Among their courses of instruction was one in English, primarily taught by Baird and his two main colleagues in the department, G. Armour Craig and Reuben A. Brower. Brower came to Amherst in 1939; Craig, the next year. Brower would develop a sophomore course in the interpretation of literature, which he later recreated at Harvard as Humanities 6. Craig, who had been Baird's student and who returned to his alma mater to teach for more than forty years, was Baird's main support in the composition course and brought to it an interest in philosophical-analytic discourse, particularly (and recently) as it was conducted in the writings of Kenneth Burke. Burke's "perspectivism," as he expounded it in *Permanence and Change* and *A Grammar of Motives,* was an important validation for the kinds of questions the composition exercises were asking, the kinds of situations they invited students to write about. Varnum quotes some remarks by Craig about how, in a typical assignment, the freshman was directed to

> "do thus and so about X; describe as thoroughly and carefully as you can what you did when you did something about X. . . ." We would always at the end say, "Now, define X. . . ." We frequently had assignments that asked one way or another, "You are in a situation where you're at a loss. What does it feel like? How do you know you're at a loss?" Or in a situation in which you don't understand something that somebody says to you, what is the experience of not understanding? What is the understanding of being at an impasse? How does this differ from the experience in which you were stuck, but you got out of it? How did you get out of it?

For even the best students, who had been congratulated in high school for their literary talents, this was something new, though Proust would have found it old hat. If—as Craig pointed out—students had been brought up to think of "good" English as belletristic, an "effusion," something else seemed to be wanted in this composition course. Puzzled freshmen, he recalled, would ask, "What do you want, sir? Do you want me to talk about metaphor?" The answer, not inevitably helpful, would be something like "tell me what you know, tell me what you did when you did X"—served a tennis ball, found yourself at a loss, used the right or wrong name for something, read a map, drew the skyline of the Holyoke Range.

I don't think it accidental that, as Craig's remarks suggest, the emphasis in the assignments was frequently on being at a loss, an impasse, being stuck, not understanding something. For the challenge in writing was to run some sort of a compositional order through experience, which William James called a blooming, buzzing confusion. In this confusion or chaos one was engaged in doing something other than being a writer: one was getting lost, or playing tennis, or taking out the trash, or being rear-ended by a careless motorist. There is an analogy here with the novelist's problem, insofar as unhappy families prove a better subject than happy ones, and "evil" characters seem more interesting than good ones. As Adams put it: "Chaos is the law of nature; order the dream of man," and nature rather than dream turned out to be the stuff of English 1 assignments.

The expense of energy on the part of both students and teachers in the course was truly prodigious: at each class meeting—three times a week first semester, twice a week in the second—a short paper was submitted, responding to an assignment handed out in the previous class. The instructor took the paper home, read and commented on it (all were ungraded, although teachers kept track of how the individual student was doing), then made it the subject of the following class. A "class" consisted of individual papers, or selected parts of them, being distributed, read aloud, then discussed and argued over. (The authors were not identified.) In the course of the first semester the student wrote thirty-some times; if (as I did) an instructor taught two sections of the course (M, W, F and T, Th, S) he read thirteen hundred or so papers over the semester. The pressure was always there, for better or worse: worse, when the student behaved lazily or cynically or just plain didn't have an idea; worse when the teacher couldn't figure out what to do in a class and ended up juggling or faking while trying to sound in control. But better when a student felt challenged and extended by the difficult questions he was being asked to consider; very much better when the instructor suddenly noted, under his tired eyes, a piece of writing come to life—an individual voice, so it seemed, asserting itself.

As an Amherst freshman in the fall of 1949, I struggled with this strange course, never knowing what "they wanted," and only occasionally writing a sentence or two that elicited praise. In fact it wasn't until a couple of years later, when I read an article Baird had written about English 1 for the alumni magazine, that I saw more clearly the way in which the questions asked had been about words and the wordless. Baird gave an example of a typical assignment that asked the student to write about something he knew how to do, like the good tennis player describing what it is to serve a tennis ball:

> He knows he knows what he is writing about, yet as he begins to address himself to his subject he immediately encounters the inescapable fact that his consciousness of his own action contains a large area of experience quite beyond his powers of expression. The muscular tensions, the rhythm of his body as he shifts his weight, above all the feel of the action by which he knows a stroke is good or bad almost before the ball leaves the racquet, all this and much more lies beyond his command of language, and rendered almost speechless he produces a mess. He knows in the sense that he can perform the action, but he does not know in the sense that he can communicate this action to a reader.

At which point the teacher invites him to distinguish between these two "levels of experience" and to generalize about them.

Varnum devotes a good deal of space in her book to accusations that "mystification" was being practiced; that while the student was being told there were no answers, told it was up to them, the English staff—handing out these daily assignments and handing them back with acid, ironic, or just plain mysterious comments—looked as if *they* knew what things were really about, what the Real Answer was. There's some truth in this, insofar as a section teacher "knew" more about, say, "levels of experience" than the typical freshman did but never handed out such knowledge as something to take notes on. Nor would it have done any good if he had, and it would have foreclosed on the sort of game both teacher and student were engaged in playing. It must be admitted that some students, and even some members of the staff, disliked playing the game and responded with various degrees of hostility or indifference. But why should such divergence come as a surprise? To believe that the course had a doctrine or secret behind it, and that once you'd unmasked that secret (once you knew there were difficulties in writing about how to serve a tennis ball) you could then retire in possession of the truth—that was surely not the point. The point was rather to make your knowledge the occasion for a more subtle, effortful, and interesting use of words, a more artfully composed composition. Baird put it neatly in a communication to Varnum: "The problem is, when you face a class of freshmen, you find they are not used to playing with language. They don't have that sense of play. I would say the purpose of our course was to make their lives richer."

From the beginning, Baird attempted to put together a teaching staff that wasn't exclusively "English." The classicist Wendell Clausen once taught the course, as did a physicist, an economist, a historian, a mathematician—perhaps there were others. Thus the "general education" component of the whole enterprise was confirmed. Upwards of fifty different people taught in English 1-2 until its conclusion: aside from Craig, a regular participant (Brower occupied himself with the sophomore course in close reading), there were, preeminently, Walker Gibson, Benjamin DeMott, John F. Butler, Roger Sale, and William E. Coles Jr. (Gibson, Butler, and Coles, subsequent to their term at Amherst, taught composition courses indebted to English 1 at other institutions, as did Jonathan Bishop and Thomas R. Edwards.) But the predominant pattern until the 1960s was for an instructor in English to teach the course for three years—perhaps two sections each term—then move on someplace else. When the pattern changed and more people got tenure, it was difficult to maintain a staff: people wanted to teach their own courses, as why should they not? As Baird moved toward retirement and the college faculty voted to replace the New Curriculum with a watered-down substitute that included required courses neither in English nor in Math-Science, things fell apart—or rather were held together only through the tenacity and stubbornness of Baird's will and commitment. Varnum tells this story well. But rather than dwell on it here, and without forgetting that the staff course was a cooperative enterprise to which numbers of resourceful teachers contributed, I want, by looking a little further at the character of Theodore Baird as it emerges in Varnum's book, to suggest why he *was* English 1 and how, without his intensely individual perspective on life and writing, the course couldn't exist. I'm convinced also that attempts by Varnum, and others quoted in her book, to "contextualize" and understand it as a moment in American education necessarily fall short of a more interesting truth.

In a revealing appendix, Varnum prints an exchange of letters she had six years ago with Baird, who proposed that rather than him telling her more things about the course, she should do an assignment, one involving the Emily Dickinson house in Amherst. Varnum was directed to go look at it, say what she "saw," and then define "looking at a poet's residence." A week later she sent Baird a paper in which she carefully described the house from the outside, also from the inside (a guide showed her around), and concluded with the assertion that "A house . . . can be read much as one reads a poem— as holding secrets of a human heart." To do this, she suggested, something like "empathy" was necessary. Baird responded a few days later, in a letter that Varnum admits disturbed her very much. He first apologized for the phrasing of the assignment and said that, in a class, he would have talked a bit about "seeing." He said her paper was excellent, A+, "very nicely-written, well-organized," and that no one could teach her anything about "this kind of writing." On the other hand, he continued, it was "entirely unsatisfactory." By way of explaining why, he described a visit he had made to his brother-in-law's factory that made X-ray tubes. After touring this operation, Baird said he could have written some "good English" about the factory, even used words like electron, anode, and cathode, but that, nevertheless, he wouldn't have had the faintest idea how the whole thing went together, how it worked. He continued: "I can write and write well about something I know nothing about. In other words the person who saw this building and the things in it on one floor after another did not know what he was looking at or did not know how to see what was there to be seen."

As a *writer* in that situation, Baird said, he was "just a brother-in-law, ignorant. I would say to him, 'A temple of marvels,' as far as I could go in imagining and expressing that imagining."

Then he turned to Varnum's response to the assignment:

> The Emily Dickinson house as you write about it is a museum. Define museum. Here is a cradle, E.D. may have slept in it. Here is a table E.D. may have written poems on it. Poems? Was she a poet? Where as you look at these objects do you see poetry? How do you get from the doorway, a certain style, to a poem? What do you *SEE*? You use the word *empathy*, as if that could, that word, possibly lead you to the poet.

And he wound up: "The plain fact is the person who looks at a poet's residence is really not able to express much of what he feels. That was (as I see it) the point of the assignment. And the point of many assignments we made, to bring the writer to an awareness of the inexpressible." "Inexpressible" not in the sense of some realm (like Herbert Spencer's "Unknowable") that language can never touch, but rather what words and sentences, however impressive they sound in a particular situation, fail to convey about that situation. If this emphasis encouraged students to be wary about what language could and couldn't do, it also encouraged a more open and imaginative response to the whole matter of expression. In his letter to Varnum, Baird partially recalled a sentence of Frost's: "It has always been a matter of wonder to me that Emily Dickinson—what? lived and wrote poems in Amherst? It is this wonder, the marvel of it that she did, I see when I look if I think at all about it in passing the house. Just as I called the factory a temple of wonders. This is my response to what I do not understand." Varnum tried to roll with the punch, admitting to herself that she didn't know what she meant by "empathy" and that Baird's challenge had made her "reexamine [her] responsibility as a language user and historian." Yet by the end of the paragraph she is also registering her distaste for the way the English staff "undertook to disorient students or trip them up. I would have to confess I was both repelled and attracted by the authoritarian nature of the course." She quotes another remark of Baird's to her about how there is "nothing more interesting for a teacher than making it possible—by setting a trap—for a student to talk himself into something he had not been taught, had not known, could now make an English sentence about." This notion, she says, bothered her: and well it might have, since she had fallen into a trap and failed to write the English sentences that would take her out of it.

In other words, and this is a comment on the overall thrust of her book, Varnum's liberal, enlightened, democratic sensibility really can't take in the mind of a teacher who played the game a very different way and who was, in the words of one of his students quoted here, "a tough guy . . . lively sense of curiosity . . . a very, very interesting man." To her credit, Varnum had enough sense of how "interesting" Baird and his course were to persist in writing her book; but she also feels compelled to draw back at certain points, as if to assure us, and herself, that it's not enough just to be "very interesting." To give herself intellectual support, she brings in the testimony of a member of the college's sociology department who came to Amherst in 1969, after the composition course was history. In the sociologist's hands, the course is seen not only as authoritarian but as exemplifying "the locker room mentality or . . . the drill instructor mentality." It is but a step from saying, as many have, that English 1-2 was *like* "boot camp" to the claim that it was *in fact* boot camp—a classic instance of not knowing when you've taken the metaphor too far. Varnum's own nods at sociological contextualization of the course seem to me pious and unconvincing, as when, speaking of the high standards enforced in English 1, she attributes it in part to "Cold War militance." This seems to me a dreary and vaporous way to think about a very "interesting" operation, one similar to taking the demanding and often frustrating challenge of the course, day by day, and flattening it out, as does the sociologist, into "terrorizing students." After all, there are degrees of Terror: English 1 was not run by Marat, Danton, and Robespierre.

Perhaps it is a question of how much we take it upon ourselves to understand the past and pronounce on its limitations. Varnum has trouble, in her closing pages especially, when she attempts to say that English 1-2 was an exciting course . . . but. She begins a paragraph with "It would be too easy to dismiss English 1-2 as a course designed by white males for white males." Indeed it would: why lead with that card? She goes on in similar concessive fashion to say, and rather primly, that "by today's standards" (What are they? Are they any good?) there were "distasteful" aspects of the course: it was elitist, authoritarian, and mystified many students. Yet "despite all this," the course was one in which "teachers and students seem often to have engaged in real conversation," one that enabled students "to claim authority over language and their lives." So, current teachers of composition "could learn much that would be of value" from it.

What this cautious balancing leaves out is nothing less than Theodore Baird, the man who concluded his cover letter to a set of assignments he handed out to the staff in the summer of 1960 by quoting Thoreau: "Give me a sentence which no intelligence can understand. . . . There must be a kind of life and palpitation to it, and under its words a kind of blood must circulate forever." "These strange words," Baird said, opened up the possibilities for a writer "in a way that Unity, Coherence, and Emphasis can never do," by allowing writing to be seen as "somehow the expression of the imagination, and imagination itself may be mysterious and wild." Try as she does, Varnum can't rise to the mystery, the passion, the wildness, the mischief and playfulness, that was Baird's and often the course's trademark. Looking back on his retirement in 1970, he noted "I always said I could hear the community sigh in relief." As for the burden of the course, "Nobody wants to do the kind of heavy work that we did at reading papers. The minute I got through they dropped it." English 1-2 exists now in the minds of those people who taught it, or tried to; but also in the minds of a great many students who took it. As college alumni, they gather at reunion weekend, in one symposium or another, to talk and argue about the past, particularly this strange, unforgettable composition course. Are they prey to nostalgia merely? When Baird said, echoing Henry Adams, "Education doesn't work," he meant something more interesting than "Education always fails." In remembering English 1 2, students may be remembering perhaps the only intellectual demand ever made on them that they could not meet. Knowing that they couldn't meet it, and still can't, may well be a sign, ironically, of educational success. At any rate, for some of those students, it seems, there was really nothing quite like it before or since, and who is to say they are deceived?

Raritan: A Quarterly Review, Winter 1997

Amherst English: Reuben A. Brower

On a May morning in 1953, the senior class at Amherst College, of which I was a member, gathered for Senior Chapel, an annual occurrence at which prizes and fellowships were handed out and the graduates were addressed by a member of the faculty chosen by the class. That year the one chosen—who had been actively lobbied for by the more "literary" element in the class (or so we thought of ourselves)—was Reuben Brower, Class of 1880 Professor of Greek and English, himself about to depart Amherst, after fourteen years of teaching there, for Harvard University. So when he began his talk, "An Earthly Paradise," with the opening words alluding to Dante's *Inferno* (which we had all read as freshmen) there could be detected a hint of his own mixed feelings about leaving Amherst: "We stand together in our local wood, not quite lost and yet not quite sure where we are going." In fact, a large number of my classmates were going to business school, and on from there to make a lot of money; but they doubtless tried to respond to Brower's claim that "we have been in an Earthly Paradise all along" and his suggestion that "before we leave it, we had best give it a thoughtful look." This, Brower proceeded to do, and what I remember most from the rest of the talk, aside from the easy grace and mellow playfulness of its tone, appropriate to the slightly self-important occasion, were two sentences he quoted from Jane Austen. They would, he hoped, help us strike a balance between sentimentality and cynicism: "Think only of the past as its remembrance gives you pleasure," was the first; "One does not love a place the less for having suffered in it," was the second. I never encounter these sentences from *Pride and Prejudice* and *Persuasion* without hearing a special ring of authority and wisdom, and though Jane Austen has plenty of both, I hear instead the voice of Reuben Brower.

Rereading the speech thirty years later confirms what I sort of knew at the time: that, although I was being addressed by a learned man who was not

only an Amherst professor but about to move (was it to graduate?) to the
fabulous Harvard, it was above all else the tone of voice that captured me.
This voice spoke to the assembled classmates—few of whom, including
me, were students of Greek or of more than high-school Latin—about how
the great mistake in the teaching of Latin had been for teachers to tell students (as I was told in high school) that we should study it in order to gain
a better command of English syntax and vocabulary. To this advice Brower
replied:

> The cricket-like voices of the elders have grown more strained as fewer and
> fewer listen, while the unanswerable answers are forgotten. We learn Latin
> to read Virgil and Catullus, to find out what it was like to be Julius Caesar,
> to die on the slopes of Vesuvius with the elder Pliny.

The ironic curl in the voice naming the elders' folly, then the "simple" answer "to read Virgil and Catullus," with a serious heightening of tone as it
moved up to Pliny and the slopes of Vesuvius—it was wonderfully exhilarating. Even if I was never to learn to read Latin with any skill, or Greek at all,
I knew why I should have learned to read them.

At this point I had never officially enrolled in one of Brower's courses,
though he had once substituted for an ill colleague in our section of the
sophomore literature course of which he had been the architect. That day
consisted of his leading us through Keats's "Ode to a Nightingale," a strenuous go-around as I dimly remember. Brower's upperclass course in literary
criticism was rumored to be tough, with good grades hard to come by;
meanwhile, I was indulging in political science (thinking that's what incipi-
ent lawyers did), with a major in philosophy (thinking, mistakenly, I might
become a teacher of it). At any rate I missed Brower until the fall of my senior
year, when he offered a new course called "English Poetry: Pope to Tennyson," which I determined to audit. In fact, the course began with John Dryden, a poet unknown to me and one whose poems in the fine-looking
eighteenth-century anthology edited by R. S. Crane were forbidding—at
least until Brower began to read aloud "To the Memory of Mr. Oldham":

> Farewel, too little and too lately known,
> Whom I began to think and call my own;
> For sure our Souls were near ally'd; and thine
> Cast in the same Poetick mould with mine.

Much of his talk about Dryden had to do with what he referred to as "allu-sive irony," and Brower in a published essay had already done a memorable job with the couplet from "Mac Flecknoe" about Shadwell ("His Brows thick fogs, instead of glories, grace, / And lambent dullness plaid around his face"), showing how it parodied a line from the *Aeneid* in which a lambent flame spreads around the brows of Ascanius. In the tribute to Mr. Oldham, the allusion was simpler, an extravagant comparison of a dead English poet, wholly forgotten today, to the nephew of the Emperor Augustus:

> Once more, hail, and farewell; farewel thou young,
> But ah too short, *Marcellus* of our Tongue;
> Thy Brows with Ivy, and with Laurels bound;
> But Fate and gloomy Night encompass thee around.

These lines did not own the complicated, richly verbal texture I had learned to admire in Shakespeare or Keats, nor did the classy classical reference to Marcellus make that much difference. Rather it was, I now see, Brower's calm but sonorous and sympathetic rendering of the lines that made them so telling—the controlled passion of his performance made Dryden, for the first time, a presence to me. A year or so later, when I read T. S. Eliot's asser-tion that "to enjoy Dryden means to pass beyond the limitations of the nine-teenth century into a new freedom," that seemed a noble way for me to imag-ine what by then I thought I had done.

What Brower had done in opening the eighteenth century to me, and what so much of his teaching did, was to instruct by example, especially by the example of the performing voice making a piece of old poetry come alive. His assurance about the worth of what he was reading was so strong, his love—in Robert Frost's phrase—for the particular "figure" made by the poem at hand so great, that you felt yourself to be a peculiarly heavy clod if you could not (as most of us surely could not at the time) participate con-vincingly in the experience. Yet by trying to like Dryden, by going through the motions of imitating the professor's admiration right down to imitating his tone of voice, something eventually happened, and one day, lo and be-hold, there was Dryden on his own, seen plain and heard with pleasure. Of course there were amusing side effects to the whole procedure, as in a mo-ment when, while dealing with some boring piece of eighteenth-century meditative verse about Fancy or Poesy and probably by Gray or Joseph Warton, Brower asked the class whether any of them had read Milton's

"L'Allegro" or "Il Penseroso," poetic sources of the later, undistinguished meditation. Two, at most three, members of the class raised their hands as I shrank lower in my humble auditor's seat. An impatient, slightly put-off, though not terribly surprised look came over Brower's face, a look that I was to see more than once in later years: "Well, for heaven's sake," his voice rising just enough to sound a shade petulant, "go home and read them." I have since tried out this technique on a class, with, I'm afraid, nothing like the success Brower's imperative had on me; for I went home and read, though with less than ecstatic pleasure, the two Milton poems.

I was a small-town boy from upstate New York (Johnson City, right on the Pennsylvania border), full of excitement about uplifting my way out of provinciality by demonstrating that I could respond to the likes of John Dryden. Of course I had no idea at the time that Reuben Brower had grown up twenty miles or so to the south of me in Lanesboro, Pennsylvania, and indeed had graduated from Binghamton Central High School, our rival up the highway. His father worked for the railroad, and I remember hearing Brower later say that he prepared his lessons while commuting back and forth from Lanesboro to Binghamton on the Erie Railroad. As an undergraduate at Amherst College, he majored in Greek and English, graduating with the quite unbelievable average of 97.3—to my knowledge the highest average recorded for any graduate of the college before or since. He also acted in various theatrical productions and was said to have cut a good figure as Bluntschli in Shaw's *Arms and the Man* (his later regard for Shaw was high). But his most notable moment, at least in legend, occurred when Robert Frost, teaching at Amherst at the time and visiting a colleague's class, asked if any student would care to read aloud an Elizabethan poem by Richard Edwards that began, "In going to my naked bed as one that would have slept." Brower volunteered, and years later in an interview Frost remembered "the way his voice fell into those lines, the natural way he did that very difficult poem with the old quotation 'the falling out of faithful friends is the renewal of love.'" After he finished reading, Frost announced, "I give you A for life."

It seems to me a representative anecdote, not so much for the clever A-for-life business as for the emphasis it puts on the centrality of the vocal performance of poetry to Brower's teaching. In my final semester at Amherst, I sometimes attended his section of the introductory literature course. T. S. Eliot was the subject of study, and I wanted to be enlightened about "Prufrock" and *The Waste Land*. But instead Brower began with "Portrait of a Lady," and what remains in my memory is his reading of parts of it aloud with a quite exquisite (the word must be used) control of satiric nuance:

> We have been, let us say, to hear the latest Pole
> Transmit the Preludes, through his hair and fingertips.
> "So intimate, this Chopin, that I think his soul
> Should be resurrected only among friends
> Some two or three, who will not touch the bloom
> That is rubbed and questioned in the concert room."
> —And so the conversation slips
> Among velleities and carefully caught regrets . . .

Expecting to hear about how Eliot was the poet of modern civilization in its decline, presider over twentieth-century chaos, I was introduced instead to tones of voice strung together with aplomb so as to create this sound-portrait of a lady. The teacher whose voice held these tones together in a natural way (as Frost put it) was giving a difficult modern poem more ease of access than I had expected. Moreover, he seemed to be enjoying himself, and so did we.

After graduating from Amherst, Brower took a degree at Cambridge in the early 1930s, studying English and classics. It was a heady time to have been there, since I. A. Richards's *Practical Criticism* had just been published, while in 1932 F. R. Leavis's *Scrutiny* began its twenty-one-year career as a magazine. The influence of these two presences on the young man from the provinces (upstate New York, western Massachusetts) was profound; yet he never became prey—at least in my knowledge of him, admittedly years later—to the extremes of Richards's enthusiasms for this or the other linguistic and cultural "project," or to Leavis's aesthetic and cultural bullying— "This is so, isn't it?" (And you'd better believe it.) To Richards's and William Empson's (also in Cambridge at the time) resourceful dealings with the poem as words on the page, unencumbered by the author's name or place in literary history, Brower brought his own philological and classical training. He could "do" a poem at length and in dazzling ways: one of his lectures in the Harvard "slow reading" course he taught many years later consisted of an all-stops-out, fifty-minute treatment of Wordsworth's "Mutability" sonnet. But he also cared about history, particularly about the history of genres; and the course that began by focusing minutely on the sonnet or quatrain would not only expand to a consideration of other genres, such as poetic drama and the novel, but would trace the fortunes of pastoral or the heroic through a sequence of writers and literary periods. To Leavis's insistence on the importance of evaluation, the making of reasoned judgments about why X was preferable to Y, Brower assented, and could on occasion denigrate with verve some piece of inferiority. But he never seemed to care all that much about ranking, and never confused himself, as Leavis did, with a scourge of mass culture or of aesthetic dilettantism. He was no dilettante— he worked too hard for that—but he liked lots of things besides reading and criticism: art, music, theater, the cinema (remember Leavis's scorn as be re-ferred to "the cinema"), just to name a few. Evaluation could also be prac-ticed as a less than life-and-death matter. A friend of mine once wrote to me describing Brower as "a pleasant guy to be around, whether you're talking about Literature and Life or just about something minor and fun like Bea Lillie . . . or the generally bad quality of *canned* green tomato pickles as over against the real article bought in a good delicatessen."

This is a personal account of Reuben Brower's importance as a teacher, rather than a survey of his career and works. Yet any account of his most fa-mous accomplishment as a teacher—the Harvard humanities course called "Interpretation of Literature" (familiarly, Hum. 6)—must be at least partly genetic. Brower had returned to Harvard from Cambridge, England, written his Ph.D. dissertation on Dryden's *Aeneid,* and in collaboration with Brooks Otis, another graduate student at Harvard, edited a lively, short-lived mag-azine called *The New Frontier,* which combined criticism of literature with criticism of American culture. He taught at Harvard until 1939, when he moved back to Amherst, replacing Harry DeForest Smith in the classics de-partment, but holding the joint title of assistant professor of Greek and En-glish, an unusual—still unusual—title to hold. Brower insisted upon teach-ing in the English department and at the outset gave a course in literary criticism; then he joined Theodore Baird and G. Armour Craig in a staff course called "English Composition"—surely an odd thing for a classicist to teach. Early along he offered a course in the classics department called "Greek Literature in English," also something out of the ordinary, and in 1942 he directed a staff course (which included his English department col-leagues Baird and Craig) called "Reading Poetry and Prose." It was to be Brower's deepest commitment as an English teacher: "The course is devoted to slow reading and detailed analysis of poetry and of prose," said the Amherst catalogue. What it did not mention, but what was to remain the

single most significant aspect of the staff courses in literature Brower insti-
gated at Amherst and Harvard, was the devotion to a common reading list
and to the exercise method. This meant, first, that no matter whom you had
for "section" (the course at its beginnings met partly en masse for lectures),
the same book would be under discussion; second, there would be a written
assignment on it, not in the form of some free-floating invitation to "discuss" ("An invitation to chaos," said Theodore Baird), but in the shape of a
carefully directed exercise.

The "exercises," which I first encountered ten years later and found
mainly terrifying, invited, nay demanded, that one locate oneself in relation
to specific expressions in the text, as, in the example Brower used in a later
essay, to Othello's "Put out the light, and then put out the light." The exercise would consist of a carefully planned series of questions; queries about
parallel words and phrases from earlier in the play; an invitation to the student to make connections, and eventually to conclude with a generalization
about the kind of literary experience he had undergone. Brower's assumption, on which this first staff course of his was built, was that a work of literature—as he put it later in rationalizing the course—"offers us an experience through words that is different from average, everyday experience. It is
different in its mysterious 'wholeness,' and in the number of elements embraced and in the variety and closeness of their relationship." So that when
Othello says these words just before be strangles Desdemona, "we feel not
only the horror of his intention, but also a remarkable concentration of
much that has gone on before: the moving history of the relations between
the lovers and between them and Iago, the echoed presence of earlier moments of 'lightness' and 'darkness.'"

This was what Brower ultimately cared about—these wonderful experiences of literature that were to be shared with students who would be guided
to them by careful demonstration, coaxing, reading aloud, leading them to
a consideration of words and relationships among words. In "Reading in
Slow Motion" (from *In Defense of Reading,* a collection of essays by teachers
in Hum. 6, edited by Brower and Richard Poirier), Brower described the
course most fully. But what couldn't be put down in any essay was the extent
to which its cooperative nature provided continuous edge and vitality. The
weekly staff meetings in which the class plan was decided upon (very much
a "game plan," as the football coaches have it) and the exercises revised and
argued over—and *really* argued over in the early days, as Theodore Baird re-

calls—were absolutely at the heart of the enterprise and kept both students and teachers on the up-and-up. At Amherst after the war, the course was enhanced by C. L. Barber's presence, and there was an important contribution from John Moore of the classics department; later on younger instructors such as Walker Gibson, William R. Taylor, Julian Moynahan, Jonathan Bishop, and Benjamin DeMott did some of their first teaching in it. As the enterprise was a shared responsibility, different people were responsible for guiding different units of a term's syllabus; when your turn came round for six classes on Tennyson's poetry or seven on *Coriolanus*, or three weeks on *The Education of Henry Adams*, you were expected to come up with something interesting, usually in the form of a possible exercise, but also with written-out suggestions for the conduct of individual classes ("poop," as it ingloriously came to be termed) for use by the other members of the staff who just might not approve of your basic approach, taste, tone, and so forth. Of course students had little idea that such things went on behind the scenes; all we knew was that the exercises magically appeared, each one more complicated than the previous. The year I took "Introduction to Literature" at Amherst, we read during the whole first term "only" some lyrics by Wordsworth and Frost, *King Lear*, Jonson's *Volpone* and *The Alchemist*. With three discussion meetings a week, there was time to live with and experience these works in a way that was both leisurely and intense.

It was this thoroughly "Amherst" course that Brower took with him to Harvard when he was appointed professor there in 1953. He took from Amherst not only the spirit and ideals of the enterprise, but also a fat backlog of exercises and other materials useful for the lectures he now had to get up (at first twice, then once a week) for the large body of Harvard undergraduates, mostly freshmen, who soon began to elect "Interpretation of Literature" as their required humanities course. The other courses had titles such as "Epic and Novel" or " Ideas of Good and Evil" or "Man and the World" or "Crisis and the Individual," and they covered a lot of ground, doling out great ideas about Western civilization to the freshmen—with Dostoevsky as the inevitably featured star—and concerning themselves very little with critical method and scarcely at all with the activity of reading. So Brower's "slow-motion" focus on reading was looked at with condescension and annoyance by other teachers of literature at Harvard. Some thought it murdering to dissect; Perry Miller simply referred to it as "Remedial Reading"; and I remember a joking reference to it as a course in "How to Talk about Literature without Actually Knowing Anything." It was suspect also because of the composition of its staff, which, especially in the early days, was still an Amherst operation, filled with graduates of the college. Richard Poirier and Thomas R. Edwards were instrumental in the early planning of the course; Armour Craig chaired it for a semester when Brower went on leave; and William R. Taylor came back from Amherst and taught it. Old boys (back then it was very much an old-boy network) from Amherst, like William Youngren, Thomas Whitbread, Neil Hertz, Floyd Merritt, Piers Lewis, and me, also taught in it. We were arrogant (I was, anyway) and defensive about the course, feeling that—unlike the rest of benighted Harvard English—*we* were vehicles of truth, bringers of light, at least of the Right Method for going about things. We hadn't, some of us, read all that much, nor had we published. But we certainly liked to talk, to argue, and here the staff course once again took on its life.

Brower now had to lecture much more frequently than he had at Amherst, and to large audiences in the lecture room of Sever or Longfellow Hall. He was not considered, and probably was not, a stunning lecturer; at least there was no spellbinding, not much personal magnetism, almost no joking and jollying-up of the students. His lecturing voice (unlike his reading voice) was unexceptional and could on occasion approach a drone. You had to listen, had to pay attention to the book, which should have been in front of you if you had brought it as instructed, and had especially to be attentive during the five or so minutes *after* the bell had rung. For it was then that Brower "tied things together," which meant, in fact, that he made all sorts of connections in somewhat of a rush. I remember trying to scribble down some of them and wondering whether he really saved up his most challenging remarks for that flustered time when the undergraduates were champing at the bit, eager to get to lunch, and snapping their notebooks shut with impatient authority, as if *that* would put an end to things academic for a while. Meanwhile Brower's absorption in what he was doing—putting the last touches to his remarks about Marvell's "On a Drop of Dew" or to the end of James's *Portrait of a Lady*—was complete, and lasted well after the lecture had finally concluded.

The course lasted for twenty years, until Brower's death in 1975, and through it passed some extraordinary students and a good many interesting teachers. *In Defense of Reading* shows some of the variety of interest and concern among its contributors, but—as with Brower's own writing—something has been lost in the process of creating the written, rather than the spoken, word. Frost, a major influence on Brower's notion of "voice" in poetry, said that poetry was what got lost in translation. (Brower himself was a lifelong student of translation and edited a volume of essays on the subject, of which his own, "Seven Agamemnons," is a notable one.) In the translation from spoken to written word, from "what went well in class" to its attempted expression on the printed page, something was assuredly lost: the immediacy, the actuality, the intimacy of reading something aloud with a class, pausing here, trying something out there, questioning that inflection and substituting another one—even as skillful a writer as Brower found this a little more than he could get into print.

Another teaching alumnus of the course—and a non-Amherst one—Paul De Man, noted in the *Times Literary Supplement* that "the profession is littered with the books which the students of Reuben Brower failed to write." If it does not sound too much like an excuse for laziness, I would hazard that there may be a connection between a scrupulous concern for "voice" in poetry and the teacher's doubt that he can ever be adequate in his own writing to convey the vocal discriminations he may have made in class. "Good readers are often spare writers," as De Man put it. Yet Brower himself wrote a number of books—on Pope, on Frost, on Shakespeare, and (in his first one, *The Fields of Light)* on the whole matter of "slow reading."

De Man's essay, "The Return to Philology," boldly attempts to link the procedures of Brower's humanities course with those of literary theory as viewed over the last decade or so. In each, De Man argues, there was practiced "an examination of the structure of language prior to the meaning it produces." This practice was subversive of other practices by those who moved too quickly to paraphrasable meanings and who treated literature as a substitute for disciplines such as theology or ethics or psychology or the history of ideas. Certainly the interests of the Harvard English department in those days were miles away from "close-reading"; one learned instead about Elizabethan drama or Christian humanism or American romanticism. Yet in emphasizing Brower's subversiveness and praising the course that expressed it, De Man's polemic in defense of theory leaves out something important. For not only (as he admits) were the course and Brower's major assumptions as a reader-critic of literature "remote from high-powered French theory"—or from any other high-powered theory, for that matter—they were totally different in the "positive" direction they took. A concern with "philology," with the structure of language in a poem or poetic drama, was where things began, certainly. But as De Man also notes but then ignores, Brower approved of the "ethical" interests he found in Richards and Leavis. He believed further that some poems, some works, were better than other ones and that an objective account of their value could be given and could, indeed, be taught. Though it was never done overtly or even acknowledged, the effect of consistently selecting certain writers and texts for study in the staff courses (Donne rather than Spenser, Keats rather than Shelley, Twain rather than Howells, Jane Austen rather than Charlotte Brontë, Fenimore Cooper never) was to establish a canon. *These* (the works chosen for study) were the ones that "taught" well, about which there was a lot to say, much to demonstrate. Brower's subversiveness, that is, stopped well short of theoretical onslaughts on the notion of a canon or on the validity of objectively determinable preferences. To put it in the unlovely language of literary theory, Brower didn't mind "privileging" or "valorizing" certain works of art, and there was very little "slippage" in his operations. Indeed, as they say these days, it was "elitist"—and that was half the fun.

Brower was an acute reader of one's essays, and when in my second year at Harvard I finally signed up for a course with him—a seminar in Alexander Pope, about whom he was writing a book at the time—I found beneficial the detailed and incisive, if barely legible, remarks he made about particular sentences, not just my paper as a whole. Such remarks often took the form of check marks in the margin, signifying his assent to a sentence or idea, and giving me the feeling that somebody was actually reading what I had written. Here was the "philological" concern De Man speaks of, and it was in sharp contrast to the casual, brief expressions of approval that passed for comments from many Harvard English professors (Douglas Bush and Albert J. Guerard were important exceptions). There were also some amusing side effects of such close reading: I strove in my own prose to emulate the man's style and procedures; so since one of the things Brower was, was urbane—I think I first heard the word used by him in relation to Dryden's "Absalom and Achitophel"—I decided that my own urbanity content should be increased. Once I tried out a favorite formulation of his, the sentence that begins "We are reminded of" and then produces some apt allusive reference. When I tried out a rather farfetched comparison that presumably "we" were "reminded" of, he scribbled in the margin "*Perhaps* we are." This unsettled me, so next time I began the sentence with "Perhaps we are reminded of . . ."

This didn't work either, as Brower noted parenthetically, "Evidently *you* were!" Outfoxed twice, I realized I would have to adopt other means of demonstrating my allusive urbanity: the structure of language was letting me down.

I had often heard Brower lecture on Frost's poetry, and his love of it carried weight for me beyond the local Amherst connection, since Brower loved Yeats, as well, and deeply admired Eliot—though he made interesting demurs about parts of *Four Quartets,* probably resisting what the Anglican concern did to the poetry (Brower was very much a secularist in matters of belief). When I determined to write my dissertation on Frost, I asked him to be principal reader and director. At the time I didn't know he was contemplating a book of his own on the poet, which he published soon after I completed my thesis. His remarks about what I handed him were invariably directed at the writing, rather than at my "readings" of individual poems, and I think this was all to the good, since I tended to treat the slightest Frostian lyric as if it were a dialectical struggle to be described in language appropriate to *Hamlet* or *Paradise Lost.* He helped me moderate my solemnities and taught me to wince at some of the critical jargon I employed, such as "structure" used as a verb. And when the dissertation was done and submitted, he helped free me from the guilty worry of how much of it was my own, how much of it, somehow, his, when he wrote to say: "Can I express one final note of relief? I had feared that our readings might sound too much alike if we both presented them to the world. (We reflect so much of the same "Amherstian" experience.) Fortunately they don't, even when we focus on the same poems. Your emphasis and reading is—I'm happy to say, *yours.*" Could it be true? I was encouraged to believe so, at any rate, and still feel grateful for his releasing and assuring me.

After I returned to teach at Amherst, I saw Brower infrequently and heard from him only occasionally. But the voice, as it had done from the first, carried authority that was deepened when it struck the personal note that he did not often strike. I found teaching at Amherst a full-time activity, most of it focused in the two composition sections that met Monday through Saturday and presented me with a set of twenty or so papers to read each night for the next morning's class. In the fall of my second year I suddenly and mysteriously contracted pericarditis and had to spend a week in the hospital. Scared and depressed as I felt, a letter from him arrived at just the right time and told me what I needed to bear: "Every young teacher has these moments when the burden seems mountainous. I hope you're not finding 'rest' torture. I have always liked being told I had to be good; it is lovely to have someone else responsible for one's conscience." The part about liking to have to "be good" was fun, but the deeper note came through in the wisdom about the young teacher. Nobody had said this to me before, and as with his response to my dissertation, I said, "Could it be true?" At any rate it provided a new way to look at and partially to free myself from "the burden."

He found himself mainly puzzled and disheartened, I think, by the "student unrest" of the late sixties and early seventies. I remember the tone, though not the details, of a long and troubled account he gave me in 1970 or so of a young woman from Radcliffe who was in his "Modern British Fiction" course and who told him in no uncertain terms that Forster's *Howards End* (always one of Brower's favorite books) was "irrelevant" to whatever the going relevance was at the time. Other turmoils were written about in ways that made them something more than the complaints of age and historical situation:

> Believe it or not, I've been having phlebitis in one leg—terrible nuisance. Was in Stillman [the Harvard infirmary] for a week, but now back in classes, & on limited activity. How much can you do with one leg stretched outright? I feel like a gouty country squire 18c style—And maybe I am!

Here the exclamation was beautifully transforming, the physical nuisance converted into a literary asset. In the bad spring of 1970, after Lionel Trilling had delivered one of his Norton Lectures at Harvard, Cambridge police and dissidents mixed it up with grievous results, and Brower wrote

> We were tear-gassed (via windows) in A. House S.C.R. [the Senior Common Room of Adams House, of which Brower was a notable Master] while having party for Trillings the night after the riot. Everyone very warm, very brave (& afterward very depressed—I was).

One does not love a place less for having suffered in it, however, and two years later, while speaking at a Harvard ceremonial occasion, Brower concluded his address with the best, and perhaps the only real, account of the ties that bind at Harvard or Amherst or any undergraduate educational institution: "We are held together," he said, "by our common bond with these charming, challenging, invigorating youngsters, who are the true end of all our efforts . . ." At present, when pious academics are careful always to refer to their students as "men and women," lest they be denying them their human rights, the word "youngsters" is especially to be welcomed; and "invigorating" they were, too, even when they told you that *Howards End* was irrelevant.

I have said nothing here of Brower's continuing interest in classics and the way he infused those interests into the teaching of English literature, particularly vital when the object of study was a genre, such as pastoral or epic. My silence in this regard stems from my own ignorance, so that even as Brower carefully and lovingly described the allusions to Homer or Horace in the poetry of Pope, I felt very much on the outside, looking on wistfully and never doing what had to be done to remedy the situation. But it is my suspicion, though it may be only my provinciality, that his warmest memories of teaching classics—perhaps of teaching anything—date back to his years at Amherst. The suspicion is given some backing by sentences from a letter of 1972, written after the sudden death of John Moore, a much-revered teacher of Greek and Latin and a sometime colleague of Brower:

> His death was a real blow. It marked an end to one whole part of my Amherst life. John, Wendell [Clausen], and I—and later Milman P. [Parry]—were joined in that odd little Classics world, in the far end of Converse Library. *There* we were—& I visualize my Amherst office & study life in & out of those two offices. John shared mine & he was always putting his head in the door, on one side, hopping on one foot, in high form or low. Most clearly I see him at the Greek typewriter, cursing & moaning as be hit another wrong key. He was a person easy to love, and much loved, yet terribly alone.

Three years later Brower himself died, also suddenly. On the program of the service held for him at Harvard's Memorial Church, there were included some lines from Horace's satire, in which he alludes to a Sabine farm:

> quandoque licebit
> nunc veterum libris, nunc somno et inertibus horis,
> ducere sollicitae iucunda oblivia vitae?

Underneath the Latin was Brower's rendering of the lines:

> Oh my Sabine farm when shall I see you, when again
> With old authors, with sleep and lazy hours
> Can I find sweet forgetfulness of painful life?

Leaving Amherst, he had spoken of "An Earthly Paradise"; now the theme returned to memorialize his final leave-taking. I was unable to attend that service but treasure as his real last words to me—even though I spoke with him subsequent to receiving them—this flash of truth in a letter thanking me for something I'd written on Virginia Woolf, another favorite of his:

> Your admirable review—very much appreciated. Life goes too quickly, Increasingly I find myself saying—"Was that it?" I can't quite get over Yeats's feeling that it is about to happen.

That he never got over that feeling, and that he could find such right words for it, was testimony to his continuing restlessness as a reader and scholar, but preeminently as a teacher.

American Scholar, Spring 1985

Name Index